CASSIUS X

Stuart Cosgrove, originally from Perth, was a fanzine writer on the northern soul scene before he joined the black music paper *Echoes* as a staff writer. He became media editor with the *NME*, a feature writer for a range of newspapers and magazines and a television programme executive at Channel 4. Stuart is a prominent radio broadcaster in his native Scotland, has won numerous awards for his work at Channel 4, and is the author of several critically acclaimed books on music, most notably his trilogy of books on soul music and social change.

PRAISE FOR STUART COSGROVE'S SIXTIES SOUL TRILOGY

HARLEM 69: THE FUTURE OF SOUL

'Cosgrove's impressive, dogged groundwork is matched by a deep
devotion to the music that is the backbone of the narrative . . .
An essential read for anyone interested in the politics and culture
of the late 60s, when soul music reflected the momentum of a
tumultuous era that resonates still.'
Sean O'Hagan, *The Observer*

'An impressively granular month-by-month deep dive
into Harlem's fertile musical response to a time of social
and political upheaval.'
Financial Times, Best Books of 2018

'Not only a gripping socio-cultural history, it feels truly
novelistic. Harlem throbs thrillingly . . . and Cosgrove captures
it vividly: heroin, civic decay, gravediggers' strikes, gender-fluid
gangsters, Vietnam vets, Puerto Rican boxers and all . . . *Harlem
69* makes startling connections across time and place.'
Graeme Thomson, *Uncut*

'The best music writing this year is about black music. Cosgrove's
deep dive into the year's events is an epic feat of archival research
that has been expertly marshalled into a narrative that joins the
dots between Donny Hathaway, Jimi Hendrix, the Black Panthers,
police corruption and the Vietnam war.'
Teddy Jamieson, *The Herald*, Best Music Books of 2018

'Cosgrove's series can be read separately, but to read them as a
trilogy gives a real sense of black music and social movements
. . . paints a vivid, detailed picture of the intensity of social
deprivation and resistance, and also the way that's reflected in,
but also affected by, the music of those cities. Reading *Harlem 69*
made me want to do two things – dig out and play some of the
records mentioned, and fight the powers that be.'
Socialist Review

MEMPHIS 68: THE TRAGEDY OF SOUTHERN SOUL

Winner of the Penderyn Music Book Prize, 2018
Mojo – Books of the Year #4, 2017
Shindig – Book of the Year, 2017

'Offers us a map of Memphis in that most revolutionary
of years, 1968. Music writing as both crime reporting
and political commentary.'
The Herald

'Cosgrove's selection of his subjects is unerring, and clearly
rooted in personal passion . . . an authorial voice which is as
easily, blissfully evocative as a classic soul seven-inch.'
David Pollock, *The List*

'Highly recommended! Astounding body of learning.
Future classic. Go!'
SoulSource.co.uk

'As ever, Cosgrove's lucid, entertaining prose is laden with detail,
but never at the expense of the wider narrative . . . A heart-
breaking but essential read, and one that feels remarkably timely.'
Clash Magazine, Best Books of 2017

'Stuart Cosgrove's whole life has been shaped by soul
– first as a music journalist and now as a chronicler of black
American music's social context.'
Sunday Herald

DETROIT 67: THE YEAR THAT CHANGED SOUL

'The subhead for Stuart Cosgrove's *Detroit 67* is "the year that changed soul". But this thing contains multitudes, and digs in deep, well beyond just the city's music industry in that fateful year . . . All of this is written about with precision, empathy, and a great, deep love for the city of Detroit.'
Detroit Metro Times

'Big daddy of soul books . . . weaves a thoroughly researched, epic tale of musical intrigues and escalating social violence.'
TeamRock

'Cosgrove weaves a compelling web of circumstance that maps a city struggling with the loss of its youth to the Vietnam War, the hard edge of the civil-rights movement and ferocious inner-city rioting . . . a whole-hearted evocation of people and places filled with the confidence that it is telling a tale set at a fulcrum of American social and cultural history.'
The Independent

'The story is unbelievably rich. Motown, the radical hippie underground, a trigger-happy police force, Vietnam, a disaffected young black community, inclement weather, The Supremes, the army, strikes, fiscal austerity, murders – all these elements coalesced, as Cosgrove noted, to create a remarkable year. In fact, as the book gathers pace, one can't help think how the hell did this city survive it all? . . . it contains some of the best ever writing and insight about Motown. Ever.'
Paolo Hewitt, *Caught by the River*

'Leading black music label Motown is at the heart of the story, and 1967 is one of Motown's more turbulent years, but it's set against the backdrop of growing opposition to the war in Vietnam, police brutality, a disaffected black population, rioting, strikes in the Big Three car plants and what seemed like the imminent breakdown of society . . . You finish the book with a real sense of a city in crisis and of how some artists reflected events.'
Socialist Review

Cassius Clay counts down the last few days of 1962. Unknown to the world, he has quietly joined the ranks of the Nation of Islam and is already wearing the sober dark suit and tie that reflects his choice. It will be another fifteen months before he will be universally known as Muhammad Ali.

CASSIUS X

The Making of a Legend

STUART COSGROVE

First published in Great Britain in 2020 by Polygon,
an imprint of Birlinn Ltd.

Birlinn Ltd
West Newington House
10 Newington Road
Edinburgh
EH9 1QS

www.polygonbooks.co.uk

1

ISBN 978 1 84697 476 2
eBook ISBN 978 1 78885 297 5

British Library Cataloguing-in-Publication Data
A catalogue record for this book is available on request
from the British Library.

Typeset by 3btype.com
Printed and bound by Clays Ltd, Elcograf, S.p.A

I am America. I am the part you won't recognize.
But get used to me. Black, confident, cocky; my name,
not yours; my religion, not yours; my goals, my own;
get used to me.

—Cassius X, 1964

The common goal of 22 million Afro-Americans
is respect as human beings, the God-given right to be a
human being. Our common goal is to obtain the human
rights that America has been denying us. We can never get
civil rights in America until our human rights are first
restored. We will never be recognized as citizens there until
we are first recognized as humans.
—Malcolm X, 1964

CONTENTS

FOREWORD

Cassius X is the story of an extraordinary human being, but more importantly it is the story of the many social forces that shaped Muhammad Ali.

The book is largely set in 1963 in the run-up to Cassius's first title fight with Sonny Liston in Miami, and focuses on the months when he was using the name Cassius X. He was yet to complete his conversion to Islam, at which point he was given the name Muhammad Ali.

At one level it can be read as a prequel to my soul trilogy – *Detroit 67: The Year That Changed Soul, Memphis 68: The Tragedy of Southern Soul* and *Harlem 69: The Future of Soul* – in that it details the emergence of soul music as one of the dominant popular musical genres of the sixties, but, at heart, it is about the complex political and religious backdrop that created Cassius X and, in turn, Muhammad Ali, and the remarkable sorcery he brought to boxing and the world of entertainment.

Many good biographies have been written about Muhammad Ali that span his entire life: that is not what this book is about. *Cassius X* portrays a man in compression, in the days when the young fighter was exploring his identity, moulding his image and forging advantageous friendships with Malcolm X, Sam Cooke and the media. It is about his role as a witness, not simply to the divisive racial landscape of America, but to the new, self-confident forms of music and entertainment that enlivened his youth.

I owe a huge debt of gratitude to my publisher Polygon, particularly my editor Alison Rae, and to my American publisher Chicago Review Press.

My personal thanks to my friends and family and, as ever, to the weird academy of northern soul.

Stuart Cosgrove
Glasgow
2020

Cassius takes a break from training in Chris Dundee's gym on 5th Street in Miami.
He is wearing a T-shirt designed by his father, who was a signwriter back in their native
Louisville, Kentucky. Photographer Flip Schulke took hundreds of photographs of the boxer
between 1961 and 1964, including the iconic swimming-pool shots. Cassius had boasted that
he trained underwater to strengthen his jabbing, but it was a fabrication concocted
by Cassius and his trainer. He didn't know how to swim.

MIAMI

Where Neon Goes to Die

In the first bleary-eyed days of 1963 Miami woke up to a raging hangover. The city was crammed with well-wishers, con artists and the walking dead. Snowbirds, in their colourful Hawaiian shirts, had flocked to the Florida beaches from Chicago and Detroit, to escape the deafening sounds of the big industrial cities and the unforgiving northern weather. Hotels bulged at the seams and disappointed guests could be seen dragging their bags along Collins Avenue in the vain hope of a late vacancy. Inside the permafrost lobbies, where high rollers escaped the heat, men in unseemly shorts swaggered around the shimmering casinos, leaving crumpled cash tips and suspicion in their wake.

Cassius Clay had been in Miami for over two years now and he had never witnessed such levels of edgy nervousness. The city was restless and rotting to its core. According to the beat comedian Lenny Bruce, who damned urban America with faint praise, Miami was the place where 'neon went to die'. Across whole swathes of the city neon flickered on and off, signage unsteadily jumped to life, and broken glass littered the sidewalks. The garish signs that looked so alluring on postcards were wheezing their last breath and advertising nothing more than a city facing decline. Decay had infected palms in the most shaded parts of the city, and bud rot, the lethal fungal disease, had attacked the once majestic trees, staining their drooping hands an ugly shade of nicotine yellow.

Miami had enjoyed an unrestrained growth after the war, driven by cheap air flights and the rise of air conditioning, but the boom was unsustainable. Work was short-term and unpredictable, unemployment surged and ebbed with the seasons, and the influx of immigrants from Cuba and the Caribbean put unmanageable pressure on social services. Many mid-priced hotels had struggled to keep up with refurbishment plans and repairs to hurricane damage, so swathes of the city looked grubby, dysfunctional and unloved.

Despite all of that, the myth of Miami thrived, and the city's sunshine reputation somehow shook off harsher realities. In her insightful book *Miami*, the celebrated author Joan Didion claimed that 'Miami seemed not like a city at all but a tale, a romance of the tropics, a kind of waking dream in which any possibility could and would be accommodated'. But wrapped up in the dream Didion also saw a city situated at the geographic end of a pistol, an American city 'populated by people who also believed that the United States would betray them'. And the man the Cuban denizens of Miami believed had betrayed them most deeply was the president himself.

John F. Kennedy was in town and his presence had added increased tension to the tumultuous self-indulgence of New Year. The year 1963 was destined to become one of dark conspiracy, the year the president was assassinated. But something else was stirring, hidden away on the other side of this segregated city.

Soul music was rippling beneath the surface, barely audible at first, but about to break across America like an electric thunderstorm and dominate the eventful years yet to come.

It was in Miami that Cassius Marcellus Clay, a lanky youth from Louisville, Kentucky, had fashioned an outrageous dream – to become the heavyweight champion of the world. Cassius and his advisers in Louisville had identified the veteran trainer Angelo Dundee as the man most likely to advance the young boxer's career. Dundee had left his native Philadelphia and was based at his brother Chris Dundee's Gym on Miami's 5th Street. So an eighteen-year-old Cassius had arrived by train from Kentucky in November 1960 to join the claustrophobic boxing academy in 'a steamy, scruffy loft above a liquor store', as the *Miami Herald* described it, on a crumbling corner downtown.

Reticent and unsure where he was going, Cassius was met at the station by his new trainer and an effusive group of Cuban boxers who drove him to an unfamiliar and heavily curtained home. The residents spoke only Spanish and the young boxer retreated deep into himself, unsure of how to communicate. As night descended, he was shown to a cluttered room near the Calle Ocho strip in the Little Havana neighbourhood, where he dumped his training bags and faced an ignominious baptism. He shared his first uncomfortable night in Miami sleeping nose-to-foot with Luis Rodríguez, the brilliant Cuban boxer who once boasted that he had the longest nose in America (his fans in Cuba called him 'El feo') and could fire snot that would kill Fidel Castro. In a darkened room infested with mosquitoes and the piercing smell of sweat, Cassius lay awake listening to distant Hispanic voices and Rodríguez's thunderous snores.

An avowed enemy of Castro's regime, Rodríguez was a lynchpin in Miami's many hives of conspiracy and a close friend of Ricardo 'Monkey' Morales, the former Cuban intelligence officer who had defected to the USA in 1960, where he was contracted by the CIA as a paramilitary officer to fight secret wars and connive with his exiled compatriots, including the boxers who trained with Cassius in the 5th Street Gym. Rodríguez played the role of patriot; a propagandist to the core, he often tried to interest a distracted and disinterested Cassius in the latest gossip sweeping through the exiled Cuban community. Rodríguez had taken on the role of the gymnasium elder, showing visitors around, issuing locker keys and trading jokes with the swarm of boxers who huddled around the ring and concealed ammunition in the ramshackle lockers. It was here amid the sawdust and the whispering Cuban middleweights that Cassius perfected his trademark shuffling dance style and the rhyming ebullience that made him famous.

Rodríguez and the restless kid from Louisville formed a close and unlikely bond, and throughout their odd friendship, they shared a belief that boxing was first and foremost part of the entertainment industry, dangerous and deadly, but entertainment nonetheless. Unsuccessfully coaching him about the warring enigmas of Cuban politics, Rodríguez recounted the names of remarkable generation of expatriates, the great Cuban boxers who had escaped Cuba and were shaping a new story for boxing. Cassius would come to know them, and share training facilities with them in the weeks and months to come. Each of their names sounded so sweet, so satisfying – Kid Chocolate, Kid Gavilán and the elegant featherweight Ultiminio 'Sugar' Ramos. Rodríguez convinced Cassius that if he spent a day watching the quixotic Cubans move on the canvas, he too could learn to dance like the wind. Cassius listened and smiled. He warmed to Luis Rodríguez and saw a flicker of his own personality reflected in the Ugly One's gregarious antics. 'Rodríguez is a clown, a friendly clown,' Robert H. Boyle wrote in *Sports Illustrated*, as if the era of the quixotic clown was about to revolutionise the world of boxing.

Spooked by his first sleepless night in Miami, Cassius vowed to find his own people, and within less than thirty-six hours he had convinced Angelo Dundee to stretch the 5th Street Gym budget and fund a cheap hotel room away from the Beach in the teeming Overtown ghetto. He initially stayed at the Mary Elizabeth Hotel on North West Second Avenue – described by his gym doctor Ferdie Pacheco as 'a den of thieves, pimps and prostitutes' – and after another week of uncomfortable nights he moved to the Sir John Hotel, the coolest R&B venue in Overtown. The Sir John was a landmark, the epicentre of Miami's fledgling soul scene and a much more comfortable hotel, with its own swimming pool and a late-night soul club, the Knight Beat. It was to become Cassius's on-and-off home throughout much of the next three years, and the place where his life took on a new direction. It was here in an otherwise modest hotel room that he began to transform his image, his religious beliefs and, eventually, his name.

On his first night in the hotel, he had unpacked his gym bag, the meagre contents giving a clue to his personality. Bundled in amongst the familiar boxing paraphernalia (gum shields, bonding tape and a tin of Vaseline) was the primitive kit of an amateur conjurer – a magic wand, a pack of dice, playing cards and battered top hat. A trick spider clung to the inside of the bag to be used as a practical joke in the stormy days and stifling months to come. He unfolded his 1960 Olympic vest and hung it over a chair, a showy reminder of his success so far. It was in Rome that Cassius had racked up his first significant victory, when he won the light heavy-weight gold medal by defeating the Pole, Zbigniew Pietrzykowski.

Floyd Patterson, heavyweight champion of the world in the early sixties, told *Esquire* magazine that when he first met Cassius Clay, 'his public image was so different. It was in 1960. I was the champion then and was travelling through Rome. I'd had an audience with the Pope, then visited the American Olympic team there and met Cassius Clay. He was the star boxer for the American team, and he was very polite and full of enthusiasm, and I remember how, when I arrived at the Olympic camp, he jumped up and grabbed my hand and said, "C'mon, let me show you around." He led me all around the place and the only unusual thing about him was this overenthusiasm, but other than that he was a modest and very likable guy.' Cassius came to realise that modesty was a weak currency and that the dollars seem to favour those who demanded attention. He became known as a boy with a near desperate desire to entertain and an adolescent whose demeanour often veered towards an irritating swagger. When he first arrived in Miami, he was largely unknown out on the streets, but his instincts served him well and his showy personality, however much it was contrived, would come to shine.

In the Orange Bowl Stadium, west of downtown, 75,000 spectators crammed in to watch a spectacular opening ceremony and witness President Kennedy and the First Lady, Jacqueline Bouvier Kennedy, being unveiled as the guests of honour at the city's most famous sporting event – the annual Orange Bowl. The president descended from the skies by helicopter before emerging onto the field surrounded by a Praetorian guard of Secret Service agents, their wired professionalism hidden behind sunglasses in the glaring Florida sun. Clint Hill, unknown and unrecognisable, stuck to the Kennedys like glue, his edgy stillness and dark glasses giving out the silent brooding menace of an undercover operative. Hill had spent the late fifties as a Special Agent in the Denver field office before being assigned to the elite White House Detail. Later in the year, he would form part of the motorcade in Dallas and was seen running from the limousine behind the president to shield Jackie Kennedy as the assassin's bullets rained down on them.

By the first days of 1963, a tangible paranoia had tightened around the president. The Secret Service had scoured the Americana Hotel in Bal Harbour for a full week before his arrival, securing a block of rooms on a lower floor instead of the harder-to-protect penthouse suite. Hotel workers were instructed to take sledge-hammers to a wall to create a secure doorway to allow President Kennedy to enter and leave under protection. Out in the exposed bleachers of a high-profile football game, nerves were shredded as the momentum of the crowds separated Kennedy from his security. His celebrity was irresistible. Surrounded by congressmen, political leeches and delighted tourists, the president tossed a coin from the stands prior to the start of the game. Historian Paul George describes him looking 'cool in what appeared to be Ray-Ban sunglasses while puffing on a cigar'.

The Kennedys were at the height of their fame and had brought political allure to a city already reeking of cheap glamour. As the opening parade passed, Miss Florida was carried on a float of giant alabaster oranges, and marching bands dressed as characters from ancient Rome paid tribute to the movie *Ben Hur*. Hundreds of locals from Miami's expatriate Cuban community crowded into the stadium. Teresita Rodríguez Amandi, who was ten at the time and had fled from Cuba to Miami with her parents the year before, told the *Miami Herald*, 'I remember seeing him from the bleachers I was sitting in with my family. It was a very important day for us. It was the first time I would see the President before my very eyes.' In front of him in the stadium were the two competing teams – Alabama and Oklahoma – and the massed ranks of their college marching bands. The game would become known to football aficionados as the 'Bama Show', in which Alabama linebacker Lee Roy Jordan almost single-handedly destroyed Oklahoma.

In an act of presidential manipulation, pride of place in the stadium had been reserved for an unorthodox group of VIPs, the ragged paramilitary army of Brigade 2506, the CIA-sponsored group of Cuban exiles who in 1961 had invaded their homeland and spectacularly failed to overthrow Fidel Castro's revolutionary government. The invasion had ended in bloody defeat with 114 dead and 1,189 Cuban exiles captured. Reflecting on their humiliation, the surviving members of Brigade 2506 were either sceptical of or, in some cases, the sworn enemies of President Kennedy. Whatever he tried to do to accommodate them was never enough. The Cuban counter-revolutionaries held the president in part responsible for their demeaning retreat and blamed him for failing to provide air cover at a critical moment in their assault. One by one, the Cubans grudgingly shook hands with Kennedy, unsure whether their presence would look like courage or capitulation.

Kennedy's main reason for travelling to Miami was neither the sun nor the sport. He hoped to reframe the catastrophic Bay of Pigs invasion and turn it into a heroic military adventure. It was set up so that he could honour the fighters on live television. A packed arena watched him accept delivery of a canary-yellow battle flag, handed to him by two local veterans, Erneido Oliva, the deputy commander of Brigade 2506, and Manuel Artime, a one-time member of Castro's revolutionary army, who had been recruited by American counterintelligence to lead the attack on the island. At a podium near the field of play, surrounded by red gerbera daisies and supported by his wife Jackie, who was dressed in a powder-pink summer suit, Kennedy told the crowd and the bristling brigade leaders, 'This flag will be returned to this brigade in a free Havana.' It was powerful theatre, which tried gamely to rescue a propaganda victory from what was a horrendous defeat, but they were words that would be deliberately misinterpreted in Miami, seen as a coded clue that another invasion was imminent. This was not the case, and so the open sore festered into a more malicious resentment. Kennedy's charm worked almost every-where but not among the Miami Cubans where he was seen as a two-faced, conniving little shit.

The Bay of Pigs was to remain an open wound in American politics for many years to come, with Cuban exiles frequently implicated in the flood of conspiracy theories that surrounded Kennedy's assassination. President Lyndon Johnson, who took up office as a consequence of Kennedy's murder, once claimed that, together with the CIA, Kennedy had run a 'damned Homicide Inc. within the Caribbean'. Unbelievably, a generation later, a cadre of Cuban exiles, survivors of the Bay of Pigs disaster, was among the burglars who broke into the Democratic National Committee Headquarters at Watergate. Their resentments were slow to subside, if they ever did. Subsequent histories of the invasion have tried to pluck honour from the humiliation – historian Theodore Draper called the invasion 'the perfect failure' and author Jim Rasenberger called it 'the brilliant disaster' – but there was nothing either perfect or brilliant about the Bay of Pigs, and its fallout had a devastating impact on Miami, turning it into a cloistered hive of intrigue, conspiracy and criminal plotting. Armed with guns, bombs and battered pride, the Cuban ex-patriots believed that history had sold them short. As the full extent of the failure of the Bay of Pigs invasion struck home, a deal was struck with Cuba.

Less than two weeks before Kennedy's arrival in Miami, the US Government had donated $62 million worth of food and medicine to the impoverished island as a form of ransom for more than 1,100 Brigade fighters captured in the invasion. What the president could not disguise was that Cuba had stood up to America. A humanitarian crisis had been forced on the embattled island and floods of refugees left to seek citizenship in the USA, changing the urban character of Miami for ever. Large-scale migration into Miami exploded after 1959. Most Cubans arrived in the city via special humanitarian provisions or political asylum, citing Communist oppression at home. The feeling was mutual. Cuba waved goodbye to families it described as 'undesirables' and took the opportunity to empty the jails of criminals of every description. Some chose to leave, others were encouraged, and caught up in the

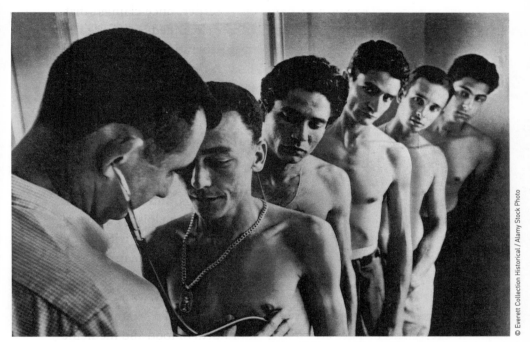

A group of volunteers receive a physical at one of the CIA's recruiting offices in Miami. Cuban refugees volunteered to fight against Fidel Castro in what became known as the Bay of Pigs invasion of April 1961. The 5th Street Gym where Cassius trained was home to one of the greatest generations of émigré Cuban boxers and a hotbed of anti-Castro sentiment.

diaspora were genuinely needy families who took the calculated risk that life in America would be better for them and their children.

Cassius's training partner, Luis Rodríguez, had been the Cuban welterweight champion back in January 1959, when the Batista Government was overthrown by Castro's revolution. Then, when professional sport fell out of favour with the new Communist regime, he emigrated to Miami to become one of the mainstays of the 5th Street Gym. Waves of Cuban immigration had been given the gloss of free-world propaganda, the weekly charter flights from Varadero to Miami flew twice a day, and a converted army barracks on the perimeter of Miami International Airport was branded 'Freedom House' and provided makeshift bunk-bed accommodation for arriving families. The Cuban population in the United States grew almost sixfold within a decade, from 79,000 in 1960 to 439,000 in 1970. Miami became the capital city of Cuba in exile, and in time Cubans constituted 56 per cent of the population. In the words of a reporter for the *Miami Herald*, they became a 'teeming, incomprehensible presence'.

In the meantime, the tourists who clung to the beaches and the lobbies of their grand hotels were largely ignorant of the incomprehensible Cubans and the underground sounds rallying in the bars and nightclubs of the Overtown ghetto. This was the other Miami, a mess of pastel-coloured concrete homes, jerry-built rooftops, pool halls and illegal bars, hidden away beneath the towering canopies of the I-95 highway. Firecrackers burst in the skies, fried oysters blackened on the grills, and sickly cocktails were cut with raw alcohol. Vials of intense Colombian cocaine were sold furtively on corners and the debris from Hurricane Donna still littered the side streets. Cassius found himself surrounded by squalor, fast living and temptation, but he vowed to resist it in the pursuit of discipline and success in the ring.

Each afternoon after his intensive training sessions Cassius and his brother Rudy, who had come to join him in Miami after high school, would walk over to The Stroll, the stretch of 2nd Avenue in Overtown, an African-American area populated with barbershops, record stores and all-day bars. Cassius ran a tab up at the Famous

Chef restaurant next door to the hotel and hung out at Sonny Armbrister's barber shop, where he quickly established a reputation for speaking the dozens, the rhyming rap game that was the mouthy pursuit of young African-Americans. It was here that Cassius witnessed the first days of soul music close up and met three men who to various degrees would all play a role in the development of his life. Coincidentally, they were all called Sam. Sam Saxon would recruit him into the Nation of Islam, the controversial religious group that would shape his ideas and attitudes to life; Sam Moore, a Miami soul singer and ex-convict, was an MC at the Knight Beat and within a few years would be half of Stax-Atlantic's famous male duo Sam and Dave; and Sam Cooke, the legendary gospel-pop star, would arrive in Miami to record one of the most controversial live albums in the history of black music and later use his formidable contacts book to secure a recording deal for Cassius with New York's Columbia Records. Cooke was one of a group of friends from the world of soul music whom Cassius carefully cultivated. Among the others were the twist-craze showman Chubby Checker; his label mate Dee Dee Sharp; Motown's blind prodigy Little Stevie Wonder; the R&B star Lloyd Price; the East Orange, New Jersey, singer Dionne Warwick; Veronica Bennett, lead singer of The Ronettes (later to become known as Ronnie Spector); and Ben E. King, the Harlem soul crooner whose famous hit 'Stand By Me' Cassius covered on his debut album.

Cassius's friendship with Sam Cooke burned bright at a time when black music was at a crossroads: gospel was spilling from churches across the nation into the bedrooms of the young, transforming love for the Lord into a more sexual and secular kind of romance. The record producer Jerry Wexler once described the former gospel star Sam Cooke as the personification of soul music's journey: 'It was all there, the exquisite exact intonations, the sovereign control of tone and timbre, the control of the subtlest pitch shadings, bends and slurs.' Sam Cooke's was the voice that gave birth not only to a new form of music but to a way of doing business, pioneering his own labels, running his own management agency, and controlling his own publishing copyright. He was a beacon of progress in an industry that had brutally exploited black artists for decades. Cooke was charismatic, ambitious and determined to control his own career, and so became a critical influence on Cassius and his thinking.

Since his early childhood Cassius had been taught the value of self-reliance. His father had lectured him on the teachings of Marcus Garvey and his mother had instilled in him a much simpler credo of good behaviour and crime avoidance. By the time he met Sam Cooke, there were numerous successful African-American businesses, in pharmacy, the funeral trade and local taxi firms, but it was in entertainment where the message of ownership and self-reliance was at its most dramatic. In the soul studios of Detroit and the gospel stores of Chicago's Southside, Cooke and his contemporaries were very public exponents of taking control. It was a message that Cassius witnessed close-up and began to apply to his own life.

Most important of all his acquaintances was the squat Sam Saxon, a former pool-hall hustler who moved to Miami and ran the toilet and shoe-shine concessions at Hialeah Race Track in central East Side. Saxon was something more than a shoe-shine boy, though. He was a renowned street captain of the Nation of Islam, sent to Miami to recruit young men in the dilapidated streets of Overtown and to offer hope to the ex-prisoners from the 'Flat Top' in Raiford Prison who had drifted back to their old ghetto haunts. Saxon had been born and raised in a troubled community, in the John Eagan Homes Projects, a tough complex built for black families in Atlanta, Georgia. He had converted to Islam as a teenager and after intensive study won the accolade of 'Rock of the South', valued as one of the Nation's most successful 'fishers of men'. Sometime in March 1961, soon after Cassius had arrived from Louisville, Saxon made his first contact with the young boxer. It was a fleeting conversation at first, but they talked frequently thereafter, and it was Saxon who first invited him to abandon his slave name and adopt the temporary name Cassius X. They met for longer and deeper conversations in a darkened room, behind the sun-parched blinds of the Sir John Hotel, as guests and visiting soul musicians lounged by the pool. It was in these inauspicious settings that Saxon laid the first paving stones on Cassius's path to Islam and his historic transformation into Muhammad Ali. Saxon, whose Muslim name was Abdul Rahaman, recounted the moment in some detail. 'My job was to see that that the men in the Temple were trained to be good providers for their family, made physically fit, and taught how to live right . . . There weren't many members who attended regularly. Realistically, in Miami there were only thirty . . . I met Ali in the March of 1961 when I was selling *Muhammad Speaks* newspapers on the street. He saw me, said, "Hello, Brother," and started talking. And I said, "Hey, you're into the teaching." He told me, "Well, I ain't been in the temple, but I know what you're talking about." And then he introduced himself. He said, "I'm Cassius Clay. I'm going to be the next heavyweight champion of the world."'

After their chance meeting on a street corner on 2nd Avenue, Captain Sam and Cassius forged an unlikely friendship. On the day they first met, Saxon spent the afternoon looking through the boxer's scrapbook, mostly cuttings from the *Courier-Journal*, his local newspaper back home in Louisville. 'He was interested in himself and interested in Islam and we talked about both at the same time,' Saxon remembers. 'He was familiar in passing with some of our teachings, although he had never studied or been taught. And I saw the cockiness in him. I knew if I could put the truth to him, he'd be great, so I invited him to our next meeting.' Cassius remembered his first day at the modest storefront mosque and from the outset was nervous about the impact on his boxing. 'For three years up until I met Sonny Liston, I'd sneak into Nation of Islam meetings through the back door. I didn't want people to know I was there. I was afraid, if they knew, I wouldn't be allowed to fight for the title but the day I found Islam, I found a power within myself that no man could destroy or take away. When I first walked into the mosque, I didn't find Islam . . . it found me.' 'The first time I felt truly spiritual,' Cassius told his biographer Thomas Hauser, 'was when I walked into the Muslim temple in Miami. A man called Brother John was speaking and the first words I heard him say were, "Why are we called negroes? It's the white man's way of taking away our identity."'

Race had shaped his young life. He had grown up against the backdrop of the most divisive civil rights campaigns in modern times. During his impressionable teenage days in high school, he had lived through the lynching of Emmett Till (1955), the Montgomery Bus Boycott (1955–6) and the desegregation of Little Rock High School (1957). Then, as a young man training in Miami, he learned of James Meredith's enrolment at the University of Mississippi (1962) and as he trained to fight Sonny Liston for the heavyweight title, a bomb blast at the 16th Street Baptist Church in Birmingham, Alabama, dominated the television news. By 1963 more than half the southern and border states were navigating the challenges of desegregation in the education system. Woolworths had announced that it would no longer operate segregated counters in its stores and the Howard Johnson company reported that of its 297 restaurants nationwide only 18 were still segregated.

Political change was palpable, but in the churches, recording studios and late-night juke joints, a more subtle revolution was underway, one that paralleled and commented on the story of civil rights but which also reflected the realm of the personal: love, romance, jealousy and betrayal. By the early sixties, the music of the African-American experience – jazz, the blues, gospel, R&B, doo-wop and pop – were starting to come together like tributaries into one great gushing river, becoming a new genre of music which became universally known as soul. It was the music of Cassius's young life, and in those first days of the new music he became one of its most famous observers.

According to his younger brother and fellow boxer, Rudolph 'Rudy' Clay (aka Rahman Ali), the family had grown up in a comparatively sedate town: 'Louisville was segregated, but it was a quiet city, very clean and peaceful.' It was shaped by segregation but with none of the ugly and overt violent racism that one saw in Memphis or Birmingham, Alabama. The brothers grew up in a carnation-pink clapboard house with an overgrown lawn on Louisville's West End, with a caring mother, Odessa, whose Baptist religion shaped their younger days. One magazine feature described Odessa Grady Clay as 'a sweet, pillowy, light-skinned black woman with a freckled face, a gentle demeanour and an easy laugh. Everyone who knew the family in those days saw the kindness of the mother in the boy.' She instilled in Cassius a love for the soaring gospel singers of his infancy and with no great success she tried to cajole her sons into joining local choirs.

His father Cassius Clay Sr was very different. An artist with some talent who painted murals for local churches, his name was often abbreviated to 'Cash'. He was a garrulous man, mostly funding the family income through his job as a commercial sign-writer. 'Odessa gave Cassius Jr. her kindness and generosity,' writer Dave Kindred claimed; 'the father was the son's wellspring of manic energy and sense of theatre.' Although Cassius's father was arrested twice for assault and battery, he was a strict but far from violent man who showed no great interest in boxing. He was known locally as something of a fantasist, occasionally dressing as an Arabian sheik or Mexican peasant, and exuded a showiness that his son adopted. His younger son Rudy once described their father as having 'a showman's spark'. Cash's most notable feature was a thin, black, sabre-styled moustache which earned him the nickname 'Dark Gable', and he was a well-known character in Louisville's black bars, jazz nightclubs and pool halls. It was his father who first ignited Cassius's interest in racial politics – tucked away in the family sideboard was his father's membership of Marcus Garvey's Universal Negro Improvement Association, the first significant black nationalist movement. Cash tried to influence his sons to pursue the road of self-reliance but he was not a fan of boxing and deep down he wanted Cassius to follow in his footsteps, pursuing art, cartography and flamboyance.

Cassius's parents were a coalition of opposites. According to biographer Jonathan Eig, his father was an extrovert, his mother more reserved. 'He was rambunctious; she was genteel. He was tall and lean; she was short and plump. He railed against the injustices of racial discrimination; she smiled and suffered quietly. He was a Methodist who seldom worshipped; she was a Baptist who never missed a Sunday service at Mount Zion Church. He drank and stayed out late; she stayed home and cooked and cleaned. Yet for all their differences, Cash and Odessa both loved to laugh, and when Cash teased her or told his stories or burst into song, Odessa would release herself completely in a beautiful, high-pitched ripple that helped inspire her nickname: 'Bird'. Cassius's mother was a formidable gospel singer, never pushy enough to sing professionally, but one of the Deep South's expansive conservatoire of devoted church singers. His father was more attracted to jazz, jump-blues and anything that aroused the crowds in local nightclubs. So the family, like many before and since, straddled the great divide between the Lord and late-night entertainment: the breeding grounds of soul.

Back home Cassius had attended Central High School, where he was a below-average pupil. One of his early girlfriends, McElvaney Talbott, now an author, journalist and educator, who was in the same class as his brother Rudy Clay, remembers Cassius shadowboxing in the school corridors as he made his way from one class to the next. He was smart but never applied himself in school. 'He was a cutup,' she told *The New York Times*. 'I just remember he was a lot of fun.' His enthusiasm was boundless; each day he would try to beat the school bus, racing along the sidewalk as his peers cheered him on. Cassius was a show-off, a prankster and a hurricane of practical jokes. In a later era, his antics might have been diagnosed as an attention deficit disorder, but the more his hyperactivity was channelled into pummelling the punchbag, training with skipping ropes, and sparring in the ring, the more it was subsumed into ritual and routine. *Sports Illustrated* once referred to him as 'an original, sui generis, a salad of improvisations – unpredictable, witty, mischievous, comical,' whereas his senior-class English teacher, Thelma Lauderdale, described him as a daydreamer. 'Most of the time, when he wasn't paying attention, which was often, he'd be drawing . . . But he never gave me any trouble. Shy and quiet in my class. Meditative.'

Cassius was never a successful school student. Another *New York Times* reporter, Gerald Eskenazi, having been impressed by the young boxer's ingenuity, quick wit and loquaciousness, remembers the sense of disbelief that Cassius failed the low level of attainment necessary to join the US Army. Dumbfounded,

Eskenazi called the principal at Central High School looking for clarity. 'He revealed to me that Ali's IQ was 78. That's right, the most irritating, charming, irascible athlete in America, someone quoted every day, already a world-wide figure, had an IQ that was 22 points lower than the norm,' he wrote. He also disclosed that Cassius had ranked 367th in his high school class of 391 students. The principal explained that it wasn't unusual for young black students to do poorly in a test designed for white kids, and that Ali was someone who got nervous when he had to take a test. (What the principal failed to say was that the students who surpassed him were black too.) It was a nervousness he tried to mask with flashy self-confidence.

At high school, Cassius had been a novice skater, attracted to the rink for teenage friendship more than sport. He was friends with his fellow boxer, the quiet and overshadowed Jimmy Ellis, the son of a local cement labourer turned Baptist minister, who had once beaten Cassius as an amateur. Jimmy Ellis was an easy man to like, not only because of his humility and his tolerance of Cassius's bragging but because of a deeply held spirituality. He was one of many great singers who stayed devoted to gospel and refused to move over to soul music; for much of his young life he was a featured tenor singer in the Riverview Spiritual Singers, one of Louisville's top gospel acts. Ellis eventually signed a recording deal with Atlantic Records.

Another junior high-school friend was the soul singer Buford 'Sonny' Fishback, who throughout much of his career sang under the name Sonny Fisher. His early career captures some of the seismic changes that he and Cassius were exposed to. While still a starry-eyed teenager, Fishback, also an accomplished church singer, began performing in Louisville bars. He dropped out of school and ended up working in local nightclubs alongside older musicians at the Top Hat, Charlie Moore's, the Crosstown Café and the Diamond Horseshoe. Fishback eventually came under the influence of the notorious Don Robey. Some of the major gospel artists of the day were shelving their Christian obduracy and crossing over to more commercial forms – rock 'n' roll, R&B and the secular love songs of doo-wop – and Robey was waiting for them. Robey was a scheming master of the devil's music and the owner of the famous Peacock Nightclub in Houston, Texas. Like many pioneers of the first generation of independent labels, Robey was a vaporous character who was known to cheat his artists by stealing their copyrights and using strong-arm violence on those who resisted. His famous Duke-Peacock group of labels reflected the changes that music was ushering in, and Fishback would end up recording for Peacock in 1967.

Fishback left Louisville when Cassius moved to Miami. He seems to have had a peripatetic career, trying to make his way through the maze of small independent labels that were sprouting up in black neighbourhoods. Like many aspiring soul singers, he moved north to Harlem to be in touching distance of the bigger black-music indies – Atlantic, Wand, Calla and Fat Jack Taylor's Tay-Ster Records – staying there for nearly twenty years while recording for labels that were nominally based in Houston, New Orleans, Chicago and Los Angeles. Most significantly, Fishback recorded for Allen Toussaint's Tou-Sea Records in New Orleans and was the voice behind the pounding underground R&B record 'Heart Breaking Man' (Out-A-Site, 1966). His fitful career in the independent soul scene finally stalled and he was incarcerated for a series of crimes, eventually returning to Louisville to reconnect with the Christian gospel roots he had left behind. He is now a flashily dressed widower, tour co-ordinator and a local civil-rights activist who claims that even from childhood, Cassius was anointed with a special gift, 'the power of words'.

Another one of Cassius's contemporaries was the jazz-soul musician Odell Brown, a virtuoso organist whose band Odell Brown and the Organizers performed locally in Louisville. After being drafted into the military and a short spell in Vietnam, in 1966 Brown's group won *Billboard*'s 'Best New Group' award. He graduated to become a staff musician at the Chess Records Studios in Chicago where he worked with the great Chess school of blues and soul musicians, among them Muddy Waters, Howlin' Wolf, Rotary Connection, Ramsey Lewis and the underground duo Maurice and Mac. Their paths occasionally crossed on the road as Cassius's career soared and Brown was working as the musical director for standout Chicago artists like Curtis Mayfield and Minnie Riperton. Odell Brown was one of soul music's great tragedies. In 1982 he co-wrote 'Sexual Healing' with Marvin Gaye, but a year later, after a period of deep depression, he was living in a skid row hotel in Los Angeles. When the Grammy Awards were on television, he was sitting in a bar watching, despite being nominated four times and winning the category for best R&B instrumental for 'Sexual Healing'. He told a stranger next to him that he'd just won a Grammy and the stranger understandably responded: 'Yeah, right.'

Despite his woeful academic record, Cassius wove many myths around his teenage years. There was the stolen bike that led to a chance meeting in the city's Grace Community Centre, where a local policeman, Joe E. Martin, guided him to the Golden Gloves Championships. There was his gold medal victory at the Rome Olympics, which supposedly ended with Cassius throwing the medal into the Ohio River after he had been refused entry to a white-owned restaurant in Louisville. It was a story that resonated in the era of civil rights and one he told repeatedly, but it has become the subject of much speculation. His brother, Rudy Clay, is adamant the story is true and has always claimed the incident happened near a burger restaurant and that Cassius threw the medal into the torrents of the river. Others have claimed he still had the medal two years later in Miami and often flaunted it to the kids who followed him on the sidewalks of Overtown, and Sam Moore claims he saw him wearing the medal round his neck like a pendant as he strolled the hotel corridors by the entrance to the Knight Beat club. He may well have been mistaken, and the myth of the gold medal has thrived on the back of claim and counter-claim.

Cassius made his professional debut in October 1960 in the Freedom Hall State Fairground, at the local Louisville Arena, where he defeated Tunney Hunsaker on a unanimous points decision. Cassius had been training locally at Bud Bruner's Headline Gym and supposedly arrived at the Fairgrounds in a pink Cadillac, an idea he had copied from the Harlem-based boxing star Sugar Ray Robinson. He had not earned any money to afford a car, let alone a pink Cadillac, and so the most likely explanation is that his equally flamboyant father had hired it for the day. It was one of the first of many showy statements that Cassius would display in the years to come. Bizarrely, his opponent, Hunsaker, was the more newsworthy of the two in the folksy way that attracts attention in local media. He was the Police Chief of the small town of Fayetteville, West Virginia, and had taken leave from his police duties to travel to Louisville. Hunsaker earned a pitiful $300 for the fight while Cassius had negotiated a purse of $2,000.

After the fight Cassius signed an $18,000 contract to be managed by a consortium of eleven Louisville businessmen, a crucial move that secured his credibility in the early years. In contrast to many of his opponents, The Louisville Sponsoring Group were mostly distinguished citizens who, unusually for heavyweight boxing, had no known criminal connections. Ten of the members of the consortium were millionaires, and each invested $28,000 to back Cassius. The deal was signed off by Cassius's lawyer, the formidable Alberta Jones, the first female African-American prosecutor in Louisville, Kentucky. Jones stipulated that 15 per cent of Cassius's winnings should be held in a trust until he turned thirty-five, an enlightened negotiating point in a sport that paid primarily hand-to-mouth, with a horrific track record of impoverished, washed-up and brain-damaged ex-fighters. Jones was a civil-rights advocate who was active in her community as a member of the National Association for the Advancement of Colored People (NAACP) and a prominent figure in the voter-registration movement. She was subsequently appointed to the Louisville Domestic Relations Court, where she was a prosecutor on behalf of abused women. In 1965, Alberta Jones was murdered, beaten and thrown into the Ohio River. It was first assumed that she had drowned but blood was found in her abandoned car near the Sherman Minton Bridge, and witnesses claim they saw three unidentifiable men throwing something or someone into the river. Police reports suggest she may have been dumped from a boat ramp, but her purse was not found until three years later, near the bridge. Many theories exist as to who the killer or killers were, yet the case remains unsolved. The fingerprints of a young seventeen-year-old local boy were found on Jones's car but no substantial case could be built against him and the investigation drove into the sand. Two theories have predominated ever since: that she was killed by a white supremacist group retaliating against her civil rights work, or that she was a victim of a Nation of Islam assassination squad, at a time when the organisation was seeking to exert legal control over Cassius's boxing career. Neither theory has ever come close to being verified.

In his adolescence, long before he left Louisville, Cassius had become fascinated by the myriad of dance craze records that were then sweeping the pop charts. The shifting rhythms and the daft incantations of dance craze sounds chimed with his own gregarious style, and he was known to dance in the school corridors, turning, spinning and side-shuffling to the imagined beat. Dick Sadler, a trainer with the legendary boxer Archie Moore, claims that he spent a long and frustrating rail journey with Cassius, when Chubby Checker's 'The Twist' and Dee Dee Sharp's 'Mashed Potato' were dominating the national teen charts. According to Sadler, Cassius stood up in the train corridor, from Los Angeles to Texas, imitating the dances and singing novelty songs over and over again to the annoyance of fellow passengers. It was a hint at his hyperactive personality and the first signs of his growing fascination with music, a hobby he shared with his brother Rudy. Fame brought them into contact with many prominent stars in the years to come, and ironically, although the young boxer's celebrity outshone almost all of them, he was visibly nervous, intimidated and in awe in their company.

His friend, the photographer Howard Bingham, who worked at the black newspaper the *Los Angeles Sentinel* when he first met Cassius, claimed that he was like a child in the company of R&B singers. He once said, 'Ali loved Fats Domino, Little Richard, Jackie Wilson, Sam Cooke, Lloyd Price, Chubby Checker, all those guys . . . It's like he's still a kid, looking up, and they're the ones on the pedestal.'

His fascination with musicians began long before he was famous. Late in 1958, Cassius was hanging outside Louisville's Top Hat Lounge, on 13th and Walnut Street, owned by a corpulent local entrepreneur, Robert 'Rivers' Williams. Although his mother had banned him from going near the Top Hat, he supposedly broke through a crowd of well-wishers and introduced himself to the R&B star Lloyd Price, whose song 'Stagger Lee', about the adventures of a St Louis pimp, was about to storm the chart. 'Stagger Lee' became one of Cassius's favourite songs, although the shady world it was set in was far from his own loving, relatively settled upbringing.

As Cassius's self-confidence grew, so too did family concerns; his mother was particularly fearful that his flamboyance would lead to trouble, and in the hypocritical way that family discipline often works, his father was worried that some of his own wayward habits would rub off on his son. There was a powerful context to their concerns. When Cassius was only thirteen, the September 1955 edition of the celebrity magazine *Jet* had been delivered to the family home. *Jet* was a compact glossy publication which featured stories of black achievement and profiles of famous African-American stars from the worlds of sport, cinema and R&B music. The comedian Redd Foxx once described *Jet* as 'the negro bible', and for many households, it was a populist window on the emergence of soul music, civil rights and black self-improvement. For this groundbreaking issue of the magazine, which was referenced again and again throughout Cassius's later teen years, *Jet* had broken with their normal diet of celebrity entertainment and carried a truly disturbing set of photographs of the mutilated and disfigured face of Emmett Till, a young Chicago teenager who had been abducted and lynched in late August 1955 during a summer vacation to his grandfather's home near the township of Money, in the Mississippi Delta. Till had been accused of being over-familiar with a local white woman and was then brutalised by her family and friends. Historian David Halberstam has since described the photographs as 'the first great media event of the civil-rights movement' and the Reverend Jesse Jackson called it the movement's 'Big Bang', an issue of savage social injustice that all reasonable people could rally around.

The editorial decision to run with the photograph at the height of the trial of Till's killers was a masterstroke in magazine publishing and repositioned *Jet* as a magazine that took risks, stood on the side of civil rights, and invited parents to discuss lynching and racial violence with their teenage children. Crammed in between features on the top musical acts of the time – Duke Ellington, Louis Armstrong, Nat King Cole and Bo Diddley – were some of the most disturbing documentary photographs ever committed to print. 'Mutilated is the word most often used to describe the face of Emmett Till after his body was hauled out of the Tallahatchie River in Mississippi,' wrote *The New York Times*. 'Inhuman is more like it: melted, bloated, missing an eye, swollen so large that its patch of wiry hair looks like that of a balding old man, not a handsome, brazen 14-year-old boy.'

What resonated most for the Clay family was the horrific curtailment of Till's teenage ambition. Emmett Till was a voluble and excitable member of a doo-wop group in Summit-Argo, Illinois, and had frequently appeared on stage at local amateur nights in Chicago's Cabrini-Green, in amateur contests against Curtis Mayfield and The Alphatones and another local rival, Jerry Butler, in the days before the two singers joined forces with the Northern Jubilee Gospel Singers. Till's body was returned to his parents in Chicago, where, at the grieving mother's request, local morticians were told not to try to disguise the boy's injuries. Simeon Booker, the Washington, DC, bureau chief of *Jet* and *Ebony* magazines, was in Chicago when he heard that the young man had disappeared; he went to Till's home and earned the trust of his mother. Booker accompanied Till's mother to the funeral home, where she overruled objections from the funeral directors and insisted on seeing her son's dead body as it was removed from a rubber bag. His mother claimed that she 'wanted the whole world to see' and so the dead boy was laid to rest in an open casket at A.A. Raynor's undertaker's morgue on Roosevelt Road. In single file, 600,000 people passed the coffin. It was a gruesome awakening that brought rage to the streets of Chicago and gave traumatic impetus to the civil-rights movement.

The Clays were among hundreds of thousands of families troubled by what they read. Petrified that their older son was cheeky and prone to opening his mouth, they sat down with

Cassius, showed him the photographs, and warned him about his conduct in a society still deeply intolerant of self-confident young black men. In *Muhammad Ali: His Life and Times*, Thomas Hauser's definitive biography, Cassius reflected on his own life and the story of Emmett Till. 'When I was growing up, a colored boy named Emmett Till was murdered in Mississippi for whistling at a white woman,' he told the author. 'Emmett Till was the same age as me, and even though they caught the men who did it, nothing happened to them. Things like that went on all the time. And in my own life, there were places I couldn't go, places I couldn't eat. I won a gold medal representing the United States at the Olympic Games, and when I came home to Louisville, I still got treated like a nigger.'

Cassius was not alone. In the early days of both boxing and soul music, there are many recorded examples of the same basic story. Motown boss Berry Gordy, who at the time was in his early twenties and running a failing jazz record shop in Detroit, remembers his father, Pops Gordy, gathering the family round the kitchen table and showing the photographs of Till's disfigured face and the old gin-tire that was tied round his neck. Stevie Wonder, then only five years old and blind from birth, remembers his mother's horror when describing the photograph to him as a young boy. The Reverend C.L. Franklin, the father of Aretha Franklin, delivered several powerful sermons on the story of Emmett Till, and the R&B star Little Willie John also spoke openly of his parents' fear that he would make himself vulnerable when he left his gospel roots and took to the road as a pop singer. He was lectured constantly about his behaviour when in the company of white people.

Miami was not immune to troubled change either. Civil rights legislation was testing the mettle of hotel owners and restaurant owners alike, buffeted by opposition to Florida's long-standing racial segregation policies. As recently as 1939, blacks were not allowed on the streets of Palm Beach unless specifically required by their employment; and along Miami Beach, few blacks could be seen unless they were carrying trays of drinks or bundles of beach towels. Sam Cooke, then one of the most famous singers in popular music, fell victim to discrimination in the early sixties when he was refused living accommodation at the famous Fontainebleau Hotel, despite being contracted to perform in the hotel's ballroom. Like many visiting black artists, he too preferred to stay among his own people in Overtown.

Throughout the fifties and sixties, Florida was tense with confrontation. In 1961, Freedom Riders challenged segregated seating on buses in Tallahassee, and various cities witnessed civil-rights demonstrations in front of segregated theatres throughout 1963. The town of St Augustine would become a flashpoint in 1964, when Martin Luther King lent his high-profile support to end segregation on local beaches.

But resistance to desegregation and defiance of the new civil-rights legislation was entrenched in communities across the southern states. Many states dragged their heels and tied up change using local by-laws, with South Carolina preserving segregation at all levels of the public schools system.

Although it is now associated with the Deep South, the civil-rights movement touched every part of America, including the coastal resorts and beaches of the Florida panhandle and even down to Miami Beach. Back in 1952, fearing local resistance to the idea of integrated beaches, the Fort Lauderdale Hotel Association supported the campaign for a segregated African-American recreational beach in Florida, when the only existing 'colored beach' was bought up by developers. As a compromise, a strip of land in the Everglades was set aside to build a new segregated beach. It was an attempt to solve a problem but it had the unintended consequence of provoking even more trouble. There was no road to the isolated beach, which could only be reached by ferry. Once there, the sands had no facilities, no shelter and no toilets. The failures aggravated an increasingly tense issue and in October 1955 one hundred African-Americans from across Florida organised themselves. They drove in a flotilla of cars to the segregated Lido beach in Sarasota to stage a 'wade-in', in which people demonstrated by wading in the waters, carrying banners and singing gospel songs, in defiance of local by-laws.

On Easter Sunday, 24 April 1960, a local physician, Dr Gilbert Mason, led more than 120 people walking in single file onto beaches along a length of shoreline at Biloxi, Mississippi, a coastal town equidistant between New Orleans and Mobile, Alabama. The sands were segregated by local statute and by extended property rights. Blacks were forbidden from lying on the beach or swimming in the waters of the Gulf of Mexico. The silent protest of 'waders' was met by a vigilante mob of white men armed with clubs, brass knuckles and bricks. The violence that ensued was shocking, and the events became known locally as 'Bloody Sunday'. Although the Biloxi waders are now a short paragraph in the history of civil rights, their stance caught the imagination of movement leaders, and demonstrations spread southwards through Florida's tourist resorts and on down into Miami.

By the time Cassius had settled in Overtown, beach demonstrations were a recurring phenomenon. In September 1960, the NAACP filed a US federal lawsuit arguing that Miami's black residents should be allowed to use public swimming facilities across the city. There were several small victories but de facto segregation persisted and facility owners continued to discriminate against visiting African-American clients. Even the famous photographs of Cassius boxing underwater in the swimming pool of the blacks-only Sir John Hotel had been taken at the height of disputes about swimming pool segregation.

The Florida wade-ins would soon reach their emotional high point in 1964, in a summer-long campaign to desegregate St Augustine beach, south of Jacksonville. At the first demonstration white beachgoers barred the waders from reaching the waters by blockading the shore. The next day, African-American protestors, backed by the presence of Martin Luther King, entered the Monson Motor Lodge to swim in its segregated pool. The hotel manager poured a bottle of acid into the water and the swimmers were arrested, but images of the injustice began to circulate around the world, infuriating many as a symbol of 'barbaric racism'. The local Grand Jury asked King to leave St Augustine. The following week, police arrested twenty-two waders at the St Augustine beach. Then, three days later, in the most violent confrontations, white racists fortified by an armed police presence attacked the demonstrators during the day and in the evening a growing mob of 500 white residents continued the attack. Nineteen demonstrators were hospitalised.

George Wallace's campaign to become Governor of Alabama personified the resistance to civil rights. Once dismissed as the most dangerous racist in America, Wallace personified a populist resistance to change. In his inaugural speech on 14 January 1963, he defiantly proclaimed: 'In the name of the greatest people that have ever trod this earth, I draw the line in the dust and toss the gauntlet before the feet of tyranny, and I say "segregation now, segregation tomorrow, and segregation forever." Let us send this message back to Washington, that from this day we are standing up, and the heel of tyranny does not fit the neck of an upright man.'

The same day in Washington, President Kennedy delivered his State of the Union Address announcing a series of tax reductions. He had only recently returned from his Miami trip. If nothing else, Kennedy's speech was rich in poetic metaphor: 'My friends: I close on a note of hope,' he told Congress. 'We are not lulled by the momentary calm of the sea or the somewhat clearer skies above. We know the turbulence that lies below, and the storms that are beyond the horizon this year . . . For 175 years we have sailed with those winds at our back, and with the tides of human freedom in our favour. We steer our ship with hope, as Thomas Jefferson said, "leaving Fear astern".'

As soon as he settled in Overtown, Cassius began to shape his daily routines. An early morning run from the Sir John took him across MacArthur Causeway towards the 5th Street Gym on Miami Beach. The first phase of his morning training regime was designed to wake him up, to loosen up and to save on cab fares from Overtown. Cassius usually jogged before sunrise, pausing for a rest at a halfway vantage point, where he had a near-perfect view of the man-made Venetian Islands below. Inexperienced in the ways of luxury, he gazed down on the aquamarine pools and varnished jetties of the wealthy. He had never seen such a picturesque concentration of suspicious dollars, where crime, faded glamour and paranoid anti-communism sat incongruously side by side. Miami's stifling archipelagos were where Al Capone died of syphilis surrounded by his family and where the New York record mogul and vinyl crook Morris Levy, the owner of Roulette Records, hid out in the winter months. Turning around, Cassius could look south to Key Biscayne. Hazy in the distance was the self-styled 'White House by the Beach' on Harbor Drive, where President Richard Nixon would purchase his Miami home. Further south in the hazy distance was the luxury apartment at Governor's Lodge on Sunrise Drive, where the Texas loan shark and car insurance millionaire Jacques Mossler was bludgeoned to death and wrapped in a blanket, the victim of a murder stoked by greed, sex and incest. But more important to the dreamer inside Cassius's mind was the 16-room rental villa that Sonny Liston and Joe Louis hired when they stayed in Miami. A Miami Police Department patrol car sat ominously outside, not to protect Liston and Louis but to calm the nerves of local residents spooked by the arrival of such unlikely and intimidating neighbours.

Miami was now his home, and Cassius's first two fights there brought him face to face with the dark underbelly of the city's criminal underworld. Two days after Christmas, on 27 December 1960, he knocked out Herb 'Bowlegs' Siler, on the undercard of a Willie Pastrano bout at the Miami Beach Auditorium. Siler was jailed in 1972 for manslaughter and served a seven-year stretch, although in later life became a devout Christian and successful businessman. A month later, in January 1961, on his nineteenth birthday, Cassius knocked out another Miami hard man, Tony Esperti, an enforcer for the Miami Beach mob and Liston sparring partner with multiple arrests for burglary, assault, extortion and, eventually, murder. Although 'Big Tony' hung out at the 5th Street Gym, he was seriously out of shape and strapped for cash when he agreed to fight Cassius. The fight ended in a technical knockout (TKO) in the third round when the referee intervened as blood streamed down into Esperti's eye and he faced serious injury. It was almost certainly a mismatch set up to bolster Cassius's fight record. When his boxing career ended, Esperti devoted himself to criminality and, according to the Miami Herald, was arrested eleven times for assault and battery. On Halloween, in 1967, Esperti arrived at the Place for Steak restaurant on the 79th Street Causeway in North Bay Village and was assassinated in a mob hit by Thomas 'The Enforcer' Altamura, a member of the Gambino crime family. The coroner described it as the perfect execution – a single lethal bullet to the brain.

A month later, in his third Miami fight, Cassius was scheduled to fight Willie 'Shorty' Gullatt but when he failed to show up the promoters drafted in a stand-in boxer, 'Sweet' Jim Robinson, a washed-up pro and failed soul singer from Overtown. Robinson was paid cash in hand to take a beating and was summarily dispatched in 94 seconds only to drift back into the pool halls of Overtown and then into homeless anonymity.

Curiously, in a city more synonymous with beaches and lounge bar music, one of the unforeseen drivers of black music was America's growing transport systems. Henry Flagler, the founder of the giant conglomerate Standard Oil, had pioneered what was to become the Florida East Coast Railway Company. By 1896, it stretched south from Jacksonville, through the coastal resort of St Augustine and down through Miami to Biscayne Bay, then the largest and most accessible harbour on Florida's east coast. Many black people came to work on railway construction and were consigned to cramped living quarters in a highly segregated community known colloquially as 'Colored Town'.

According to local journalist Paul George of the *Biscayne Times*, the residents were 'victimized by segregation and discrimination, and policed by a white force with "Deep South" mentalities. Colored Town was characterized, on the one hand, by crime, congestion, and disease, but on the other by a bustling business community, a small cadre of professionals, fraternal orders, civic and business organizations, a number of entertainment offerings, and numerous churches.' It was this neighbourhood, rich in late-night entertainment, that eventually became known as Overtown, and immigrants arriving from Cuba, Haiti, Jamaica, Trinidad and Tobago, Barbados and the segregated southern states gave the neighbourhood a unique, almost Caribbean character.

By the early sixties, transportation had moved forward again, and Miami like many American cities became a slave to the car.

A massive road construction project was underway and the skeletons of a new era stretched out like concrete bones high in the skies above downtown. In 1956, Congress had passed the Federal-Aid Highway Act that kick-started a national road-building boom. Plans were laid to facilitate the westward expansion of the Miami Business District, which meant routing Interstate 95 through Overtown and the inner city's old ghetto neighbourhoods, which now had a population of over 34,000 residents. It was a decision tense with racial connotations. Miami's network of banks, high-rise offices and downtown condominiums were to be developed at the expense of the city's poorest neighbourhoods. Similar strategies were developed elsewhere too. In 1959, construction had begun on the $54 million Chrysler Freeway in Detroit, wrecking the old Hastings Street, the beating heart of Detroit R&B, and the city's oldest black residential district. Families were scattered to new projects and inner-city ghettos, among them the Franklin family, whose daughter Aretha was already a child prodigy on the national gospel circuit. In Las Vegas, most blacks lived on the city's west side behind what was called the 'concrete curtain', the network of roads and railway underpasses that separated the area from the downtown business district.

A strange segregation was separating old neighbourhoods from new dreams. While Detroit's Black Bottom slums disappeared, Overtown somehow survived, hemmed in by freeways, overpasses and intersections, a clustered ghetto beneath an umbrella of concrete.

Never as globally famous as Motown or as brutally tragic as Memphis, Overtown was one of soul music's hidden heartlands, a place where a new era in music was emerging. Miami's soul clubs were dotted along the main streets of Overtown – some legal and some dashing undercover when the police patrols arrived.

The king of them all was the Knight Beat. It was owned by one of Cassius's many local associates, a remarkable man and amateur social historian called Clyde 'The Glass' Killens, a ghetto entrepreneur and pool-hall owner, who had earned his nickname because of his limitless passion for whisky and soda. Killens prowled Overtown's nightlife with a tumbler of Scotch seemingly stuck to his hand, making the bogus claim that he was a descendant of the original Lord Calvert, the distant aristocrat who had been an early coloniser of America.

Killens was born in Valdosta, Georgia. He left home at fifteen and moved to Miami to run a gasoline station, which was little more than a front for selling moonshine liquor. For most of his life he lived at NW 2nd Avenue and 11th Street in the heart of Overtown, and remained loyal to his community and its many attractions for decades. Killens was neither a criminal nor a gangster, but he was part of soul music's shady demi-monde, who by his own admission had to work in a society that was intolerant of his music and suspicious of his venues. So he bent the law and eked out an existence as a soul music promoter at a time when the music was underground, forbidden and yet to explode into life. Killens became something of a local bard in Overtown. According to Sharony Andrews, a staff writer at the *Miami Herald*, 'He can tell you about when the tracks were just being laid for streetcars to go through Overtown, about being one of the first blacks to vote in the 1920s, about getting air conditioners in the old Colored Town theaters, about the hurricane of 1926 that ripped through the houses of affluent whites in Miami Beach but couldn't beat down the shotgun shacks of Overtown.'

Killens was a curly-haired ball of enthusiasm who became a magnet for talent. There was Willie Hale, whose protruding front teeth bequeathed him the nickname 'Little Beaver', and there was Paul Kelly and his backing group The Spades hustling for a contract with anyone who would listen. Kelly enjoyed some success with a timeless soul record 'Chills And Fever' (Lloyd, 1965) and a few years later recorded one of the most controversial records in the history of sixties soul, 'Stealing In The Name Of The Lord' (Happy Tiger, 1970) – a hugely divisive record that spoke out against corrupt religion and which some have claimed all but ended Kelly's career. Cassius liked his garrulous style and plagued him for details of how the old Chitlin' Circuit of R&B shows worked economically. Quietly and with increasing calculation he was storing up tales of how business worked and how to ensure he was paid in line with his talent.

By 1962, Clyde Killens had turned O-Town into Miami's mini-Harlem, and owned a string of nightclubs across the ghetto, among them the Knight Beat, Harlem Square, the Island Club and Mary Elizabeth's Hotel Fiesta Club. He had a trusted reputation on the often distrusted live performance circuit and this came with the ability to book the best: Mary Wells, James Brown, Aretha Franklin, Major Lance, Garnett Mimms, Dionne Warwick, Jackie Wilson, Patti LaBelle and the Bluebelles and Sammy Davis Jr all performed regularly in Overtown, many of them after a show at whites-only stages in Miami Beach. Killens would arrange for them to be driven across the Bay to play Overtown into the small hours for a cash lump sum that would never be reported to the tax authorities.

According to a memoriam in the *Miami Herald*, 'Killens's genius was recognizing that it took more than big names to keep audiences happy. On "Ladies Night", he gave out free panty hose and dresses. Sunday's door prizes were grocery carts filled high with offerings like neck bones and cans of black-eyed peas. His "Night in Nassau" was big with South Florida's Bahamian population; patrons brought native dishes like stewed conch, conch salad, conch fritters, pigeon peas and rice and fried fish.'

Cassius's room at the Sir John was on the ground floor, not far from the entrance to the Knight Beat, facing a shimmering azure swimming pool with cracked tiles and creaking diving boards. Months later, he would move with Rudy to a cramped grey-cinder apartment on NW 7th Avenue near Alapattah, called the Alexander Apartments, which was next door to his favourite eatery, the Famous Chef restaurant. But he came back to the Sir John. It was only when his success soared in 1963 that Cassius and Rudy bought a small family house at 4610 Northwest 15th Street in Liberty City, where they lived together with a teenage runaway and keen welterweight boxer, Grady Ponder from Sylvania Georgia, whom Cassius took pity on when he arrived homeless and broke at Miami's Greyhound bus station.

The swimming pool at the Sir John became a curiously important landmark in the career of the young boxer. It was by the pool that he met visiting singers like the razor-sharp Jackie Wilson who had been forced to stay in Overtown after being refused entry at the glamorous beach hotels. He was shaping his own energetic style with hits like 'Baby Workout' (Brunswick, 1963) and 'Shake, Shake, Shake' (Brunswick, 1963), offering a slick, new dimension to black music which still had its feet firmly planted in traditional rock 'n' roll. This new style was increasingly referred to as 'uptown', a term which variously referred to the Harlem district of New York and the Uptown Theater in Philadelphia. It was by the pool in February 1963 that Cassius met his first real girlfriend, the Philadelphia soul singer Dee Dee Sharp, already a seasoned performer and yet still only nineteen years old. She was in residency at the Knight Beat, and he was sharing a room with his brother, sleeping away the afternoons after intensive morning training sessions at the 5th Street Gym. Since his teenage days several women had been attracted to Cassius's extrovert personality but some were turned off by his breath. He had developed a training technique of drinking fresh water and crushed garlic, ostensibly to control his blood pressure, but it was not his most attractive habit. Nonetheless, Dee Dee Sharp fell briefly in love with him and their relationship continued off and on throughout the dramatic months to come. Sharp has since claimed they had agreed to marry, but it never happened, and when Cassius did marry it was to another young woman he met in Miami, a cocktail waitress called Sonji Roi, who also had ambitions to forge a career as a soul singer. Using Cassius's growing fame as collateral, she eventually released three records later in the sixties, one for the Pittsburgh indie American Music Makers, and another two on her personal label Sonjee Records.

For three intermittent months in 1963, Cassius and Dee Dee hung out at their hotel with DJ Butterball from Miami's tiny AM radio station WMBM, one of an irrepressible generation of men who did much to shape and promote soul music in its infant days. DJ Milton 'Butterball' Smith – aka 'Mrs Smith's 300 pound boy' – was a Miami institution and one of a generation of radio broad-casters who were transforming musical taste. A Korean war veteran, who began playing records in the days of 78rpm, he pioneered black music on air, championing the new era of independent soul and connecting the music to civil-rights and anti-poverty campaigns.

Using his cackling laugh and larger-than-life personality as a broadcasting gimmick, 'Butterball' originally came to prominence at the fledgling WFEC radio station under the name 'Fat Daddy' and was drawn to Cassius through a love of boxing. They often talked together by the hotel pool, verbally jousting, swapping indiscretions and talking about sport and music. According to Butterball's inventive memory he claims to have shadow-boxed with Cassius to promote a James Brown concert.

Since his teenage days back home in Louisville, Cassius had cultivated an interest in local radio and was a fan of the irrepressible Jack 'The Rapper' Gibson, the madcap maven of Radio Station WLOU, in Louisville. It was Jack Gibson who kindled Cassius's teenage love of comic rhyming couplets and primitive rap. Gibson also played the role of 'Jack the Jockey', a larger-than-life persona who came to life during the Kentucky Derby, dressed in jockey silks and a riding helmet and carrying a comedy whip. Gibson was an unaccredited character in the formation of Cassius's cartoon personality. Born in Chicago, Gibson's first experience on the crackling radios of the post-war era was as an actor; he played supporting roles in short radio dramas where his skin colour was an irrelevance in the segregated days of popular entertainment. He subsequently moved south to Atlanta where he broadcast for a local radio station from a makeshift studio above the offices of the Southern Christian Leadership Conference (SCLC), the civil-rights organisation led by Martin Luther King. Gibson became a prominent political figure in the campaign to secure improved pay and conditions for black DJs as the influence of R&B spread.

In his book *Redemption Song*, the author Mike Marqusee saw in Cassius the qualities of a new media age, one in which radio and television were increasingly shaping public attitudes. 'Of course, the swagger, the bragging, the manic competitive zeal had always been part of the subculture of big-time sports; but it was Cassius Clay who brought those qualities out of hiding and fashioned them into a saleable image. His egotism was bold and risky, but above all playful, and always softened by the undercurrent of self mockery.' It was, according to Marqusee, 'a playground foolery orchestrated for the modern media'. Cassius had grown up with the urban radio stars of the fifties, and drew heavily on their rhyming and self-aggrandising style. He was self-evidently a boxer and the product of the Columbia Gym in Louisville but his personality was shaped by black radio as much as by boxing. As he travelled America, promoting his fights and psychologically stalking his opponents, Cassius came to know the very best black broadcasters of the era – there was Jack Gibson and Larry Dean (who called himself 'Long, tall, lean, lanky Larry Dean') from his childhood in Louisville; DJ Butterball from his Miami days; and Shelley the Playboy, Johnny Jive and 'Tall Paul' Dudley White from Birmingham, Alabama. Chicago was the home-base of Pervis Spann, Herb Kent ('the cool gent') and the formidable E. Rodney Jones, an early exponent of funk and rap, who broadcast for WVON, the self-styled Voice of the Negro. There was Spider Burks in St Louis, the Magnificent Montague in Los Angeles (who coined the phrase 'Burn, baby! Burn!') and the Ace from Outer Space, Douglas 'Jocko' Henderson, who managed to outdo Cassius's theatricality when he appeared nightly in a kitsch astronaut's outfit at the Apollo Theater in Harlem. The irrepressible 'Frantic Ernie' Durham, who had a master's degree in journalism from New York University, broadcast on WJLB in Detroit from a custom-built studio in the Gold Room of Motown's local playground, a nightclub called the 20 Grand.

Every sizable urban area had an R&B radio station that brought black music to teenage homes, creating local stars who moved effortlessly from nightclubs to broadcasting. What they shared with Cassius was a flashy playfulness, comic arrogance and a relish for black dance music as it progressed from R&B to soul. In his leisure time, Cassius often pretended to be a DJ and stored up rhyming couplets from the radio to be used in his own life as he boasted his way up the rankings; at midday, when the sun was at its hottest, he sometimes took to the darkened stage of the Knight Beat to play the role of in-house MC. In March 1963, after his fight with Doug Jones, his management team lived up to a promise and bought the young boxer a tomato-red Cadillac Eldorado – 'Big Red' – which was fitted with a record player, sold under the brand name Norelco. The device could take a single 45 slid into its thin gaping mouth.

As Cassius drove, he cheerily rapped his own introductions to the latest soul records, while his loyal brother Rudy acted as the technician, feeding the next single into the Norelco.

Official biographies of the rise of Muhammad Ali frequently cite the influence of the professional wrestler George Wagner from Butte, Nebraska, whom Cassius met in a radio studio in June 1961, the week before Cassius's fight with the Hawaiian heavyweight Duke 'Kolo' Sabedong in Las Vegas. By his own admission, Cassius was shy by comparison with the outrageous 'Gorgeous George', who threw all manner of insults at his opponents. George's pantomime claims to be 'The Greatest' was a masterclass in sporting narcissism. He entered the ring in frilly purple attire accompanied by a valet, to the sound of Elgar's 'Pomp And Circumstance'. Cassius was so impressed, he bought tickets to see Gorgeous George perform in a Las Vegas hotel later that week and something clicked. If he could combine the rhyming boasts of the radio DJs and then add Gorgeous George's claims to greatness, he would attract attention in ways that no boxer had done before. He could popularise the old ghetto game of the 'dozens' – a game, or rather a subcultural form, common in the backstreets of ghetto America and in the hardened prison yards of the post-war era. While Cassius was never jailed, nor even remotely the product of a deprived home life, like most teenagers he played the dozens. As his reputation soared, many of his boasts were shamelessly stolen from street talk: 'I'm so mean, I make medicine sick'; 'I should be a postage stamp. That's the only way I'll ever get licked'; 'If you even dream of beating me you'd better wake up and apologise'; and 'I am the astronaut of boxing. Joe Louis and Dempsey were just jet pilots. I'm in a world of my own.' They were slick, self-aggrandising and clearly tongue-in-cheek. He was the soul DJ lost to radio but heaven-sent to boxing promoters.

In July 1961, Cassius defeated Alonzo Johnson, an orthodox heavyweight from Aberdeen, Mississippi, at a bout in Louisville's Kentucky Fair and Exposition Center. He won narrowly on points, and with this fight he racked up eight successive heavyweight victories. It was the first national television coverage of one of

Cassius's fights and the first significant clue that the media were waking up to his potential. Slowly but surely, Cassius was emerging on national radar. *Life* magazine and *Sports Illustrated* both commissioned a Miami freelance photographer called Flip Schulke to photograph Cassius at the 5th Street Gym. Schulke struck up a good relationship with Cassius and took him shopping to Burdines, the department store on Flagler Street, where Cassius tried on shirts, a jacket and smart shoes. The manager took the photographer aside and despite Schulke's protestations told him that the store did not allow 'Negroes' to try on clothing. Schulke, who had travelled extensively across the states of the Deep South as a photographer with Martin Luther King's Southern Christian Leadership Conference (SCLC) and was accustomed to stories of segregation, was taken aback by the store's policy of discrimination in a major US city. He argued vociferously with the manager, informing him that the boy he was excluding from the premises was an Olympic gold medallist. Cassius calmed him down and guided him out on to Flagler Street and they returned to Overtown to buy the clothes.

The two men talked excitedly about photography, and Cassius asked what kind of photograph would get him onto the cover of *Sports Illustrated*. Schulke described a photo session he had recently completed that had been shot underwater. Without skipping a beat, Cassius told him that he trained underwater every morning in the pool at the Sir John. It was a complete fabrication improvised on the spot but the idea excited Schulke and he rang round his editors to place the photographs. *Sports Illustrated* declined and asked for more conventional gym shots, but *Life* responded positively and gave Schulke enough encouragement for him to drive a car loaded with scuba-diving equipment, underwater cameras and diving weights to the Sir John swimming pool for what turned out to be a landmark moment in boxing history. Cassius, who could not swim and had never trained underwater, took to the pool, punching furious uppercuts through the water. The photographs, now known as 'The Arc of Bubbles', featured in a spread in *Life* magazine and became classics of sports photography – and the beginning of Cassius's realisation that photography was a key to visibility in America's burgeoning magazine industry. He began to befriend photographers as if they held a special power and in the years to come became the most photographed sporting personality ever.

What was unique about Cassius was his instinctive feel for publicity and his prescient understanding of how the media worked. He once explained his approach to the press to a *Miami News* reporter. 'Now take those Associated Press reporters,' he explained, showing a grasp of syndication, 'I always talk to them. Some of them send to thirty-eight papers. *Ebony* and *Jet* come around; I see them. Negroes want to know about me . . . now take *Time* . . . that magazine goes to intelligent people. People who don't go to fights much. They read about me and want to go to fights. They talk about me. And your paper. Cover all of Miami and Florida. Lots of people down there . . . networks come around. I'm glad to see them. Only ones I had to send away is those little radio stations that put you on at 4.30 in the afternoon and nobody's listening.'

Cassius's fights were meticulously stage-managed to progress his name up the heavyweight rankings. Trainer Dundee, a wily operator, rarely risked the prospect of a damaging defeat or a major career setback and so opponents were diligently screened and fights chosen with caution. In February 1962, Cassius fought Don Warner, a heavyweight from North Philadelphia, who became the sparring partner of Cassius's future rival Joe Frazier. Fight magazines led with the headline 'Watch Out, Cassius, A Knockout Specialist Is On His Way', a response to Warner's pre-fight hype that he had a way of defeating the rising star. Some boxing aficionados were already convinced that Dundee was shielding Cassius from the real heavy hitters. In the days before the fight at the Miami Auditorium, Cassius had complained about toothache and Warner boasted that he would deliver a punch that would remove the sore tooth. It proved to be an empty boast. Despite an energetic first round, in which Warner looked briefly to have the upper hand, he faded badly and Cassius won through a TKO after the referee stopped the fight in the fourth round.

Virtually unknown beyond hardcore fight fans, many of Cassius's famous characteristics were by now falling into place. A UPI wire report had previewed the fight two days previously. 'Cocky Cassius Clay, who calls himself "the greatest", promised Tuesday to dispose of Don Warner in five rounds or less. "So I can go on to bigger things." Former Olympic champion Clay turned 20 a month ago and has only 11 months left to live up to his vow to be champion by the time he's 21. "This fight won't go more than five rounds . . . He's just got to fall, and that's all there is to it. I have to go on to bigger things."' Cassius was already predicting when his opponents would fall, a piece of promotional shtick that made him a dream character for magazines, newspapers and the emergent television networks. (Later, Warner also converted to Islam; he became known as Hasan Muhammad. He briefly fell under suspicion in Joe Frazier's training camp, who thought he was spying and feeding information back to Cassius.)

Predicting the outcome of fights had become a media-friendly stunt. In November 1961, before a hometown crowd in Louisville, Cassius had defeated the German heavyweight Willi Besmanoff. Before the fight, he told a TV interviewer, 'I'm embarrassed to get in the ring with this unrated duck. I'm ready for top contenders like Floyd Patterson and Sonny Liston. Besmanoff must fall in seven!' Enraged by the prediction, Besmanoff came at Cassius with furious lunges, but his overreaction played to the young fighter's arrogant style. Clay danced around him and ridiculed the German for six rounds, then knocked him out in the seventh, making good on his prediction. The press loved it and cajoled Cassius to deliver more fantastical predictions. In May 1962, Cassius travelled north to New York's famous St Nicholas Arena to fight Billy Daniels, an Air Force veteran who now owned a barber's shop in Brooklyn. The St Nick, which was nicknamed 'The Cradle of Champions', was a world-famous arena but by now was on its last legs, having hosted over 30,000 professional fights and provided a stage for Jack Johnson, Rocky Graziano, Kid Chocolate and Floyd Patterson. It closed nine days after Cassius's victory there, a direct victim of the rising popularity of domestic television. ABC bought the building and converted it into a TV studio, a development in the story of boxing and the media that fortuitously came just as Cassius's fame exploded.

His instinctive ability to self-promote brought journalists, photographers and eventually television crews streaming to the 5th Street Gym, and others periodically trailed him to Overtown, where Cassius interrogated their plans and made his own sometimes preposterous suggestions. The photographs and short clips that have survived from Cassius's early years are remarkable in both their range and theatricality. Photographer Lee Betterman captured him inside a boxing ring in a bow tie and tuxedo as if he was ready to attend a black-tie dinner; the *Life* and *Vanity Fair* photographer Steve Shapiro captured Cassius shadowboxing in the family home in Louisville and relaxing on a settee, playing Monopoly; Marvin Lichtner's images are more redolent of classic sports photography, capturing close-ups of Cassius sparring in his Everlast head guard; and Bob Sandberg of *Look* magazine captured charming images of Cassius performing magic tricks for local youngsters.

Of all the many perspectives that history has given us of Cassius's unique life, little is made of his obsession with close-up magic and simple tricks that would delight onlookers. James Drake, a staff photographer at *Time/Life*, took Cassius to a secluded Catholic campus at Nazareth College in his native Louisville to meet one of his greatest fans, Sister Ellen James Huff. The reunion was a photographer's dream, the nuns resplendent in traditional black-and-white robes and Cassius effervescent, loving the contrivance of the moment. Sister Ellen had once hired Cassius as a library cleaner to supplement his lowly income as a trainee boxer and said she liked his 'zest'. Years after she found him sleeping on one of the long tables in the library, she put a sign up that read: 'Cassius Slept Here'. She had been one of the first people he showed his Olympic gold medal to and the pair remained lifelong friends.

Cassius's cleverly cultivated friendships with photographers have stood the test of time. The Scottish photographer Harry Benson took The Beatles to the 5th Street Gym in 1964 and invited Cassius to pose with the group, and then participate in a cod-punching trick, flooring all of The Beatles in a row. Few photographs can lay as strong a claim to capturing stardom in the sixties quite so memorably as this one. Then, in April 1968, there was the photograph that dominated the front page of *Esquire*, titled 'The Passion of Muhammad Ali': Carl Fischer's stark and provocative take on the martyrdom of Saint Sebastian, in which the boxer stands with five bloodstained arrows embedded in his naked chest. No one did more to assist photographers than Cassius.

Understandably, it was African-American photographers who got closest to him. The grandfather of African-American photography, Gordon Parks Sr, perfected a portfolio that stretched through rural poverty, civil rights, Harlem jazz and ultimately Black Power. He took the greatest pure portrait of Cassius, drenched in sweat and stripped of the veneer of play-acting. But the man who got closest was his confidant Howard Bingham, who met him when he was a photography student in Los Angeles, and then joined the growing entourage around the young boxer. Feeding off Cassius's instinctive love of attention and fame, Bingham was encouraged to compose photographs that stood apart from the familiar punchbag and gym shots. He set up a remarkable image in which Cassius is training in the 5th Street Gym accompanied by a concert violinist. The Brylcreemed violinist carefully strokes his bow as Cassius skips furiously beside him. Behind them both are the decaying men's room and boxing posters promoting fights of the era, among them the Cuban champions who trained alongside the young contender.

But most telling of all, and those that have been pored over most in the years since, are Bingham's historically important shots of Cassius in casual conversation with his mentor, the Black Muslim radical Malcolm X.

Back in Miami, the swimming pool at the Sir John became Cassius's afternoon meeting place. He ran a tab at the Famous Chef restaurant where he ate every day and spent his afternoons resting by the pool or sleeping in his dark room, blinds drawn to fend off the sun. Then, as the sun faded, his cramped hotel room filled up with visitors who came to shoot the breeze and talk boxing or music. When their talk inevitably turned to civil rights, such as police brutality in Birmingham, or the gruesome murder of Emmett Till, Clyde Killens took a chilling pleasure in trumping every story of racial violence. One of the reasons that the teenage Killens had moved to Miami from his birthplace in Valdosta, Georgia, was the social disruption brought about by a local lynching. He never tired of recounting the saga of thirty-three-year-old Mary Turner who was eight months pregnant at the time of her murder. Turner had stood up to a local mob that had murdered her husband in a lynching rampage the previous day and threatened to pursue them in court. Local area newspapers which barely travelled beyond the locality in Lowndes County, described her threats as 'unwise remarks' and claimed that her threat of legal recourse had enraged locals. Mary Turner fled but was caught and taken to a place called Folsom's Bridge, where she was hung by her ankles from a tree and had gasoline poured over her. At the height of the frenzied attack, her stomach was opened with a field knife and her unborn child dropped to the ground, where it was reportedly crushed. Turner's body was riddled with bullet wounds and she was buried with the remains of her dead child; the site was marked with a whisky bottle with a cigar butt stuffed in its neck. These atrocities – seen, heard about, or, in the case of Emmett Till, turned into a major scandal in the black press – were buried in the shallow grave of the mind, to be remembered and resented for decades yet to come.

Cassius was permanently on Clyde Killens' guest list at the Knight Beat. He was a familiar figure to staff and visitors, and ingratiated himself with the singers, pimps and well-wishers amid the tantalising nightlife. But Cassius's self-denial was extraordinary. Despite the myriad vices surrounding him, Cassius lived a monastic existence. He once told the *Sports Illustrated* writer Houston Horn that he had to fight vigorously against temptation. 'The hardest part of the training is the loneliness,' he confided. 'I just sit there like a little animal in a box at night. I can't go out on the streets and mix with folks out there 'cause they wouldn't be out there if they were up to any good. I can't do nothing except sit. If it weren't for Angelo I'd go home. Here I am, surrounded by showgirls, whiskey and nobody watching me. All this temptation and me trying to train to be a boxer. It's something to think about.' By his own admission, Cassius would drift to sleep listening to the music nearby and was up early enough to see the last drunken stragglers as they headed home in the rising sun. He would then jog the few miles to the 5th Street Gym to train with the Cubans and subsequently with his two handpicked sparring partners, Cody Jones from Detroit and 'Dangerous' Dave Bailey from Philadelphia.

The Knight Beat was the jewel in Clyde Killens' crown and America's soul music terminus. It was the last stop on the Chitlin' Circuit, the southernmost tip of the segregated itinerary of old theatres, juke joints and speakeasies that took blues, swing and R&B artists on tour, down the curved spine of eastern America from the Regal Theater in Chicago, to the Flame Show Bar in Detroit, the legendary Apollo in Harlem, the Uptown in Philadelphia, the Howard in Washington, DC, the W.C. Handy Theatre in Memphis's Orange Mound and then the stop before Florida – the Bronze Peacock in Atlanta. It was in these venues that soul music was forged: rough, untutored and gasping for attention.

In part because of its geographical location, Miami is a unique city with its own idiosyncratic place in the history of soul music. It had an unrivalled winter-beach culture which attracted musicians to perform in clubs, bars and hotel restaurants. By the early sixties, the many threads that embroidered soul music were already in evidence – the raucous juke-joint anthems of rhythm and blues, the jagged journeys of jazz, the spiritual choruses of church music and the newly popular dance craze songs that radio had blared into teenage homes were already widely known in African-American communities.

Cassius had grown up an inveterate record collector who liked to show off his dance moves in the school corridors and at the local skating rink back home in Louisville. But the soul music he had come to relish was not just a musical synthesis, it was a product of its times and of social change – the migration north from the racially intolerant southern states, the bustling ghettos of the big northern cities, the network of bars and nightclubs that lit up the city strips, and the local entrepreneurs, some criminal and others deeply community-conscious, who determinedly built a success out of themselves, their families and their acts. Arching out across the airwaves and broadcasting the message and the music were the doyens of sixties soul, the radio DJs who spoke in tantalising tongues to send dispatches from the front line to their streetwise troops.

Lying around daydreaming in her untidy bedroom in Overtown's James E. Scott Projects was a girl named Bessie 'Betty' Wright. Her family was already a prominent force in local gospel competitions and in a number of different guises performed on the undercard at the Knight Beat. Her older brother Philip was a guitarist with Killens' in-house calypso band and her sister Jeanette was a vocalist with the underground Miami group The Twans, whose Motownesque song 'I Can't See Him Again' (Dade, 1965) became one of sixties soul's all-time obscure classics.

Betty Wright had grown up on the streets of Overtown, a stone's throw from Cassius's hotel room, and was discovered at thirteen years old in Johnny's Records, a tiny vinyl store in Liberty City owned by Johnny Pearsall and his wife, the soul singer Helene Smith. Pearsall was a graduate of Florida A&M University. He regularly employed members of the university's famed marching band as backing musicians and then trawled the clubs of ghetto Miami for lead singers. At the rear of the store were the offices and makeshift recording studios of Deep City Records, one of Miami's pioneering independent soul labels, which was busily cutting corners and leveraging deals to bring out records by The Diamonettes, Frank Williams and His Rocketeers, James Knight and The Butlers, Helene Smith, The Rising Sun and Lynn Williams. (Lynn Williams was the teenage daughter of the R&B juggernaut Hank Ballard, whose original version of the dance craze record 'The Twist' begat both a new form of popular dance music and a global pop hit for Philadelphia's Chubby Checker.)

It was in and around Deep City's impoverished studios that Betty Wright would become the unrivalled First Lady of Miami Soul, an artist of towering brilliance who never enjoyed the visible success of her gospel contemporaries Aretha Franklin and Gladys Knight – in part because she had been born in Florida rather than in the clattering northern industrial cities of Chicago and Detroit, where opportunities were greater.

Another prominent soul music entrepreneur in Miami was the

Merlin-like Henry Stone, whose pointed beard gave him the look of a wizard. Stone was a white Jewish army bandsman from The Bronx who was born Henry David Epstein in 1921. On his demobilisation from the military he set up the Florida record distribution company Seminole. By the fifties he was working with Ray Charles and James Brown as their de facto distributor in Florida and was the local beef behind national labels Atlantic, Motown and Stax. While distribution was Henry Stone's main business, it was another one of his local independent labels, Dade Records, which identified the wealth of talent congregating in Overtown. Dade drew on a reservoir of Florida-based musicians, among them former teen idol Steve Alaimo, Nat Kendrick and the Swans (a pseudonym for James Brown and his Famous Flames), the radio DJ 'King' Coleman, the vocalist Yvonne Fair (of 'It Should Have Been Me' fame), Clarence Reid, the soul singer who doubled as X-rated rapper and comedian Blowfly, and latterly the great southern soul singer (Benny) Latimore. In 1963, George McCrae disbanded his local group The Jivin' Jets to join the US Navy, and on his return to Miami, with his wife Gwen, he grew to become one of the international stars of Miami Soul. Among the many fine records that Dade released to obscurity was Jimmie 'Bo' Horne's 'I Can't Speak' (Dade, 1969), a stunning mid-tempo soul sound that might have been a national hit had it been released on a major or a more readily available New York label. Later known as Jimmy, Horne was a sociology graduate. He had to wait until the seventies disco boom before he had even a modicum of success.

Sam and Dave were Miami's most successful discovery and unquestionably the greatest male duet to emerge from the classic era of sixties soul. Their energetic partnership was founded on an underlying tension: they hated each other. When Sam Moore and Dave Prater first met, they were rivals on the Miami amateur-night scene, trying to hack out a professional contract in one of soul music's outlying cities. Moore was a character on the edge, yearning for a career as a singer but perilously close to being dragged back to his troubled teenage years. As a child, he had been obsessed with local Miami gospel star Marion Williams and had followed her career when she became a featured lead singer alongside Clara

Ward with the famous Ward Singers. He had been brought up by his grandmother, but swerved off the rails and spent time in a youth reformatory before serving a jail term in Raiford Penitentiary, upstate near Jacksonville, for procuring prostitutes. Before being locked up, Moore had made tentative progress as a backing singer for the Dizzy Jones Band, local Miami rivals to James Brown and the Famous Flames. On his release he returned to Miami and hung out in the bars in Overtown and Liberty City, hustling work as a singer and compere. Like so many of his generation, Sam Moore was torn between the music of the church and the music of the juke-joint.

He met Dave Prater in a crime-addled nightclub called the King of Hearts, which was situated beneath the diseased palm trees on the intersection of 20th Avenue and 62nd Street. Gradually, they found work on the circuit and performed as a duo at the Sir John Hotel, along the corridor from Cassius's rented bedroom. Sam Moore knew Cassius as well as he knew his partner. They met when Moore was working as the club's MC and Prater had shown up as an amateur-night contestant. It was by improvised mistake – filling a void in the evening's entertainment – that they came to sing together. Even their trademark trick of dropping the microphone and catching it again came through error rather than stagecraft. Neither knew the other well and they were never temperamentally suited but what they lacked in synergy they more than made up for with sheer unbridled energy. Sam and Dave growled like rabid dogs, barked at each other across the stage and performed acrobatics punctuated by thunderous R&B. They became known as 'Double Dynamite', 'The Dynamic Duo' and briefly 'The Sultans of Sweat'.

That early testosterone was quickly replaced by animosity; despite global success, they became irreconcilable enemies for the rest of their lives, forced to work with each other in a double act that seethed with unfathomable rivalry.

By January 1963, Cassius was in the final days of preparation for his next match and due to travel north to Pittsburgh to fight Charlie Powell of Logan Heights, San Diego, in the newly opened Pittsburgh

Arena, in front of 17,000 fans and a nationally televised audience. His family had travelled to be there with him and to celebrate his twenty-first birthday. As he predicted, Cassius knocked Powell out in the third round. Remarkably, he had by now predicted the result in thirteen of his fourteen knockout victories and his reputation soared.

Powell was in many respects the greatest athlete Cassius had ever faced. He ran one hundred yards in under ten seconds and had played seven seasons of pro-football with the San Francisco 49ers, becoming at the time the youngest NFL player in history. Somehow, in the off-season he had also managed to build a respectable career as a Top Ten heavyweight boxer.

The fight took place on 17 January 1963, a little more than two weeks after President Kennedy's appearance at the Orange Bowl, and an agreement was made with Cassius's Louisville Sponsoring Group that a percentage of his purse would be donated to the families of the miners who had lost their lives at the US Steel Corporation's Robena mine disaster in Greene County, Pennsylvania, three weeks before. Methane gas had exploded in the mineshaft, killing thirty-seven men and injuring many more. It was a gesture that momentarily wrong-footed the press; increasingly used to writing about Cassius's arrogance and boasting, they were forced to acknowledge his support for a very local cause. Having dispatched Powell, Cassius returned to Miami to light training at the 5th Street Gym. By mid-afternoon he was back in Overtown, avoiding the sun, relaxing and resting up.

Just a few days before the fight, though, in the stuffy heat of a Miami nightclub, he had met and befriended the legendary Sam Cooke.

Sam Cooke was not only famous, he was a successful and pioneering music business entrepreneur who exemplified the virtues of taking control and self-improvement. He had set up his own record company, the visionary SAR Records, which acted as a bridgehead between traditional gospel and the newly emergent soul scene. In his own performing capacity, Cooke had signed a lucrative recording contract with RCA Victor and was only the second

African-American to sign to the label after the calypso star turned actor Harry Belafonte. RCA, like many major labels both then and since, struggled with black music, never fully getting to grips with its authenticity and pace of change, and never fully understood the subcultures that fed its novelty and innovation. That vacuum was filled by the urban independent labels of Detroit, Chicago and Harlem.

Cooke had only just returned from a now historic tour of Britain, where he co-headlined with Little Richard. His itinerary meant that he missed out on the first and last nights of the twenty-one-city tour. On the final night at the Liverpool Empire, Cooke had already flown back to America, and so the promoters drafted in a promising local group, The Beatles, who cited Little Richard and Sam Cooke among their many musical influences.

Despite his credentials as a highly marketable singer with an international reputation, Cooke's return to Miami was personally humiliating. He was refused entry to the segregated beach hotels and so had to be driven daily by Society Cabs, the only black-owned taxi firm in Miami, to Overtown, where he stayed in a blacks-only hotel. It was a recurring story in Cooke's life. In October 1963, he wrote his civil rights anthem 'A Change Is Gonna Come' after he was jailed for refusing to leave a whites-only Holiday Inn in Shreveport, Louisiana, when the hotel management refused to honour a reservation because of his race. In the altercation that followed, Cooke was arrested, along with his wife Barbara and two others, for disturbing the peace.

Over the holiday season in Miami, Cooke had two major engagements. By night he was fulfilling a lucrative residency at the glamorous Fontainebleau Hotel and by day he checked out the facilities at the Harlem Square Club in Overtown, where he recorded a live album on 12 January. It turned out to be one of the most remarkable recordings in the early history of soul music, an album considered so raucous and so drenched in the spirit of the ghetto that it was hidden away and remained unreleased for over twenty years.

RCA had cultivated Cooke as a nightclub crooner, someone who could play the supper club circuit from the Catskills to Las

Vegas and then during the winter months fulfil holiday residencies at major Miami beach hotels like the Deauville and the Fontainebleau. The aim was to attract well-heeled audiences, particularly those that were settled in their tastes and uncomfortable with the pace of change. What they got was the polar opposite – a more intense and authentic performance than the commercial market was ready for. Entry tickets to the Harlem Square Club had been oversold and staff had to hurriedly remove tables and chairs to let more people in; what was initially set up as a relaxed cabaret-style venue soon became like the stalls of the Apollo on a Saturday night. To hold back crowds outside, the management hastily rigged loudspeakers on a block along 11th Street, and the vicinity became a boisterous outdoor festival.

Cooke built an immediate rapport with the noisy local audience. 'Don't fight! We're going to feel it!' he shouted as the band musicians, drawn from one of Harlem's finest bands, King Curtis and the Kingpins, struck up a relentless groove. Cooke began his set with 'Feel It', followed by a version of his timeless 1960 hit 'Chain Gang', which he delivered with all the turbo-charged power of a sixties soul storm. For most of the audience, familiar with the syncopated pace of the original, this was like a new version completely and closer to the later Memphis electricity of Otis Redding and Sam and Dave than the sophisticated nightclub style RCA had been banking on. Cooke showcased his classics – 'Cupid', 'Twistin' The Night Away' and 'Bring It On Home To Me' – before climaxing with the near-perfect song for a now lawless Miami night, 'We're Having A Party' and an extended medley of party memes before leaving the stage, his dress suit drenched in sweat and his band exhausted in the stifling heat.

Everyone who witnessed the show claims it was one of the outstanding performances of early soul music, matching the energy of James Brown and the vocal charisma of Marvin Gaye. But in the cold light of day, when the tapes arrived in New York, senior managers were unnerved by the ferocity of what they heard – a performance of such intensity that it was deemed too dangerous for the radio airwaves. Put simply, RCA considered the recording to be too black. They shelved the tapes and abandoned the project.

Cooke's masterpiece, *Sam Cooke Live At The Harlem Square Club, 1963*, remained hidden away in record company vaults, unknown and unloved for decades. (Cooke's experience was not unique. Many major labels struggled to make sense of the first days of soul and recordings deemed unsuitable were left to gather dust in studio vaults.) Cooke's album only came to light when it was discovered by chance. It was finally released in June 1985, by which time social attitudes had changed. It is now universally acclaimed as one of the greatest live albums of all time.

In the same week that Sam Cooke recorded his raucous *Harlem Square Club* album in Miami, the venerable *Saturday Evening Post*, which since the late nineteenth century had been a mainstay of middle-class American publishing, published a six-page exposé of the Nation of Islam entitled 'Black Merchants of Hate'. It was written by Alfred Balk and Alex Haley, the emergent African-American writer who later became the collaborative author of *The Autobiography of Malcolm X* (1965) and the great back-to-Africa genealogy classic *Roots: The Saga of an American Family* (1975). The article savaged the Nation of Islam and undermined its credibility by questioning whether it had any connection whatsoever with the mainstream of Islam, and more importantly exposed the dramatic disagreements that were to follow. The feature profiled Malcolm X to the detriment of his insecure and less charismatic leader Elijah Muhammad, the head of the Chicago-based movement. It was a wound that would fester as the two men drifted further apart. 'Articulate, single-minded, the fire of bitterness still burning in his soul, Malcolm X travels the country, organizing, encouraging, trouble-shooting,' Balk and Haley wrote. 'While Muhammad appears to be training his son Wallace to succeed him when he retires or dies, many Muslims feel that Malcolm is too powerful to be denied the leadership if he wants it.' It was a vindictive and divisive piece, which may well have been directed by the FBI, who provided Balk with briefing notes and may even have funded some of his travel arrangements.

Initially, the article completely passed Cassius by. He never read the *Saturday Evening Post*, and nor did the Cubans at the 5th

Street Gym, but it was delivered weekly to the homes of Cassius's sponsors, the confederation of Louisville millionaires drawn from the ranks of local businessmen and conservative-leaning families. The chairman of the sponsoring group, Bill Faversham, was among the first to suspect that his protégé was involved with the Nation of Islam and concluded that it would have two consequences: it would endanger his investment and expose Cassius to the rage of middle America. For three years, Cassius had kept his faith hidden from his manager, his sparring partners and even his own father. Curiously, for a boxer who became famous for his big mouth, he was guarded about his faith and went quietly to prayer, avoiding attention and keeping counsel with himself. His silence was a powerful antidote to his garrulous public persona.

After the live recording of the Harlem Square Club show was over, Sam Cooke returned to the Sir John for a private after-show party. It was by all accounts a continuation of the show itself, a spirited and celebratory affair, as if New Year had never ended. Cassius was among the throng briefly, visible and congratulatory. It was difficult to talk above the music but Sam promised to recommend a good agent in the music business and to suggest contacts that could convert Cassius's raw potential and turn him into a recording artist. Then, mindful of the time and his commitment to early morning training, Cassius simply disappeared, back to his room and his single bed, where he slept through the din next to Rudy. It was a clue to how Cassius managed the commotion of being a public figure: his entrances into crowded rooms were often grand and overstated, his exits quiet and unnoticed.

Sam Cooke's party was a premonition of what was to come. A year later, the victorious Cassius would return from Miami Beach to Overtown as the undisputed heavyweight champion of the world. Close by his side would be Sam Cooke, the football star Jim Brown and his mentor, Malcolm X, the most famous Black Muslim in America and a figure who not only divided opinion but brought tumult and controversy in his wake. The four men – the boxer, the football star, the singer and the firebrand political leader – crowded into the Hampton House Motel on 27th Avenue, a landmark

The Louisville Lip. It is February 1963, and Cassius, holding a copy of *Sports Illustrated* magazine with heavyweight champion Sonny Liston on the cover, is waiting to meet his promoters, the consortium of eleven businessmen who call themselves the Louisville Sponsoring Group. The original contract between Cassius and the group gave him a $10,000 bonus and a guaranteed minimal annual salary of $4,000 for two years. His backers paid all his training expenses, and everything he earned was split 50:50. 'Some of us wouldn't cross the street to see a concert,' said one, 'but we'll go hundreds of miles to see Cassius in the ring.' Another commented that the group were behind Cassius to 'improve the breed of boxing, to do something nice for a deserving, well-behaved Louisville boy and, finally, to save him from the jaws of the hoodlum jackals'.

African-American venue in Brownsville. They mingled with locals, gorged on bowls of vanilla ice cream, and then slipped into a guest room to discuss music, racism and religion. It was a meeting that not even the prying eyes and ears of the FBI were party to, but all four men were now under surveillance on a daily basis, and through the dark arts of spies, informers and bugging devices, the first days of soul were surrounded by a growing paranoia.

Cassius's days of discretion were over. He was being lauded, watched and stigmatised in equal measure. Quietly at first, he had eliminated the slave name Clay and begun to call himself 'Cassius X', but even that was a short-lived staging post on the way to becoming universally known as Muhammad Ali.

A remarkable and controversial future stretched ahead of him, but the clock was already ticking down on the lives of his friends Sam Cooke and Malcolm X. This was America – get used to it.

Malcolm Little aka Detroit Red (his distinctive red-tinted hair gave him his early nickname) was in prison for burglary when he converted to Islam. Born in Omaha, Nebraska, in 1925, the fourth of seven children, he'd been a pot-smoking, zoot-suited street hustler as a teenager, uninterested in politics and increasingly drawn into a world of violent crime, pimping and drug-dealing. As the black nationalist Malcolm X, he became a powerful, sophisticated orator and leader within the Nation of Islam, promoting the separatist teachings of Elijah Muhammad until his assassination in New York in 1965.

DETROIT

Detroit Red and the Sound of Young America

Cynthia Scott lived on Edmund Place, a desolate street of boarded-up Victorian mansions hidden away behind the grand churches of Woodward Avenue. A once-fashionable neighbourhood, by 1962 its grandeur and fine architecture had been worn down by crime, poverty and unforgiving social decay. Drug-related violence was rife, and police brutality was commonplace. An article in *Time* magazine described blight 'creeping like a fungus through many of Detroit's old proud neighbourhoods', fertilised by 'substantial and persistent unemployment'.

Scott's size set her apart and marked her out as one of Woodward Avenue's most visible street prostitutes. She towered over six feet and weighed 193 pounds in an era when women were expected to be petite and demure. Dressed in an ocelot jacket that was stretched to bursting point by weightlifter's shoulders, she had a voice that could be heard above the foghorns on the misty Detroit River. Over the years, she had been convicted eleven times for accosting and soliciting, and while many prostitutes feared violence from pimps or drunken customers, Scott guarded her own money and was more concerned by police and vice officers who habitually robbed sex workers of their earnings, or demanded sexual favours. Of all the many problems facing Detroit in 1962, the most alarming was a total breakdown of trust between a predominantly white police force and the African-American communities that were beginning to dominate the crumbling inner city.

In June 1962, when Cassius set foot in Detroit for the first time, he only knew it as a city of automobiles and the distant hometown of one of his favourite heavyweight boxers, the legendary Joe Louis. The music of Motown was not yet part of the national consciousness and barely known to Cassius except for a few vaguely familiar tunes. Scott was not on the street either – she was in DeHoCo, the Detroit House of Correction, serving a jail sentence for soliciting. Within a matter of months she would be dead, shot in the back by a white police officer, the prequel to a decade of tense community relations which were to catastrophically erupt in the long, hot summer of 1967.

Two weeks after he had defeated Billy 'The Barber' Daniels in Harlem's St Nicholas Arena and five weeks before his next scheduled bout, in Louisville, Cassius was back home with his parents when the phone rang. It was Captain Sam Saxon. He was planning to drive north from Miami to Detroit to attend a major Muslim rally in the Motor City. He extended an invitation to the Clay brothers to accompany him. By now Cassius and his brother Rudy were regulars at the mosque in Miami and had attended several Nation of Islam meetings there, but the Detroit rally was something else. It was being touted as one of the biggest and most urgent ever, and a unique opportunity to see the leader of the Nation of Islam, Elijah Muhammad, in person.

It now seems that Cassius may have been aware of the Nation of Islam as far back as his teenage days growing up in Louisville. His aunt Mary, his father's sister, has claimed that he began to show greater interest in the movement after he returned from an amateur Golden Gloves tournament in Chicago in 1960. His brother and their school friend, the boxer Jimmy Ellis, were by then keen record collectors and often spent time hanging around record stores and buying up new releases. His aunt claims that the boys brought several records home from Chicago, one of which was a picture-disc 45. It was an independent pressing of Louis X's 'The White Man's Heaven Is A Black Man's Hell' (A Moslem Sings, 1960), an early release by the Black Muslims. It was a record that stood out among the racks and racks of Christian gospel by artists like Mahalia Jackson, Albertina Walker and the Caravans, the Highway QCs, the Salem Travelers, and the Soul Stirrers featuring Sam Cooke. Louis X was the Nation of Islam preacher Louis Farrakhan, then a twenty-seven-year-old singer who had been raised in Roxbury, Boston, by immigrant parents from the Caribbean. For much of the fifties, Farrakhan had been a relatively successful calypso singer, known as 'The Charmer', who toured extensively throughout the Caribbean communities from Miami to New York and recorded several comedy classics, many of them risqué party songs.

It was not until 1961, while training in Miami to fight Utah chicken farmer LaMar Clark, that Cassius began to engage with Islam more deeply. He had been attending Miami's Mosque 29 for over a year when the Detroit Rally was announced, but this was his first significant sight of the leader Elijah Muhammad, and his first encounter with the movement's charismatic preacher Malcolm X.

The Detroit Rally had been urgently convened to contest the shooting of a group of Nation of Islam members by Los Angeles Police officers weeks before. Gruesome newspaper coverage described the body of one of the victims, suited, face down, swimming in a pool of his own blood. Malcolm X called the shooting 'cold-blooded murder' and the anger provoked by the killing brought over 3,500 supporters of the Nation of Islam to Detroit's Olympia Stadium to register their support.

The Olympia was a beast of a building on Grand River Avenue. It was robust and reverential, stylish and steadfast. The stadium's former general manager Lincoln Cavalieri once said, 'If an atom bomb landed in Detroit, I'd want to be in the Olympia.' It could accommodate 11,000 spectators over four levels, was home to the Detroit Red Wings ice hockey team and was known in the city as the 'Big Red Barn'. One reason that Cassius was excited about Saxon's invitation to the rally was that the Big Red Barn occupied an importunate place in boxing mythology. It was the home venue of 'The Brown Bomber', boxing legend Joe Louis, and it was the dramatic stage for Jake LaMotta's back-to-back fights with Sugar Ray Robinson in 1943. Those fights screamed of boxing's greatest rivalry, pitting the roughhouse LaMotta – urged on by his Mafia owners – against the elegant craftsman Sugar Ray, a rivalry that came to be portrayed as 'the matador versus the raging bull'.

In readiness for the rally, the hall was bedecked in dramatic chiaroscuro. Forming a stunning backdrop behind the main speakers were ranks of men in black suits, crisp white shirts and black bow ties and women resplendent in pure white tunics and headscarves. Banners were draped along the balconies with slogans bearing the core values of Islam – 'There is No God But Allah' – and capturing the mood of political self-improvement – 'We Must Make Jobs For Ourselves'. The latter was a unifying principle at the heart of the civil-rights era and one that had widespread appeal across Detroit, where a blue-collar work ethic and a buoyant self-improvement movement had laid the foundations for black-owned businesses.

Foremost among Detroit's local entrepreneurs were the Gordy Family. Berry 'Pops' Gordy Sr owned a string of shops, building contractors and a printing firm; mother Bertha had broken down barriers in the segregated housing market and set up the first insurance company aimed exclusively at the African-American community; and their son Berry Gordy Jr, having failed with a now-bankrupt jazz record shop, had recently set up an aspiring R&B label – the Motown Corporation. Gordy had built Motown on the back of an $800 loan from the family's small investment fund, the Ber-Berry co-operative loans company. It turned out to be one of the most visionary loans in the history of corporate America, producing a billion-dollar business that showcased Smokey Robinson, Marvin Gaye, The Four Tops, The Supremes and The Temptations. By the mid-sixties Motown had given birth to an instantly recognisable fusion of popular gospel, up-tempo backing-tracks and joyful teenage narratives which came to define modern soul, or what Gordy confidently promoted as the Sound of Young America.

All of those many tributaries – jazz, gospel, R&B and independent production – had come together in Stevie Wonder's debut studio album, *The Jazz Soul Of Little Stevie*, on the Motown subsidiary label Tamla. Recorded in 1962, it was already being touted to local DJs before its official release in September, when Cassius arrived for the Nation of Islam rally. Although they were both emergent stars in the firmament of African-American popular culture, neither Cassius nor Stevie Wonder knew each other. It would be another year before they met, backstage at the Apollo in Harlem, where Cassius had gone with his girlfriend Dee Dee and her friends the Ronettes to see Dionne Warwick in concert. By then, Stevie Wonder's single, 'Fingertips Parts 1 & 2' (Tamla, 1963), was a major hit and Cassius was noisily climbing the heavyweight rankings. A mutual interest in magic and practical jokes brought the two young men together in what was always an unlikely friendship: Little Stevie was a thirteen-year-old blind boy and Cassius was now a twenty-one-year-old adult with a deepening interest in Islam. The two men's lives intertwined on many subsequent occasions: Ali sang with Stevie Wonder at the Regal Theater in Chicago in the late sixties and the Motown superstar performed at the ailing boxer's seventieth-birthday celebrations in Las Vegas in 2012, a fundraiser for research into Parkinson's.

Sam Saxon had driven alone for over fifteen hours from Miami. When he stopped in Louisville to pick up Cassius and Rudy at the family home, there was tension in the air; it was clear the brothers were going to Detroit without the blessing of their parents. Cassius's mother was suspicious of Saxon from the outset and resented the idea of her sons travelling to Detroit for a Muslim rally. But the pull of the occasion proved too powerful, and the three men continued the drive north to Detroit, sharing the driving and napping in the back seat. Cassius had a phobia of flying and endured any inconvenience as long as it meant he could avoid aeroplanes. He had flown to Rome under duress to fight in the

Olympics, and was sedated when he flew to London to fight Henry Cooper, but more often than not he travelled by train or by car, and time was always built into his fight schedule to avoid even short-haul flights.

Cassius was unfamiliar with Detroit. He had fought the Detroit heavyweight Lucien 'Sonny' Banks only four months before in New York's Madison Square Garden, but they had exchanged only a few words when they met briefly for a bizarre promotional photo-session in which Cassius sat at an upright piano trying to play while wearing boxing gloves as the mystified Banks looked on. John Condon, the publicist of the Banks fight in New York, immediately bonded with Cassius and was taken aback by his willingness to promote the fight. Another thing caught his eye: Cassius was always neatly turned out, frequently wearing a thin bow tie. At the time, Condon saw it as nothing more than a fashion choice, but it was an early sign that Cassius had already started to absorb the style and disciplines of the Nation of Islam. Back home, Bill Faversham, the chairman of Cassius's sponsors in Louisville, had also noticed the bow ties, the first of many signs that he picked up on as his concern about Cassius's direction of travel increased.

On the surface it appeared as if Banks was just another fall guy dragged into Cassius's sphere and used as a dupe to sell tickets, but he proved to be a more competitive fighter than expected. Cassius was forced to take a mandatory count after being felled by Banks early in the fight, before he dispatched the young Detroit challenger in the fourth.

Like many Detroiters, Banks had been born in the Deep South, in a dirt-poor farming settlement in northeast Mississippi, near Elvis Presley's birthplace in Tupelo. He had moved north with his family in search of a better life when his father found a job at Ford's giant River Rouge Plant in Dearborn, at that time the largest integrated factory in the world. In a story by now familiar to Detroit, Sonny followed his father onto the assembly line.

By the outbreak of the Second World War, Detroit had become a crucible of industry and of racial tension. Over 400,000 immigrants – like the Banks family, most of them from the Deep

South – had moved to the city to find work in the car plants and munitions factories. Unable to fully integrate the colossal number of new arrivals, Detroit's inner city became the flashpoint for intractable racial conflict. In 1942 the city had built the 200-unit Sojourner Truth Housing Project to accommodate black defence workers and their families, but the residents in the adjacent neighbourhood, largely all-white, ethnic Polish, fiercely opposed the development. Continued demonstrations, violent clashes and hundreds of arrests prompted the mayor, Edward Jeffries, to mobilise the Michigan National Guard to support the first black families' move into their homes. White residents living on Nevada and Fenelon Streets protested to change the occupancy to white-only, and flyers were circulated in other districts asking for help: 'Help the white people to keep this district white. Don't be yellow. We need every white man. We want our girls to walk on the street not raped.' Black families who had already signed contracts and paid rent in advance were forced to run the gauntlet of over 1,000 armed white residents, crosses were burnt, and it took the intervention of armed police and the Michigan National Guard to create a path for the incoming families. Under pressure from warring communal factions, the federal authorities promised to build more new inner-city housing for black workers. The most famous new-build was Detroit's Brewster-Douglass Project, where The Supremes grew up, and which was subsequently mythologised as the spiritual home of Motown. Racially integrated housing was Detroit's frontline and at the root of many social disturbances yet to come. A year later, in June 1943, only four months after the Sugar Ray–LaMotta double-header, a riot exploded, one of the worst in the country's history.

But that was all before the Banks family arrived. By 1962, Sonny Banks was a talented prospect and a well-known fighter on the monthly invitation bouts at the Graystone Ballroom, on the corner of Woodward and Canfield.

When they reached Detroit, Cassius and his brother found a city bristling with activity and tense with racial difference, on the cusp of reinventing black music. Berry Gordy had also worked at the

River Rouge assembly plant as a young man, but now owned a small recording studio on West Grand Boulevard which he had nicknamed 'Hitsville'. One of Gordy's big ideas was to borrow the industrial strategy of 'division of labour' from the assembly plants and set up a studio system predicated on a house band who with time became known as The Funk Brothers, and a dedicated backing-singer team, The Andantes. Motown held weekly quality-control meetings, which prioritised releases or sent songs back into the system to be improved. Gordy's friend and collaborator Smokey Robinson was named vice president, placing an emphasis on songwriting and lyricism that would stretch well into the future. As Motown's success grew, they soon came onto Cassius's radar when Mary Wells had a hit with her boxing-themed love song – 'You Beat Me To The Punch', written by Smokey Robinson. It reached number one in the R&B charts and went Top Ten on *Billboard*'s pop charts.

The week after Cassius arrived in Detroit, a lesser known Motown group, The Contours, released 'Do You Love Me'. The song was written with The Temptations in mind, but when Gordy was unable to track down the group, it was given to The Contours. It was the tale of a young man rejected in love because he can't dance but when he returns to the dance floor he becomes like a demon, dancing to 'The Mashed Potato' and 'The Twist', channelling the success of Chubby Checker and Dee Dee Sharp. The song became one of many threads that connected Motown to the groups of the so-called 'British Invasion': Brian Poole and the Tremeloes, The Dave Clark Five and The Hollies all covered The Contours' hit while The Beatles were already planning a cover version of one of the group's favourite songs, Gordy's 'Money (That's What I Want)', which was already an R&B hit for the Detroit vocalist Barrett Strong. The journey that soul music was undertaking was best explained by the generational leap from blues to Motown, the former founded out of hardship and the brutal economy of the rural southern states and the latter the aspirational sound of the north. Built on the back of R&B and gospel, Motown was sprinkled with the magical allure of entertainment and by the summer of 1963, it was already poised to become the most successful black-owned musical corporation ever, dominating the charts that year with stellar hits by Little Stevie Wonder, Martha and the Vandellas, Mary Wells, The Miracles and Marvin Gaye. No one was yet talking about the Motown sound, but they would.

No family personified the change from blues to Motor City soul quite like the Ballards. Still a teenager when Cassius first came to town, Florence Ballard grew up with twelve siblings in a crowded household on the Brewster-Douglass Housing Projects. Her drunken father Jesse Ballard, who had been born in Bessemer, Alabama, and moved north to Detroit as part of the great migration, was a blues guitarist of some repute. Jesse worked locally in a General Motors plant and taught his daughter rudimentary musicianship, but her home life was chaotic, and she struggled emotionally after being brutally raped by a friend of her brother. By 1965 Florence was a founding member of one of the most successful female groups in the world, The Supremes, taking to the stage in Las Vegas in shimmering dresses and high-top wigs but constantly fighting deep-seated depression.

The exterior of the Olympia on Grand River Avenue was already busy with anticipation. Muslims had come from all across America, bussed in from Chicago and New York, and driven through the night like Cassius and his brother from the southern states. Police patrols circled the neighbourhood, alert but low-profile. Young men selling copies of *Muhammad Speaks*, the Nation's newspaper, were lined along the sidewalk and cordoning the entrance. Before the rally, Cassius walked into the Shabazz luncheonette on East Forest, a Muslim eatery whose motto was 'Every man is a builder of a temple – his body'. According to Roberts and Smith, the joint authors of *Blood Brothers*, it was the moment Malcolm X first set eyes on Cassius Clay. 'Malcolm X noticed Sam Saxon accompanied by two handsome, athletic men walking straight toward his table. Malcolm could see they were anxious to meet him,' they wrote. 'One of the brothers, a confident young man with the face of a matinee idol, pumped the minister's hands and announced, "I'm Cassius Clay," which he assumed said it all.' Malcolm X was disinterested in boxing and had no idea who the emergent heavyweight fighter was. They only spoke briefly as Malcolm X returned to preparing his opening remarks for the afternoon rally but it was the first of a number of meetings that affected both their lives in ways that were neither simple nor easily understood.

Initially, their friendship was one of a mentor and his student; 'Malcolm was very intelligent, with a good sense of humour, a wise man,' Cassius once said. 'When he talked he held me spellbound for hours.' But, as the circumstances around them changed, their relationship became strained, and finally became a lost cause ticking down to tragedy. They were close friends and confidants throughout much of 1963 but as the internecine politics of the Nation of Islam suppurated in 1964, Cassius was forced to make a choice that eventually drove them apart and precipitated Malcolm X's assassination.

Malcolm X was no stranger to tragedy. His father Earl Little had died in 1931 in Lansing, Michigan, when he slipped and fell under a streetcar in the dark of night. Little had been a black nationalist sympathiser and unsubstantiated rumours spread that he was murdered by a Michigan racist group, The Black Legion. It did not end there. After her husband's death, Malcolm's mother Louise battled to keep the family together in the face of brutal poverty and her own damaged mental health. Michigan state authorities regularly appeared at the family home questioning her ability to care for her seven children, and, after a serious nervous breakdown in 1939, she was committed to the Kalamazoo State Mental Hospital. Her children, including Malcolm, were dispersed to local orphanages and foster homes. Malcolm remained in the Detroit area until he prematurely dropped out of junior high school, where he had been a gifted and popular teenager. He drifted to Boston, where he stayed with his half-sister Ella, and by 1943 was living in Harlem as a pimp and small-time crook. Resplendent with a straightened conk haircut and fashionable zoot-suit clothes, he assumed the nickname 'Detroit Red' due to the red tinge in his hair (possibly a throwback to his white Scottish grandfather whom he resented bitterly. 'I learned to hate every drop of that white rapist's blood that is in me,' he said.) After a spate of robberies, Malcolm was arrested and charged with breaking and entering, and sentenced to an eight-to-ten-year stretch in Charlestown State Prison in Massachusetts. In prison he studied Islam and converted to the faith, returning to Michigan on his release. He stayed with his brother Wilfred in a wooden-frame home in Inkster, which coincidentally was in the same low-income neighbourhood as one of Motown's first successful girl groups, The Marvelettes.

There is now consensus that Malcolm X may have exaggerated his criminal record, in part to appeal to convicts and criminal youth who he wanted to convert to Islam, and in part to emphasise the transformative way that his own life had been turned round. His biographer, Manning Marable, claims that he 'participated in prostitution, marijuana sales, cocaine sessions, numbers running, the occasional robbery and, apparently, paid homosexual encounters'. Attuned to his audience, he would embroider facts about his eventful past, carefully selecting what to play up and what to avoid.

By the time he had returned to Michigan, Malcolm X was already on the radar of the FBI – they first opened a file on him in 1950 – who warned the Detroit office of his presence in Inkster and of 'his communist and Islamic tendencies'. From those earliest days he was under surveillance and the pressure of being watched was to intensify when he moved permanently to Harlem. Malcolm X 'is an excellent speaker, forceful and convincing', one FBI informant said in 1958. 'He is an expert organizer and an untiring worker', whose hatred for whites 'is not likely to erupt in violence as he is much too clever and intelligent for that'.

By the early sixties, Malcolm X had become the figurehead of Mosque No. 7 in Harlem, arguably the most visible and combustible of all the Nation's temples. His assistant minister was a man known as Benjamin 2X Goodman, who was ex-military and like many new recruits into the Nation of Islam had experienced bitter racism within the armed services. As the war in Vietnam intensified, disillusioned returning veterans became as important a source of recruitment as the prisons. Together, they organised weekly rallies which mobilised action about major national issues like slum

Malcolm X talks to a woman in the Halal restaurant of Temple 7, on Lenox Avenue and 116th Street, Harlem, New York. Founded in June 1954, Malcolm was the head minister, and rapidly expanded the small operation into a membership of thousands. It is early in 1963 here, and Malcolm has recently befriended Cassius, who he originally met in a similar Muslim café close to the Olympia Stadium, on Detroit's Grand River Avenue. Immediately after Malcolm's death, Temple 7 was firebombed.

landlords and police brutality but also focused on specifically local matters such as the gradual encroachment of the wealthy Columbia University onto land and property once occupied by black families. Malcolm X's rallies were often held in front of the Harlem landmark Hotel Theresa and accompanied by live music; he frequently led a contingent of supporters from the Fruit of Islam downtown to support strikes and political demonstrations. Elijah Muhammad had expressly forbidden Nation members to support Martin Luther King's mainstream civil-rights campaigns on the basis that they argued for improved conditions within an integrated America, while the Nation's avowed philosophy was separation of the races. So, as civil-rights groups assembled, Malcolm X's followers were often visible on the streets nearby, perceived as counter-demonstrators.

When Malcolm X took to the stage in the Olympia on 10 June 1962 he sat stage right on a dais, behind a low bank of Muslim women. Next to him was a vacant white leather high-backed chair, like a throne bought in a local cut-price furniture store. It was left vacant to await the arrival on stage of the Nation of Islam leader Elijah Muhammad. Next to the throne was another chair which was left symbolically vacant throughout the day. Malcolm X's opening remarks focused on the Los Angeles killings of April 1962, when Mosque No. 27 had been the grisly scene of a major police incident. Manning Marable has described the L.A. incident as a critical moment in the fractured history of the Nation. 'Just after midnight on April 27, 1962, when two officers observed what looked to them like men taking clothes out of the back of a car outside the mosque, they approached with suspicion. What happened next is a matter of dispute, yet whether the police were jumped, as they claimed, or the Muslim men were shoved and beaten without provocation, as seems likely, the commotion brought a stream of angry Muslims out of the mosque . . . Within minutes dozens of cops raided the mosque itself, randomly beating NOI members. It took fifteen minutes for the fighting to die down. In the end, seven Muslims were shot, including NOI member William X Rogers, who was shot in the back and paralyzed for life. NOI officer Ronald Stokes, a Korean War veteran, had attempted to surrender to the police by raising his hands over his head. Police responded by shooting him from the rear; a bullet pierced his heart, killing him. A coroner's inquest determined that Stokes's death was "justifiable".'

The Nation used the incident to highlight police brutality against the black community and to imply that there was a conspiracy afoot to attack and undermine the movement. Malcolm X appeared on the left-leaning radio station WBAI, once described by *The New York Times* as 'an anarchists' circus', which broadcast from an old church via a transmitter on the top of the Empire State Building. He shared his views on the incident with interviewer Dick Elman, telling him that 'in the shooting that took place, seven men were shot. Seven Muslims were shot. None of them were armed. None of them were struggling. None of them were fighting. None of them were trying to defend themselves at all. And after being taken to the police station, they were held for 48 hours and weren't even given hospitalization. We have one now who is completely paralyzed. We just got all of them free last night . . . And this happened in Los Angeles last Friday night, in the United States of America, not South Africa or France or Portugal or any place else or in Russia behind the iron curtain, but right here in the United States of America . . .'

Enraged by Stokes' death, Malcolm X vowed to avenge it and to organise vigilantes to challenge the police. It was a reaction that brought him into conflict with his leader Elijah Muhammad, who was of the more calculating view that you don't go to war over a provocation. It was the first of many disagreements that would tear their relationship to shreds and bring the Nation of Islam into a rancorous internal conflict.

Cassius saw none of this. He was keen to embrace Islam but was not yet a convert. In many respects he was naïve about the internal contradictions and personal agendas simmering within the movement.

The symbolic empty chair that Cassius stared up at was reserved for the beleaguered Detroit Police Commissioner, George Edwards Jr, who had been invited to sit with the dignitaries – in part to test his mettle and embarrass the police chief, who had at least promised to bring change to policing in the city. The bespectacled Edwards, son of a radical lawyer from Dallas, Texas, who had once been kidnapped by the Ku Klux Klan for fighting segregation, was seen as a liberal force for good in what was a corrupt and deeply conservative police force. Edwards had moved to Detroit between the wars as a socialist and a union organiser for the United Automobile Workers and had a background that did not endear him to the old guard within the city's police department. He faced an almost unwinnable battle convincing a disgruntled and predominately white police force that street-level brutality was not the answer to building a safe city. Conscious of his reputation as a liberal leader and fearing that his presence on the dais would be interpreted as support for the Nation of Islam, Edwards politely declined the offer of a top-table seat. But he agreed to attend the rally, and volunteered to be searched by the Fruit of Islam security section who were stationed in the lobby. There was a strict no-guns policy for all attendees, who were frisked at the door. It was a volatile moment, and to protect the police commissioner in the event of trouble, a back-up contingent of Detroit police officers were hidden away in a nearby warehouse ready to be mobilised if required. The meeting went off without event and Malcolm X thanked Edwards from the stage.

Commissioner Edwards was having a torrid time trying to bring a semblance of order to policing in Detroit. Recruitment of black officers had been painfully slow and had not made any impact on police–community relations. The fragile trust would soon be shattered by the killing of Cynthia Scott in July 1963. She was close to home, walking along John R. Street with a wad of money in her hand, when she was spotted by two white officers, Theodore Spicher and his scout-car partner Robert Marshall. They apprehended Scott, demanding to know whose money it was, possibly with the intent to confiscate the cash and keep it for themselves. Scott resisted, and in the altercation that followed she was shot dead. A Homicide Bureau investigation produced some evidence but not enough to convict the officers or to allay suspicions in the black community that Scott had been the victim of a 'shakedown' and was at risk of losing her 'immoral earnings'. The incident provoked widespread demonstrations by a myriad of different groups who had sprung up across the restless city arguing for greater equality. Two of the most visible groups were UHURU, who talked of 'the anti-Negro machine that is America', and GOAL, the Group on Advanced Leadership, a militant local civil-rights organisation who organised a high-profile protest in front of police headquarters at 1300 Beaubien. The latter group had been established by the black nationalist minister Reverend Albert Cleage and Wilfred X, a Minister of Muhammad's Mosque No. 1 in Detroit and the younger brother of Malcolm X.

Scott's death would become a personal setback for Edwards. He was abroad at the time, attending an Interpol conference in London, and so was accused by some of being asleep on the job. It was an unfair accusation, but unavoidable events often erode public confidence, and in the killing of Cynthia Scott, the apparent absence of the police commissioner led to a deeply held perception within Detroit's African-American community that nothing would change and that policing in the city would remain as corrupt and racist as ever. It was a mood that would darken still further until the rebellious summer of 1967, when tensions around inner-city policing became a national crisis.

On 4 May 1962, a week after the shooting of the Nation of Islam members in Los Angeles, Malcolm X held a press conference at the Statler Hilton Hotel and accused the police of murdering Stokes. It was high-octane theatre from a brilliant firebrand speaker who had built a reputation back in Harlem as one of the great street-corner orators, well versed in speaking to unruly crowds. Unaware of an already tense hierarchy within the Nation, west coast newspapers covering the press conference mistakenly described Malcolm X as the organisation's leader. It was an unwelcome error that intensified the off-stage dispute. The press coverage antagonised Elijah Muhammad, who had a habit of brooding alone at his base in Chicago under a darkening cloud of animosity towards his young acolyte. The two had once had a close father-and-son relationship, which began when Malcolm X was still behind bars and strengthened as he rose up the ranks of what was a controlling and at times paranoid organisation. But by 1962 a tension was developing that would soon hurtle out of control.

James Baldwin's famous essay 'A Letter from a Region of My Mind' appeared in *The New Yorker* in November 1962, and was republished in book form as *The Fire Next Time*. In the essay, Baldwin talks of a prolonged religious crisis during his teenage years and confronts the limited options that were available to young African-American men growing up in the ghettos of America. Baldwin portrayed the options, in binary simplicity, as being between street crime or evangelical Christianity. He finally rejected both, seeing in Christian faith another form of slavery. It was a brutal truth that many comforted by religion were shocked to hear.

'For the wages of sin were visible everywhere,' Baldwin wrote, 'in every wine-stained and urine-splashed hallway, in every clanging ambulance bell, in every scar on the faces of the pimps and their whores, in every helpless, newborn baby being brought into this danger, in every knife and pistol fight on the Avenue, and in every disastrous bulletin: a cousin, mother of six, suddenly gone mad, the children parcelled out here and there; an indestructible aunt rewarded for years of hard labour by a slow, agonizing death in a terrible small room; someone's bright son blown into eternity by his own hand; another turned robber and carried off to jail. It was a summer of dreadful speculations and discoveries, of which these were not the worst. Crime became real, for example – for the first time – not as *a* possibility but as *the* possibility.'

Although deeply sceptical of the Nation of Islam, Baldwin was impressed by its capacity to offer ghetto youth and particularly hardened criminals a way to transform their lives. Describing the power of pride preached by Elijah Muhammad, Baldwin wrote, '"I've come," said Elijah, "to give you something which can never be taken away from you . . ." This is the message that has spread through streets and tenements and prisons, through the narcotics wards, and past the filth and sadism of mental hospitals to a people from whom everything has been taken away, including, most crucially, their sense of their own worth.'

It was a hope that had been handed to Malcolm X in Charlestown State Prison when he reflected on his own mother's incarceration and his descent into crime. Some of these ideas were now swirling around in the mind of Cassius Clay, a young boxer who had never experienced narcotics or prison or mental hospitals, but had lived a comparatively good life in a settled family home where God was Christian and God was love.

Baldwin also recognised that for his parents the appeal of the Nation of Islam and the emergent politics of Black Power engendered a fear. 'The fear that I heard in my father's voice, for example, when he realized that I really *believed* I could do anything a white boy could do, and had every intention of proving it, was not at all like the fear I heard when one of us was ill or had fallen down the stairs or strayed too far from the house,' he wrote. 'It was another fear, a fear that the child, in challenging the white world's assumptions, was putting himself in the path of destruction.' This was precisely the fear that was rattling through the mind of Cassius's father: that his son's impetuousness, his clowning and his attraction to Islam, would lead eventually to his destruction or, like Emmett Till, to his savage death.

Other messages were in the air and soul music was refracting it all. In some respects the music itself was a compromise of forms, drawing on the underground and lawless power of rhythm and blues, inspired by the choral testifying of the Christian church, and honed by the confections of pop. On the surface, soul music was integrationist and so had precious little in common with the Nation of Islam. In his hoodlum days, Malcolm X had been a fan of the criminal underground and the early pioneers of R&B like Johnny Otis, but he graduated to his favourite female singer Dinah Washington. In the prime of his life, Malcolm X preferred jazz to the coarser juke-joint sounds or ghetto soul. Then, with his conversion to Islam, he backed those artists who had also converted, including the Thelonious Monk band with bassist Ahmed Abdul-Malik, the pianist Ahmad Jamal and his friend, the vocalist Dakota Staton. She had been discovered at the Baby Grand in Harlem and signed to Columbia Records before changing her name to Aliya Rabia for a period. Staton married one of Malcolm X's closest musical friends, the trumpeter Talib Dawood, and for a time she operated one of Harlem's busiest record stores, which serviced not only the local jazz but also the independent soul scene, and was a meeting place for Malcolm X's supporters. It was a further complication. Not only was Staton a high-profile supporter, her husband Talib was a vitriolic critic of the Nation of Islam and Elijah Muhammad in particular. The Nation's leader had come to believe that Dawood was Malcolm X's mouthpiece and that his scathing opinion pieces in the daily newspaper the *New Crusader* were ghostwritten by Malcolm X. Elijah Muhammad's irritation and animosity deepened. An irreparable rift was opening up, in part worsened by Malcolm X's charisma, his numerous speaking engagements and his extraordinary appeal. Elijah's more fragile ego and need for centralised control put the two men on a collision course.

Maya Angelou, then the director of the Cultural Association for Women of African Heritage, interviewed Malcolm X in Harlem in 1960, and described his sexuality almost as if it had been a teenage crush. 'His aura was too bright and his masculine force affected me physically. A hot desert storm eddied around him and rushed to me, making my skin contract and my pores slam shut . . . His hair was the colour of burning embers and his eyes pierced . . . I had never been so affected by a human presence . . . his voice was black, musical, baritone,' she said, as if Malcolm X was one of the rising stars of the new soul.

If the upper echelons of the Nation of Islam were at daggers drawn then the Christianity that underpinned soul music was not significantly better. Detroit's network of churches was a minefield – electric with disputes, liturgical differences and sexual intrigue. In the battle for the soul of Detroit, old-school Baptists, the traditional breeding ground of gospel music, were led by the ebullient Reverend C.L. Franklin, the father of the gospel prodigy Aretha Franklin, then still only twenty. The Franklins were close to the mainstream of civil rights; they lionised Martin Luther King – sometimes portraying him as 'Black Jesus' – and in 1963 would bring their formidable numbers to march with King along

Woodward Avenue, in what became Detroit's most famous civil-rights march. Black nationalists tended to support the city's Reverend Albert Cleage, a Christian preacher who was closer to the emergent Black Power movement and was the vociferous force behind the unveiling of the Shrine of the Black Madonna, a stunning artwork featuring a young ghetto mother and her baby, portrayed as Madonna and Child. They were only two prominent ministers among a myriad of churches and congregations.

Reverend Franklin lived the life of a sixties soul singer. He was a flamboyant character who favoured a sharp suit and ostentatious jewellery, and arranged his hair in the fashionable ghetto styles of the day, often shocking the staid members of his congregation by preaching the gospel in a greased conk hairstyle more readily associated with Detroit's pimps and gangsters. According to his biographer, Nick Salvatore, Franklin sported 'alligator-skin shoes, diamond stickpins, flashy rings, [and] watches, and ministerial crosses complemented his colourful neckties. While he occasionally bought clothes on the road, his regular haber-dasher was a downtown Detroit firm, Kosins.' Franklin was a legendary preacher whose loyal congregation had been displaced by highway construction and slum clearance. The original New Bethel Baptist church had been located in the old Hastings Street ghetto but was relocated to Linwood Avenue when the community was cleared to accommodate the Chrysler Freeway. Franklin was not only a high-profile figure in the civil-rights movement but also a successful gospel artist in his own right, and an influential figure in the evolution of black music in the city. His thunderous voice, crackling from the heavens, had been recorded by Chicago's Chess Records and sold in R&B stores across inner-city America. Always a showman, Franklin had led a convoy of parishioners from the site of the old church to the new one, turning gospel's caravan of love into a noisy congregation of Buicks and Cadillacs.

If anywhere could be described as the church of Motown, it was Franklin's New Bethel Baptist Church. Smokey Robinson's co-writer Warren 'Pete' Moore of the Miracles married Bonita Tyson at Bethel, a marriage witnessed by almost the entire

Motown staff. Mary Wilson of the Supremes, one of the congregation's most enthusiastic singers, once described Franklin as a 'sexual' preacher. 'Women loved him,' she said. 'He was a ladies' man! My mother adored him.' Franklin preached fire and brimstone but lived his life like a pop star. His wife had divorced him, leaving him a single father tending a family of four, but his charisma meant he was rarely alone. A string of housekeepers, many recruited from the Bethel congregation, helped out, and Franklin had unofficial wives, including the brilliant gospel singer Clara Ward, with whom he had a long-standing love affair. She in turn became Aretha Franklin's surrogate mother. Reverend Franklin had no great theological problems reconciling the restraints of the Old Testament with his adventurous sex life. This was in many respects another stepping stone on the way to soul music – the gospel according to sinners. The music was not simply a secularisation of the church choirs, it was their furtive glances, their hidden desires and, in time, their full-on sexual craving.

In May 1963, a year after the Nation of Islam rally in Detroit, two simultaneous events came to define the era and its music. Reverend Franklin was planning a massive demonstration to bring national attention to racial discrimination and civil rights. On the home front he gave permission to his supremely talented daughter Aretha to diversify away from the gospel church and take on a secular soul residency at Detroit's famous Flame Show Bar. The bar was a centrepiece venue in Detroit which hosted major names like Della Reese, Etta James, Dinah Washington and B.B. King, and became the Midwestern residency for the great Billie Holiday. For historians of Detroit music, the Flame Show Bar was arguably where soul music really began. It was where local talent like Aretha, Jackie Wilson and LaVern Baker first performed. The club's motto was 'where the smart people meet' – hinting at the ambition and upwardly mobile values that came to define the Motown era. It attracted the Motor City's most entrepreneurial young people. Berry Gordy was a regular, and his fashionable sisters Gwen and Anna ran the club's in-house photography concession, delivering on-site photos to customers. When she took to the stage Aretha Franklin was already uncomfortable with attention and burdened by her epic talent, but she kept her anxieties hidden for now and her performances across the week reached levels of emotional power that signalled that soul music had a star in waiting.

The Reverend Franklin had an ulterior motive. He was conscious that constraining his talented daughter to gospel was restricting her earning potential, so he broke with spiritual absolutism and gave her permission to fully embrace R&B. His plans for a massive civil-rights demonstration in Detroit had many more barriers to overcome. Some local ministers and politicians saw it as a provocative idea that would attract bad press and, possibly, violence; others thought it would be a damp squib that would only attract the committed and so undermine the movement for change; and many more thought it was a vanity project to boost Franklin's self-importance. Franklin was undaunted. He called in favours from his famous friends, among them the gospel superstar Mahalia Jackson, the actor Harry Belafonte and Berry Gordy's stable of rising talent at Motown. With confidence in the proposed march growing, Martin Luther King agreed to travel from Atlanta to join them. The Nation of Islam, resistant to the message of racial integration, boycotted the march, but many more surged to the city. At its height, the march swelled to over 500,000 people, row upon row linking arms as they swarmed along Woodward Avenue. King, true to type, arrived late after a delayed flight and was ferried by car by the Detroit police who calculated that his presence would bring a peaceful focal point to the day. It was on 23 June 1963, at the final gathering place by Cobo Hall, that King improvised the first version of 'I Have a Dream', the speech that would become so epochal when he repeated it at the March on Washington for Jobs and Freedom two months later.

The Detroit march was a landmark in civil rights for the populous northern industrial cities. 'It was absolutely a world statement,' Aretha Franklin told *USA Today*, 'that we could not only organize but we were healthy and wealthy in numbers.' She herself was not there, but stuck in an apartment in Manhattan suffering from agoraphobia, unable or unwilling to travel to the Motor City. On record, Aretha had yet to find her real voice; she was signed to Columbia Records, and so poorly produced she was covering jazz standards, pop songs and underwhelming material. Although her recording career was directionless, there was clarity in the contracts she had signed: her forthright father had refused to allow her to perform in any venue that operated a segregated ticketing policy.

Soul music was gestating in the streets and the start-up studios of Detroit. It was sexualising the gospels and reflecting the hopes of the civil-rights movement. Motown was an upwardly mobile form of black music, which either rejected or heavily varnished the rough surfaces of blues and old-school R&B, and delivered a more polished and aspirational sound and image. Like Cassius himself, Motown was not afraid of wealth or self-promotion.

Cassius shared many of Motown's social ambitions. He was passionate about fame and celebrity and increasingly conscious of the money he could make in and out of the ring, but there was a twist in the road. Detroit soul looked decisively towards the mainstream, while Cassius was slowly but surely embracing Islam, a religion that thrived in the prisons and in the ghettos but which had never occupied centre stage in African-American society. Casually at first, and then with growing devoutness, he began to absorb the teachings and the diatribes of the newspaper *Muhammad Speaks*, which he would buy regularly at the Miami mosque or on the street corners of Overtown. On Sunday evenings he would tune into Miami's radio station WMIE, which carried a syndicated sermon and speech by Elijah Muhammad, and periodically he would fall into conversation with local converts on his way to the 5th Street Gym and question them about Islam.

According to authors Roberts and Smith, his encounter with Malcolm X had a lasting impact. 'That day in Detroit changed Clay's life. There was something about Malcolm – his swagger, the dazzle in his smile, the way everyone in the diner watched him –

that alerted Cassius that the brother minister, who, in the words of the activist Dick Gregory, "spoke like a poor man and walked like a king", possessed an unbridled confidence and an audacity to speak to his mind in a way that no one else did.' It was the day that Cassius X came into being.

On the long road trip back from the Detroit Rally, the conversation with Saxon and his brother Rudy regularly returned to the family's surname. Cassius had always liked the name Clay – in fact it was a source of some pride to his father. For the first time that weekend, he began to seriously question it. Initially, Cassius found the name a difficult one to relinquish, having been reared for years on stories told to him by his father about his namesake's role fighting slavery. The original Cassius Marcellus Clay (1810–1903) was the son of Kentucky Revolutionary War veteran and slave-owner General Green Clay. While at Yale, Cassius had heard a speech by abolitionist William Lloyd Garrison, who influenced his anti-slavery sentiments. Unlike Garrison, who called for the immediate end to slavery, Clay was a gradualist and wanted to see emancipation evolving throughout the south. During the 1840s, he was elected to the House of Representatives, but his anti-slavery views eventually cost him his seat and almost his life. He survived two assassination attempts as the battle over slavery became more savage and according to his biographer, David Smiley: 'On one occasion, caught without his pistol, General Clay was shot above the heart by a would-be assassin. He forestalled further ado by slicing off the assailant's nose and ears with a Bowie knife.' The death threats continued when he freed his own slaves and published Kentucky's anti-slavery newspaper *The True American*. Vandals wrecked his publishing equipment, and unable to publish unimpeded, Clay relocated to Cincinnati and subsequently served as Lincoln's foreign minister to Russia. In his book *Lion of White Hall*, Smiley claimed that the original Clay was 'braggadocious and continuously talked about his military exploits in the Mexican-American War to anyone who would listen'. Boasting about his triumphs was a trait that was not his alone.

As the three men drove south from Detroit, the stories of Cassius's childhood pride were counteracted by a fiery Islam.

The Brothers X: Cassius and Malcolm at 125th Street and 7th Avenue, New York, in March 1963. Coincidentally, they are wearing styles that became synonymous with black militancy later in the decade, Cassius sporting the black leather jacket of the Black Panthers and Malcolm in the immaculate tailoring of the Nation of Islam.

Malcolm X was a passionate advocate of abandoning the legacy of slavery. 'You're nothing but an ex-slave. You don't like to be told that,' he once said. 'But what else are you? You are ex-slaves. You didn't come here on the *Mayflower*. You came here on a slave ship. In chains, like a horse, or a cow, or a chicken. And you were brought here by the people who came here on the *Mayflower*.' Cassius knew that members of the Nation of Islam were required to eliminate their surname or 'slave name', effectively crossing it out with a denunciatory X. Each mosque kept a record of these converts as they journeyed on their way to full participation. Some converts, like Muhammad Ali, even went on to achieve the status of having their 'own name'. Depending on their first name, the recruits were given a number to signify their place on the mosque's master list. Cassius and Malcolm had no one with the same first name ahead of them and so they took a single X. Others were beholden to the numbers they occupied on a mosque's list. So, for example, two men arrested by the New York police in the aftermath of Malcolm X's assassination in 1965 were members of the Nation of Islam's Mosque No. 7 in Harlem: Norman 3X Butler (Muhammad Abd Al-Aziz) and Thomas 15X Johnson (Khalil Islam).

Conversion to the Nation of Islam was an onerous voyage. New recruits had to memorise and recite verbatim the ten questions and answers of Student Enrolment, and only after memorising them were they allowed to write a 'Saviour's Letter', which was then mailed to the Nation's headquarters in Chicago. The Saviour's Letter had to be written under strict requirements and copy the hand-writing style of the movement's founder Wallace Fard Muhammad. It was only after private conversations at the mosque and troubled discussions with Rudy that Cassius began the process.

When Cassius returned to Miami from the Detroit Rally, he came increasingly under the influence of another teacher, Minister Ishmael Sabakhan, who had assumed duties at the local temple in Miami. Under Sabakhan's guidance, he began to use the name Cassius X, informally at first and then with greater self-confidence and only in company he trusted. To the majority of people, particularly those who followed the circus of heavyweight boxing, it was a barely visible change. Most people knew him as Cassius or Cass, and in his fights – overseen by Angelo Dundee and his management syndicate in Louisville – he was always billed as Cassius Clay; his contracts, too, were invariably signed in his birth name. The name Cassius X was his mosque name, a secret he kept with his brother and a few friends from the Nation in Miami.

Later in life, in a letter to his second wife, and by then universally known as Muhammad Ali, Cassius revealed how the Detroit trip had intensified feelings he had been having over several years and that he had been attracted to Islam as far back as 1961, when he was still a teenager and living in Louisville. The letter reminisces about one night in particular:

One night at a skating rink in Louisville (I was on my way home), the skating rink was located at 9th and Broadway St., while I was standing outside the building in a crowd of about 400 people, all black people, like most boys [I was looking] for a pretty girl to say something to. A black brother dressed in a black Mohair suit, [with a] white shirt and a black bow tie, was [selling] some newspapers called *Muhammad Speaks*. At that time it was the first time I had seen a *Muhammad Speaks* newspaper. The brother walked up to me and said, 'my brother, do you want to buy a *Muhammad Speaks* newspaper, so that you can read about your own kind, read the real truth of your history, your true religion, your true name before you were [given] the White Man's name in slavery?' He said, 'oh, by the way there is a meeting that we are having today on 27th and Chestnut St. at 8 o'clock this evening.' And at the time it was about 6 o'clock in the evening. I told him OK, I will be there. But I had no intention to go to any meeting. But I did buy the *Muhammad Speaks* paper. And [one] thing in the paper [made] me keep the paper, and that was a cartoon. And the cartoon was about the first slaves that arrived in America, and the cartoon was showing how the black slaves were slipping off at the plantation to pray in the Arabic language facing the east. And the white slave master would run up behind the slave with a whip and hit the poor [slave] on the back with a whip and say, 'what are you doing praying in that language, you know what I told you to speak,' and the slave said, 'yes sir, yes sir, Master. I will pray to Jesus, sir, Jesus.' And I liked that cartoon. It did something to me. And it made sense.

With the benefit of hindsight, the clues to Cassius X's conversion to Islam were already there in April 1962, when the chairman of his sponsoring syndicate, Bill Faversham, filed an application of a boxer's licence to the State Athletic Commission of California, in advance of his fight against the Boise, Idaho, heavyweight George Logan. Faversham was the son of an English Shakespearean actor and an unlikely character to be involved in the world of boxing. A stickler for procedure, Faversham, according to *Sports Illustrated*, was a 'gravelly-voiced, stentorian man' and was 'the glue that binds the syndicate to Clay and to Clay's trainer, Angelo Dundee'. He was used to seeing Cassius well dressed, often in suits and Harris tweed jackets, but he was initially unaware of the workings of the Nation of Islam. Dutifully, Faversham signed the application in the name of Cassius Marcellus Clay, but the attached photo-booth passport photograph shows Cassius in a black suit, a crisp white shirt and slender black bow tie, the uniform of the Nation of Islam. Neither Faversham nor Dundee, nor the State Athletic Commission of California made the obvious connection, although something about the photograph lingered in Faversham's mind in the months to come. The fight with George Logan, at the Los Angeles Sports Arena, ended in the fourth round, and the only controversy that it provoked was accusations from Logan's camp that Cassius had illegally thumbed his opponent's weak eye.

Cassius's deepening interest in Islam was a substantial risk to his career. In the conservative world of boxing, many including Faversham and his sponsors believed it would ruin him, although there was a counterargument that his eventual conversion gave him distinctiveness in a crowded boxing market. Gene Kilroy, his corner man and trainer, who first met Cassius at the Rome Olympics, told the British newspaper the *Daily Telegraph*: 'If he hadn't accepted the Nation of Islam, he would have been just another fighter. That put him above everything else. It gave him a

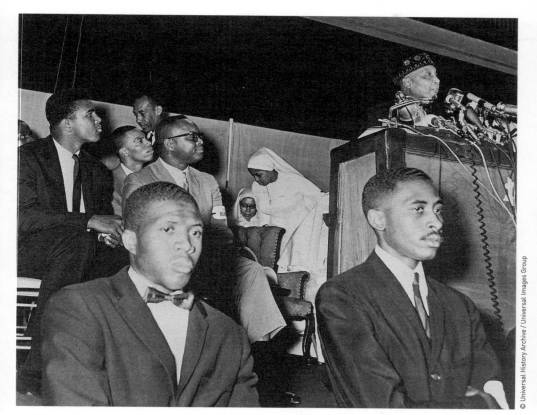

Watched closely by Cassius, Elijah Muhammad gives a speech in early 1964. By this time, the leadership of the Nation of Islam is at war with Malcolm X, who is conspicuously absent. Cassius is about to be granted the holy name of Muhammad Ali.

cause about life. It gave him a way to live. It made him a teacher.'
It was a view in part shared by Cassius's tutor, the Nation of Islam
leader for the Southern states, Jeremiah Shabazz, who had been
sent to Miami to prepare Cassius for conversion. He told biographer
Thomas Hauser that 'we had a champion in the making, a celebrity,
and everybody was very happy about that; particularly those of us
in the South, because most of the brothers in the North didn't
know about him except for the few who followed boxing . . . And
we knew that if Cassius made a public declaration of faith, he'd
never get to fight for the championship.'

Boxing authorities across the USA were cautious bodies and
fearful of bad publicity, whether that came from the malign
influence of organised crime or the personal deportment of
registered fighters. The authorities had no idea what was going on
in the private life of the charismatic Cassius Clay. They saw only
the joking young challenger with the big mouth who was racing up
the heavyweight rankings. They saw a lively and effervescent
character who could bring attention to the sport, and at no stage in
his development from winning Olympic gold to racking up wins
from his base in Miami did the authorities anticipate his planned
direction of travel.

In the autumn of 1962, a letter arrived at the offices of the
Louisville Sponsoring Group summoning Cassius to travel to
Albany, New York, to appear before the Joint Legislature
Committee on Professional Boxing at a critical time for the fight
game. Those who requested his presence had no idea about his
weekend journey to Detroit or his closeness to the Nation of Islam.
Cassius was in effect leading two lives, one spiritual and the other
pugilistic, and for many months to come he suppressed his beliefs
in public and avoided anything that would bring attention to the
new path his life had taken. He was accustomed to appearing in
dark suits and bow ties at formal boxing dinners and when he
walked out at night, most saw a smart young man. In September
1962 he appeared on the pages of *Muhammad Speaks* for the first
time and, in one of his most famous quotes, Cassius hinted at his
spiritual journey: 'I know where I'm going and I know the truth, and
I don't have to be what you want me to be. I'm free to be what I want.'

Ironically, his clowning, rapping and effusive personality disguised his faith. Most people saw only the act and were not paying much attention to his private life. That was never likely to last. The FBI's strategic infiltration of the Nation of Islam and their caseload on Malcolm X had begun many years before, and the director of the FBI, J. Edgar Hoover, was becoming more and more suspicious of this young heavyweight who was beginning to charm audiences on national television.

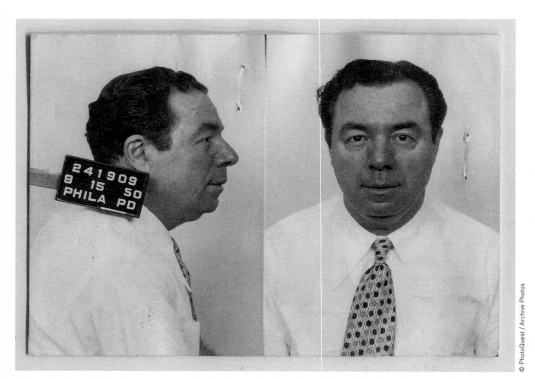

Mug shots of Philadelphia-based mobster and fight-fixer Frank 'Blinky' Palermo (1905–1996), taken on 15 August 1950, in Philadelphia, Pennsylvania. In the early sixties, he came under investigation by the Kefauver Committee, tasked to scrutinise organised crime's involvement in boxing. By 1959, Palermo and his partner, fellow Mafioso Frankie Carbo, controlled Sonny Liston's contract. He fought twelve fights under their management.

PHILADELPHIA

The Guy with the Goods

It would be a long time before Blinky Palermo walked the streets of Philadelphia again. Each day, the squint-eyed convict shuffled along the 700-foot central corridor of 'The Big House' at Lewisburg's Federal Penitentiary. Palermo was in forced retirement and his reign as one of boxing's biggest match fixers was all but over. He had been arrested eighteen times in the previous ten years on charges that included forgery, arson, impersonating a police officer, fraud and larceny. He was not a violent man but he knew people who were and, even in jail, an aura of weary threat still hung around him.

Lewisburg was the incongruous home to some of America's most dangerous inmates. From the outside, it was an imposing and solemn building, more like a cathedral than a prison, and although its splendour was lost on some of its residents, the penitentiary was an architectural marvel, based on the design of the fourteenth-century Palazzo Pubblico in Siena. For Francisco 'Blinky' Palermo it resembled the Cathedral Basilica on 18th and Benjamin, or the local churches of his childhood in Philadelphia's Southside, and as he trudged to the vast prison canteen, Palermo looked more like a clinically depressed Carmelite monk than a Mafia villain.

His most strenuous exercise was lying in his cell, reading dog-eared copies of *The Ring* magazine and conspiring to get messages back to the gyms, the bar-rooms and the pool halls of home. He'd grown up on Haines Street, in Germantown, in an Italian-American family. Throughout his childhood and adolescence, his mother Angeline worried about his sleepy and disfigured right eye, while his father Sam was more concerned about guiding him through the rituals of the family business and gaining the approval of Angelo Bruno, the man known by the epithet of 'the Gentle Don' who had led the Philadelphia mob since 1959. Bruno was a criminal with a conciliatory bent and a clear moral code: he forbade the Philly Mafia from trafficking in heroin, preferring more traditional Cosa Nostra crimes such as bookmaking, loan-sharking and fight-fixing. It was in the fight game that Blinky Palermo flourished, serving his apprenticeship by fixing local bouts and finding street bums to take a dive against rising opposition. It was through this trade that he met his friend and criminal collaborator Paolo Giovanni 'Frankie' Carbo, a product of New York's Catholic reformatory system. Working in concert, often under the Mafia code-name 'The Combination', Carbo and Palermo manipulated the outcomes of hundreds of fights by intimidating promoters, beating up managers and threatening boxers if they refused to go along with their fixes. Carbo's gentle voice and debilitating diabetes disguised a ruthless and pathological killer: he was a gunman for the Lucchese crime family and a member of the organised crime gang Murder Inc.

The Combination was often colloquially known as 'Octopus', due to the grasping tentacles that reached out into every aspect of the fight game, all but dominating the middleweight rankings over two decades. Such was the depth and complexity of the mob's control of boxing that the supreme council of the Mafia – the so-called 'Commission' – met in 1961 to deliberate on a dispute between factions in Chicago and Philadelphia, over the contractual split of the heavyweight contender Sonny Liston. The council eventually sided with Palermo and his associates. It was a decision that would soon have an impact on Cassius and his ambitions to win the heavyweight title.

After their trials for conspiracy, extortion and fixing boxing bouts over decades, the authorities ensured that the two men were separated and taken to different jails, to bring their partnership to an end. Despite failed appeals which stretched well into the sixties, Palermo slept comfortably in his cell in Lewisburg, while Carbo drew the short straw and was confined on Rikers Island, cleaning up the raw sewage that seeped into his cell with handfuls of powdered detergent. The long sentences meted out to the two Mafia hoods were designed to bring their corrupt practices to an end, but even in jail Carbo and Palermo manoeuvred and conspired and threatened to retain a slice of Sonny Liston's contracts.

According to local criminal legend, while Palermo and Carbo served their sentences, Liston's controversial career was directed on their behalf by Pep Barone, the owner of a boxing memorabilia bar in Allentown, Pennsylvania, and Sam Margolis, a leading figure within the East Coast pinball and jukebox business. At first glance Margolis fulfilled all the stock stereotypes of a pernicious Mafia fixer, his jowly face masked by wreaths of smoke from a Havana cigar. He was described by *Sports Illustrated* as a man who had an uncanny habit of shaking off criminal charges: 'Pudgy and 50, he pleaded guilty in 1937 to operating a gambling house in Chester, Pa., was fined $50 and sentenced to from one to three months in jail. In the early 1940s he was twice arrested on gambling charges in Delaware County, Pa., but not found guilty either time. In 1950 Philadelphia police arrested him for assault and battery, but he was discharged again.' Through a shady front company called Inter-Continental which controlled Liston's fights, Margolis was the man who represented the company, but his shares were most likely held in trust for the incarcerated Carbo and Palermo.

It was through Palermo's influence that Liston had left his native St Louis, Missouri, where he had been in jail off and on throughout much of his young adult life, for a new base in Philadelphia. Liston's life there was strange, to say the least. He lodged in the Hamilton Court Hotel, in the heart of the University of Pennsylvania's urban campus, where the muscle-bound boxer often played checkers with local students. His favoured hangout was the Sansom Delicatessen on South 39th Street, a local Mafia haunt co-owned by Palermo and Margolis, where Liston's wife Geraldine was employed as a kitchen assistant. When he went out onto the streets of Philly, Liston usually hung out at a pool hall at 57th and Haverford, which was owned by Palermo, or was found shooting the breeze with customers at Palermo's Mercury car dealership. It was Palermo who introduced Liston to the millionaire Morton Witkin. For a time, Witkin was at the beating heart of Philadelphia's politically sensitive 13th Ward. A hive of immigrant friction in the early twentieth century, the area was infamous for its pool halls, opium dens and brothels, and known by the nickname 'Tenderloin'. Witkin was a divorce lawyer by trade and one of a myriad of people who became tied up in the parasitic contracts that the heavyweight champion Sonny Liston was fighting amidst. A Republican Party fixer, whose horn-rimmed glasses and crumpled white linen suit gave him the appearance of a down-at-heel author, rather than an analytical lawyer, he had a reputation for securing acquittals even for the most nefarious characters. Witkin was near legendary within two radically different worlds: well-heeled Republican Party fund-raisers and Philadelphia's Mafioso. Although he helped Liston out with contacts and legal papers, he may also have inadvertently deepened Liston's associations with organised crime.

Philadelphia was a boxing city, but it was also one of the driving forces of teenage pop – home to one of the most influential independent labels of the time, Cameo-Parkway, and the hugely influential *Bandstand* television show. Cameo-Parkway was founded in Philadelphia in late 1956 by a local pianist, bandleader and songwriter Bernie Lowe, who enjoyed early success by adapting the lyrics of Big Mama Thornton's epic R&B hit 'Hound Dog' and re-recording it with a local group Freddie Bell and the Bellboys. The group were fronted by an Italian-American vocalist Ferdinando Bello and the single was issued on the Philadelphia indie Teen Records. This seemingly insignificant moment in pop history had many of the elements that differentiated Philadelphia from other cities in the first days of soul. First, the softening and appropriation of R&B for a largely white consumer market; second, the identification of a new 'teen' market; and third, the recognition that the Italian-American community in Philadelphia and New York had a reservoir of young talent that had the kind of romantic good looks that met the mainstream needs of early network television. Crooners like Perry Como, Frank Sinatra, Tony Bennett and Dean Martin had dominated post-war music but were eventually displaced by a new generation of teen-orientated Italian-Americans such as Frankie Avalon (Francis Avallone), Bobby Rydell (Robert Ridarelli), Lou Christie (Lugee Sacco), Frankie Valli (Francis Castelluccio) and the elegant white soul singer Timi Yuro (Rosemarie Timotea Auro).

Working from a base at 1405 Locust Street, Cameo Records and its Parkway subsidiary grew to become one of the biggest independent record companies of the day. Cameo-Parkway was never a black-owned label; it regarded soul music, or rather dance craze music, as one strand of a diverse catalogue, which was initially built around teen idol Bobby Rydell and the label's relationship with the television show *Bandstand*.

Bandstand began as a local area show on Philadelphia's WFIL-TV and by 1952 had evolved into a teen dance show recorded at a custom-built studio at 4548 Market Street in West Philadelphia. In 1956 producers Dick Clark and Tony Mammarella pitched the show to the ABC network, claiming it would reach the elusive and highly valued youth market. In August 1957 it was rebranded as *American Bandstand* and broadcast nationally, quickly securing its status as the pre-eminent teenage music show of its time. This was a moment of critical change in consumer habits. The daily bible of consumer capitalism, *The Wall Street Journal*, estimated that America's 16 million teenagers spent somewhere between $9 billion and $11 billion annually, and described them as 'a market that's getting increasing attention from merchants and advertisers'. *American Bandstand* reflected and profited from the phenomenon and attracted sponsors and advertisers from emergent youth-market products like 7 Up, Dr Pepper and chocolate snacks Mounds and Almond Joy.

Presenter Dick Clark's career had blossomed on the back of the teenage phenomenon. In 1950 there were approximately 250 disc jockeys in the US; by 1957 there were closer to 5,000, an increase in part due to the burgeoning radio market and the sheer quantity of new records being produced. It was fertile ground for an explosion in R&B radio. The rise of new forms of media promoting music had an obvious Achilles heel: the market's vulnerability to bribes and payola. Local DJs – working on small production margins and, usually, low pay – were susceptible to bribes and inducements that often came in the form of cash, drugs or sex. In some cases it even stretched to a share of royalties. One DJ, Wesley Hopkins of KYW in Cleveland, gave a glimpse into the extent of the malpractice. He admitted receiving $12,000 in 'listening fees' from record companies for 'evaluating the commercial possibilities' of records.

An unhealthy relationship had grown up between *American Bandstand* and several select record companies, not least Cameo-Parkway. Accusations of vested interests were rife, and Dick Clark himself came perilously close to being ruined by the Payola hearings in 1960. His television show set him apart as the only DJ with a truly national audience and he was forced to admit that he had an interest in thirty-three music-related companies – and owned a copyright share in 160 separate songs, 143 of which he had received as gifts from producers. Clark was an entrepreneur who played fast and loose with the system. He had launched a live travelling show called the 'Caravan of Stars' with a racially mixed cast, which toured small towns and cities across America, and which by the early sixties was seen as *American Bandstand* on tour. Headliners included Chubby Checker, Bo Diddley, Paul Anka, The Drifters, Duane Eddy and Dee Dee Sharp, as well as emergent soul groups from Philadelphia including The Tymes. The show cross-promoted the tour which inevitably referred back to the show – a circle that made Dick Clark a millionaire.

The teenage market was ripe for exploitation. In his ground-breaking book, *The Nicest Kids in Town: American Bandstand,*

Rock 'n' Roll, and the Struggle for Civil Rights in 1950s Philadelphia, Matthew F. Delmont describes an era of music media that was finely tuned to local markets. 'When Clark took over *Bandstand* in 1956, hit records were made on a city by city (or market by market) basis. Major record companies and large independent labels in New York, Chicago and Los Angeles had local promotion men whose job was to get their records played on local radio in smaller markets. Cincinnati's independent King Records, for example, had a network of thirty-three branch offices across the country. Record companies would track which records were "breaking" . . . in different cities, and these popular records were pushed across the country. Record companies considered Philadelphia to be a "break out" market that could influence national distribution.'

By 1960 Philadelphia was the capital city of teenage pop, the fourth largest city in America with a population of over two million and a regional reach stretching north to Wilmington, Delaware, and across the Delaware River to Camden, New Jersey. It was bigger than Detroit and had a population greater than Boston and Baltimore combined.

A less obvious by-product of the show was its camera style, a low-slung perspective which focused on the dance steps of the studio dancers as they navigated songs that were often straight steals or derivative of dances in local teenage nightclubs – 'At The Hop' by Danny and The Juniors (1957), 'The Stroll' by The Diamonds (1957) and 'Sophisticated Swing' by The Applejacks (1960). A tacit form of exploitation was in play. Dance styles pioneered at R&B clubs populated largely by young African-Americans were being appropriated by white groups, and the almost exclusively white TV shows were using the style to shape the image of teenagers on national network television.

The *American Bandstand* studios were in South Philadelphia, where Italian-Americans had settled in substantial numbers, where Blinky Palermo had his home and where some of boxing's fiercest gangsters hung out. Throughout most of the post-war period, it was an area seething with racial tension and local gang warfare.

Chubby Checker, born Ernest Evans, had just started attending South Philadelphia High School in 1954 when the landmark Supreme Court ruling known as *Brown v. Board of Education of Topeka* ruled unanimously that racial segregation of children in public schools was unconstitutional. South Philadelphia was already tensely integrated, and for a while Checker shared classrooms with Fabiano Forte, the Italian-American teenager who morphed into the heart throb Fabian, and with Cassius's girlfriend, Dee Dee. The *Brown* ruling was to have a profound impact, provoking bitter racial divisions throughout the southern states and erecting the backdrop for what became the bussing policies of numerous towns and cities, and in Philadelphia triggering a decade of civil-rights campaigns that challenged the last vestiges of segregation in the city.

Chubby Checker's name was a derivative of the famous R&B star Fats Domino, a contrivance that came about courtesy of his record company and their suffocating relationship with *American Bandstand*. Before he was known as Chubby, Evans worked in a poultry store in the Italian Market on 9th Street, where he killed, plucked and boiled chickens for local housewives. It was a nearby Italian stall-owner, Henry Caltabiano, who introduced him to Cameo-Parkway, thus setting him on an unusual path to stardom. Checker was first and foremost an impersonator capable of imitating all the big stars – from Elvis Presley and Frank Sinatra to Ray Charles and James Brown – and it was as a musical mimic that he first came to the attention of Dick Clark. One story claims that it was Clark's wife, Barbara Mallery, who came up with the name Chubby Checker. An informal deal had been struck. Cameo-Parkway would provide a conveyor belt of talent, most of them drawn from Philadelphia's black and Italian communities, and they would be showcased on television. From the mid-fifties onwards, Philly singers would wait hopefully in the back rooms of the recording studios, on standby, hoping for the day when a major star had a travel mishap or simply pulled out of the show.

It was the Twist craze that brought Chubby Checker to national prominence. The original version of the song, 'The Twist', was pure R&B, and had its origins in Miami's Overtown ghetto where Cassius lived. It had been released on the B-side of Hank Ballard's growling 1959 single 'Teardrops On Your Letter' (King, 1959). Ballard was one of dozens of R&B singers whose style and lyrics were deemed too explicit and unrefined for mainstream radio and so the more malleable Chubby Checker was coached through a recording session, in which the song was given a softer, more innocent workout. On 6 August 1960 Chubby Checker performed his version of 'The Twist' live on *The Dick Clark Show*, an *American Bandstand* spin-off hosted at the Little Theater on West 44th Street, in the heart of Broadway. The song shot to number one in *Billboard*'s Hot 100 chart, and the accompanying dance swept around the world. Unusually, in 1962, Checker's version returned again to number one in the pop charts, only the second song since Bing Crosby's 'White Christmas' to occupy the top spot twice. It remained there for twenty-five weeks as mass media coverage and celebrity endorsement turbo-charged the craze. At the time, Chubby Checker issued the most unlikely advice to his followers: 'Just pretend you're wiping your bottom with a towel as you get out of the shower, while putting out a cigarette with both feet.'

The Twist craze and the dance styles that inevitably followed played directly to Cassius's showy athleticism and inherent love of comedy. Nat Loubet, a writer for *Ring* magazine, even saw a distinct likeness between Cassius and Chubby. 'Cassius Marcellus Clay is the "utmost" as a hustler,' he wrote. 'He's a pitchman's pitchman. He'd have made a good preacher by virtue of his glib delivery. He sells Cassius Marcellus Clay most convincingly. He's often mistaken for Chubby Checker, the Twist and Rock 'n' Roll idol. Since Chubby is also his idol he files no complaints on this score.'

The most successful female singer from the Philly conveyer belt was Dee Dee Sharp. She was still only eighteen when she first met Cassius by the pool at Miami's Sir John Hotel, and for much of their time together she was accompanied by a chaperone, her strict and sometimes overbearing mother. When they met in

Dee Dee Sharp, the one-time girlfriend of Cassius Clay. Throughout the early sixties she was one of the most successful recording artists in the early days of soul music. Sharp was signed to the Philadelphia label Cameo-Parkway and for a while she was the dance craze partner of Chubby Checker, the Philadelphian artist synonymous with the Twist. And she sang in D sharp.

Overtown, Sharp – whose real name was Dione LaRue – was arguably more famous than Cassius, but that would soon change as her hit records faded and his notoriety increased. It is not clear whether Cassius was romantically attracted to Sharp, or whether she was just another of the many contacts he was accruing in the entertainment industry. When they first met, he was impressed that she had once recorded with Chubby Checker, a singer whose soulful buffoonery had always appealed to him, but despite his hyperactivity, Cassius was not confident in the company of women. In his early years as a heavyweight contender, many of the people closest to him talked about his fascination with women – whom he described in the soul parlance of the day as 'foxes' – but in their company he tended to be shy and nervous.

Between 1961 and 1963, as Cassius worked his way up the heavyweight rankings, Sharp built her career as the dance craze movement's cheerful female star. As a teenager, she had benefited from the close relationship between pop and television. Sharp became the quintessential dance craze darling. The granddaughter of a prominent Philadelphia preacher, she was a gifted pianist and an accomplished gospel singer. She had her first solo hit with 'Mashed Potato Time' (1962), followed in quick succession by 'Gravy (For My Mashed Potatoes)' (1962), 'Baby Cakes' (1962), 'Ride' (1962) and 'Do The Bird'(1963). At the height of her fame, in 1962, she was the only female artist with three Top Ten hits on the *Billboard* charts, and one of the first black teen idols in the first phase of network television.

Paradoxically, Sharp may have lost out on her greatest opportunity. As her pop success soared, aspirational songwriters composed songs for her. In New York's Brill Building, the writers Gerry Goffin and Carole King were inspired when their babysitter Eva Narcissus Boyd demonstrated a local dance called the Locomotion. They hurriedly wrote a song and sent a demonstration copy to Cameo Records in Philadelphia but heard nothing back, and so recorded it with the babysitter. Little Eva's 'The Locomotion' (Dimension, 1962) became a global hit and one of the most addictive and successful songs from the dance craze era.

None of Sharp's hits were especially innovative or challenging, nor did they give any indication of how black music would intensify in the years to come, but they were a breakthrough of sorts and her glitzy television fame attracted Cassius. Dance craze records delivered the first sustained evidence of music from inside African-American communities that could sell extensively to the mainstream. Her hits were instantly recognisable to the teenage audiences who listened to local radio in Miami and Philadelphia. When the dance craze days waned, she briefly signed a deal with the Atlantic Records subsidiary ATCO and released a plea for a new musical direction, 'Help Me Find My Groove' (1968).

Beyond his brief affair with Dee Dee Sharp, Cassius had another reason to be attracted to Philadelphia. His interest in the teachings of Elijah Muhammad and the Nation of Islam were deepening, and his first point of contact, Sam Saxon, contacted the upper echelons of the organisation in Chicago looking for guidance. Saxon was advised to seek the support of a man from Philadelphia called Jeremiah Shabazz, who had been promoted to Minister of the Nation of Islam's Temple 15 in Atlanta, Georgia, and had overall responsibility for the Deep South, overseeing the business of mosques in Alabama, Florida, Georgia, Louisiana, Mississippi and South Carolina. Shabazz was born in Philadelphia. He attended the Benjamin Franklin High School, which at the time was suspected of educational radicalism and fell foul of the McCarthy purges, when it was accused of recruiting and tolerating Communist teachers. Shabazz graduated with honours and was subsequently drafted into the US Army, serving eighteen months in Japan and Korea. Returning home, he studied at Temple University College and took government jobs in the Post Office, Navy Department, Railway Mail Service and finally the Army Signal Corps. In 1955 he was sacked by the army for belonging to the Nation of Islam and so devoted his attention to the cause, rising to become the East Coast captain of the Fruit of Islam, a powerful quasi-paramilitary role within the organisation's feared security units. According to *The New Yorker*, Jeremiah Shabazz was 'not someone you'd ever wish to offend'.

At the time he was introduced to Cassius, Shabazz was on the verge of returning home to Philadelphia to head up Temple 12, the epicentre of the Nation's many activities in the city, some of them notably illegal. They had set up base in an old meeting hall at 1319–21 West Susquehanna Avenue in North Philadelphia and waves of recruitment had swollen their ranks. By the end of the sixties, membership of Temple 12 was estimated at 10,000, and its influence in both spiritual and criminal activity boomed. Within a decade, by the end of the seventies, it would be the home of Philadelphia's most feared criminal gang – the Black Mafia. Shabazz was one of Elijah Muhammad's closest advisers and an increasingly prominent figure in Cassius's growing entourage, and he would soon become a sworn enemy of the Nation of Islam leader Malcolm X. A dispute was looming. Shabazz was not simply a spiritual mentor but a man capable of building an alternative business network around Cassius. In time this would prove threatening to Cassius's pre-existing contracts with his sponsors back home in Louisville and with the nefarious characters from the Philadelphia mob that had a vice-like grip on fight fixing. Cassius often travelled with Shabazz during recruitment drives and attended speaking events in Philadelphia, furtively at first, and then more openly.

In September 1963 Cassius travelled to Philadelphia to hear Elijah Muhammad deliver a speech, 'Separation or Death', a deeply divisive message in the evolving philosophies of the Nation of Islam. Bespectacled and wearing his kofia hat adorned with an Islamic star and crescent logo, Muhammad's rambling speech reiterated the core beliefs: that African-Americans could obtain success through discipline, racial pride and physical separation from white society. It was the ideology of separateness that set the Nation of Islam apart from the wider civil-rights movement and the wave of desegregation that Martin Luther King had masterminded in hotels, restaurants and colleges. Shabazz continued to coach Cassius on the basic tenets of the Nation of Islam's separatist philosophies and travelled with him on the road to guide his thinking. More than anyone, he addressed doubts raised by Cassius and gave him the language and arguments to challenge critics.

Elijah Muhammad's address was delivered at an arena on the corner of 45th and Market Street, where *Bandstand* had first been recorded in the fifties. According to a report in the *Philadelphia Tribune*, Cassius 'wore an expensive silk mohair suit and a sullen expression on his face'. It was the first newspaper to report his presence at a Nation of Islam rally but no major newspapers beyond Philadelphia picked up on the account and it remained buried in the anonymity of regional news. Malcolm X was in the audience that day. He watched, disbelievingly at first, as the young boxer gracefully stood to acknowledge a standing ovation.

While Cassius learned first from Sam Saxon, then Jeremiah Shabazz and latterly Malcolm X, Dee Dee Sharp took her influences from much more traditional sources: her mother's spiritual direction, the local gospel choir and the Christian bible. Sharp did not warm to Shabazz and she has subsequently insisted that she was unsure about the spiritual journey that Cassius had embarked on. Apart from the vagaries of fame, the one thing they shared was an interest in black broadcasting. Sharp was a friend of a man who was something of a maven within north Philly's teenage black community, a remarkable local DJ called Georgie Woods – 'The Guy with the Goods'.

As the politics of educational desegregation gripped the city, Woods and his radio-led campaigns picketing against segregation brought black teenagers onto the streets to challenge discrimination. Not content with simply targeting the schooling system, they turned their attention to another institution where racial bias was rife – the nation's top teenage music programme, *American Bandstand*.

American Bandstand had cultivated a reputation across the years for breaking new music, but the story behind the scenes was considerably more murky. *American Bandstand* had a policy of segregation, choosing dancers from South Philadelphia's white Italian-American communities and ignoring or discouraging young black teenagers from queuing up to join the audience. Many black performers appeared on the show but precious few studio dancers were drawn from Philadelphia's inner-city ghettos.

At the very point that Cameo-Parkway was discovering a new generation of stars and a cosy relationship with *American Bandstand* was in place, Dick Clark changed the game. He decided to leave Philadelphia and move his entire operation to Hollywood where the opportunities in film and television were substantially greater. Cameo-Parkway had already contracted Patti LaBelle and the Bluebelles, Eddie Holman, Bunny Sigler and latterly Christine Cooper and Janie Grant, most of whom would set the pace locally until the upsurge of Philly Soul in the early seventies, but without *American Bandstand* to lean on and promote its product, the label plunged into sudden and irreversible decline. Times and tastes had changed. Soul music was deepening its significance and widening its range, and the new music from the British beat scene was reorientating American pop music. Overnight, the British Invasion had rendered many of their acts old-fashioned.

Strangely, at the very moment the label lost its relevance, Chubby Checker recorded one of his most inspiring songs, the gloriously up-tempo 'You Just Don't Know (What You Do To Me)' (Parkway, 1965), proof positive that his real talent as a singer was hidden beneath the weight of his tubby identity and the straitjacket of the Twist craze. Dee Dee Sharp also made her escape. She moved to another local Philadelphia label, Gamble Records, owned by her future husband Kenny Gamble. Freed from the confectionery limitations of the Cameo-Parkway sound, Sharp recorded one of her best records, 'What Kind Of Lady' (Gamble, 1968), a song with the layered and descanting subtlety of Motown and the early orchestral, more sophisticated experimentation that would come to define the Philly Sound.

At the top of the list of the things Cassius wanted to do in Philadelphia was to sit high in the upper tier of the Blue Horizon, universally regarded as one of the greatest boxing venues ever. He wanted to work out at Champs Gym in Strawberry Mansions, the home of his friend, the Philadelphia heavyweight Don Warner. Cassius had humiliated the self-styled 'KO Artist' back in February 1962, in what was his twelfth consecutive victory. According to Angelo Dundee, the Warner fight was a milestone. 'Warner was tough, another left-hooker, from Philadelphia, but Cassius kept him off balance . . . the guy would cock his hook, and Cassius would feint, stick and move away from the punch.' Reflecting on the fight, Dundee realised that Cassius had a talent that could evade and entertain all at the same time, defending himself in the most unorthodox way with his arms by his side, and his feet like lightning. At the time, Cassius had predicted the fight would end in the fifth round, but it was all over by the fourth, with Cassius claiming that Warner had not shook his hand and 'so a round was deducted for bad manners'. It was improvised shtick which the press fell for. In reality, when the mask of boxing was peeled away, the two men were on good terms. Warner extended an open invitation for Cassius to visit Champs and hang out with him in Philly. They travelled together to London in 1963, where they fought the Cooper twins. Cassius defeated the more talented Henry Cooper and Warner lost on points to Henry's identical twin George, on the undercard at Wembley Stadium.

For Cassius, Philadelphia had substance. It was a hotbed of local boxing talent, including his future great nemesis, Joe Frazier, then an amateur, who had won the first of his three Golden Gloves championships. By the time Cassius was courting Dee Dee Sharp, Frazier was on the cusp of selection for the US squad for the Olympic Games in Tokyo. He was working in Philadelphia's meat markets, skinning cattle in a kosher slaughterhouse. In his amateur days Frazier ran in the morning before reporting to work at the meat plant, then boxed at night at the Police Athletic League gym. He won the Middle Atlantic AAU championship in 1963 and 1964, racking up thirty-seven amateur bouts and losing only twice – both times to Buster Mathis, from Sledge, Mississippi, a giant of a boy who could never quite shake off the pounds and fulfil his potential. In a 1964 article, *Sports Illustrated* memorably described the heavyweight thus: 'He wobbles. He quivers. He rolls. He shakes. He is a dripping mass of flesh, a monument to fat. He is 6 feet 3 and weighs 295 pounds. His waist is 44, his chest is 52, but sometimes in the heat of action the measurements seem the other way around. Sitting in the corner, he looks like a melting chocolate sundae.'

Frazier had arrived in Philadelphia from Beaufort, South Carolina, and when he returned victorious from the Olympic Games, he became employed as an odd-job man at the Bright Hope Baptist Church. There he formed a local soul group, The Knockouts, whom he toured with as lead singer, appearing with Sammy Davis Jr and Dionne Warwick. Frazier's singing career stretched to nine single releases on indies like Jobo Records and Cloverlay, the latter, a label funded by his boxing syndicate. In later years he briefly signed up with majors like Capitol and Motown, and whatever the outcome of his many compelling fights with Muhammad Ali, when it came to soul music Cassius was the contender and Frazier the champ. Frazier was by far the superior singer and his gruff soul voice owed much to the legacy of the growling R&B sound that flourished in the ghetto bars of the fifties.

Cassius was also keen to meet up with Chubby Checker and DJ Georgie Woods. Cassius was in many respects an R&B DJ without a radio station, delivering his playful fantasy talk like an old-school rapper: 'It's hard to be humble when you're as great as I am'; 'I've wrestled with alligators, I've tussled with a whale. I done handcuffed lightning. And thrown thunder in jail. You know I'm bad. Just last week, I murdered a rock, injured a stone, hospitalised a brick. I'm so mean, I make medicine sick.' Much of this was borrowed wholesale from the airwaves, and it was inevitable he would bond with Woods, the guy with the goods, a man who influenced almost everyone he met.

Woods was born in Barnett, Georgia, a rural crossroads that was an hour north of Macon, the township that would also give birth to James Brown, Little Richard and Otis Redding. He was the ninth of eleven children and had a dirt-poor upbringing blemished by the worst experiences of the Deep South. 'Like many black families in the area,' the writer Mathew Delmont claims, 'Woods's family faced consistent threats from the Ku Klux Klan, culminating when the Klan burned a cross in his family's yard. While his father continued his work as a preacher in Georgia, Woods's mother moved the family to Harlem in 1936 to escape this racial violence and to find better employment and educational opportunities.'

The great migration north gave oxygen to black music. From about 1915 to 1970, more than six million African-Americans travelled north to Chicago, Detroit and New York, and their journey became a key catalyst in transforming rural blues music into the more sophisticated urban forms that become known as soul. Originally based in Harlem, Georgie Woods got his start in radio with WWRL, an R&B station in New York, and then moved to Philadelphia's radio station WHAT in 1953. He eventually moved across town to WDAS, which he began to refashion as the most hip and politically connected soul station in America. In 1957 he almost single-handedly broke the now historic Sam Cooke record 'You Send Me', playing it on heavy rotation and forcing other rival radio stations to follow suit. He organised a series of black music events at the city's Metropolitan Opera House, then at the Academy of Music in Center City, and finally at the Mastbaum Theater. The sell-out shows were a hybrid of the times, with big bands, local doo-wop amateurs and the featured singer LaVern Baker, who was billed as 'Little Miss Sharecropper'. Woods was fiercely committed to civil rights and was a prominent fundraiser for Martin Luther King's movement, once arranging for thirty local buses to transport protesters from inner-city Philadelphia to civil-rights demonstrations in the Deep South and to King's famous March on Washington for Jobs and Freedom in August 1963.

Woods was an agent of change. He sensed that the young people who came to his shows were the teenagers that society was blaming for all the ills of the day and so he – with the support of another local DJ, Mitch Thomas, the first African-American man to host a soul show on US television – promoted dances aimed at combating juvenile delinquency, using local skating rinks in Elmwood and Carmen as a base. He brought The Jive Five, Bobby Bland, Lee Dorsey, and the original purveyors of the Twist, Hank Ballard and the Midnighters, to Philadelphia, inviting them to take a stance on troubled youth. He was wise to the wider changes sweeping through America and attuned to the emergent soul groups that were forming in the Philadelphia public schools system.

In August 1963, a day after King's historic March on Washington, a black couple bought a new home in a suburban community called Delmar Village, in Folcroft. Horace Baker, a laboratory technician, and his wife, Sara, a nurse, both in their twenties, wanted a safe, peaceful environment in which to raise a family. They were not making a political statement. But as the Bakers tried to enter their new home on Heather Road, all hell broke loose. They were attacked by a mob throwing bricks and bottles. Later that night, their home was wrecked –the furnace, hot-water heater and plumbing fixtures were all destroyed – and left ransacked and uninhabitable. Gamely, the Bakers made repairs and tried to move in again, but this time they were met by a bigger mob of 1,500 whites who stoned the house and showered them in spit and racist insults. Windows were broken and the doors were virtually torn off the hinges. The rioters chanted, 'Two, four, six, eight – we don't want to integrate!' and hurled eggs, rocks and a Molotov cocktail before the state police intervened. After months of harassment and a distressing episode where police found Howard Baker wandering near the airport rambling incoherently that he couldn't protect his family any more, the Bakers decided to move. They eventually settled in Philadelphia's Mount Airy section, where they tried to get on with their lives.

It was a critical moment, when the worst racist extremes of the Deep South crept closer to Philadelphia. Georgie Woods spoke out against the violence, backing the Bakers and their right to a safe home. From as early as 1954, he organised soul music events with a political underpinning and told the *Philadelphia Tribune* that 'many of the teenagers who patronize these shows find in them an outlet for their emotions. And while previous single shows have been attended by as many as 30,000 teenagers we have never had any serious trouble. This proves, as far as I am concerned, that there might be less delinquency if there was more healthy entertainment such as that offered by our shows.'

One of Woods' biggest shows – held in May 1963, and his first fundraiser – starred Jackie Wilson and a singer he briefly recorded with that year, the gospel singer Linda Hopkins. The MC was a local Philadelphia comedian, the garrulous twenty-six-year-old Bill Cosby, who was destined to become more infamous than any of the acts he introduced. According to the *Philadelphia Tribune*, it attracted over 2,000 people and had 'the flavour of an old fashioned "down-home" revival'. The event raised $60,000 for the Philadelphia branch of the NAACP, an organisation that Woods had joined back in 1955. The money was earmarked for tackling racist failings in the local education system. In March 1964 he promoted another major show starring Sam Cooke, Jerry Butler, The Shirelles and Martha and the Vandellas at the Convention Hall in West Philadelphia to benefit the NAACP Legal Defence and Education Fund. It attracted an audience of 14,000, with a further 5,000 locked outside. Sam Cooke had travelled down from Harlem, where he had been sharing a hotel with Cassius while helping him promote his debut comedy album *I Am The Greatest*.

Woods told the radio historian Jacqui Webb: 'I got into civil rights because there was discrimination against black people everywhere, and I felt it personally.' He said that he then began to use his radio shows to promote black music and to draw attention to local injustices. 'I'd go on air and tell people where I was going to be demonstrating, and a mob of people would show up and I had a microphone and I was directing people . . . When school got out all the teenagers came and got into the picket lines because I was there demonstrating for our rights.' In what was an early version of 'flash mobs', Woods encouraged young people to congregate after his show – to demonstrate at local restaurants, factories or nightclubs where there were discriminatory practices. Armed with a growing reputation and a vast army of listeners from high schools across the city, Woods became a local irritant to *American Bandstand* by organising picket lines and demonstrations outside the show's studios. The show's discriminatory policy of snubbing young blacks had not gone unnoticed. Far from being a beacon of interracial tolerance, as claimed by Dick Clark in later life, *American Bandstand* was a stubborn bastion of whites-only studio policy. Woods not only highlighted bad practice but pointed the finger at the show, bringing it unwanted negative attention and scaring core advertisers. Across America

R&B DJs were developing into something more than garrulous characters who played records. Many were deeply embedded in community politics and in some cases – such as Martha Jean 'The Queen' Steinberg, in Detroit, Jack 'The Rapper' Gibson in Cassius's native Louisville, and Georgie Woods in Philadelphia – were cogs in the machinery of civil rights.

In his pursuit of a more racially fair Philadelphia, Woods had built up a friendship with a remarkable educator, a gentleman by the name of Floyd L. Logan, who as early as 1932 had founded the city's Educational Equality League 'to obtain and safeguard educational opportunities for all peoples regardless of race, color, religion, or national origin'. Circumstances and shared values brought the DJ and the veteran educator into alliance. This was an era when the desegregation of schools was making headline news, in part because of the violence that erupted during the tense days to integrate Little Rock High School in 1957. Coincidentally, this high-profile civil-rights dispute brought another prominent DJ to the fore. Al Bell, who shaped the careers of the Staple Singers and Isaac Hayes, and rose to become the co-owner of Stax Records in Memphis, campaigned on behalf of the Little Rock families. By 1971, when soul was at its triumphant height and Cassius had become Muhammad Ali, Bell featured alongside the boxer in *Ebony* magazine's list of The 100 Most Influential Black Americans.

A number of recurring themes were in clear view: the divisive issue of schooling, the gathering power of the civil-rights movement, the communicative influence of R&B radio DJs, and the emergence of a commercially exciting form of black music, which was increasingly attracting the name 'soul'. They all merged in Philadelphia, when Logan and Woods joined forces to target Girard College, a boarding school set in a leafy campus north of Fairmount Avenue.

The Girard campaign, which gathered momentum from 1962 to 1965, became a catalyst in the story of Philadelphia soul music. Woods rallied the troops nightly, playing extraordinary new music and inviting young teenagers to take action. Listening to the radio in their bedrooms and witnessing Martin Luther King's protests on television, young African-Americans were empowered, and many would come to transform music in the city. Among their number were Kenny Gamble, then a twenty-year-old apprentice on the morning show at radio station WDAS who had recently signed as a solo artist to Columbia Records; Weldon McDougal Jr, a founding member of local group The Larks; and Howard 'Frankie' Beverly, then an eighteen-year-old who had formed his first group The Blenders and would soon form the quintessential Philly Soul group Frankie Beverly and the Butlers, and then the jazz-funk supergroup Maze. All three had been keen high-school musicians who supported the demonstrations and brought hundreds along with them for the cause.

At the core of the dispute was a far from simple issue which dated back to early nineteenth-century philanthropy, when the wealthy banker Stephen Girard bequeathed $6 million to create a residential school for impoverished children, specifically 'poor, white, male orphans'. However noble Girard's intentions were, by the early sixties, the original founding principle of the bequest was at odds with racial integration and in breach of Supreme Court laws on education. Put simply, why should poor black orphans not benefit from the college and its scholarships? Throughout the fifties local educationalists within the African-American community had tested the restricted covenants at Girard. Then, in 1954, when *Brown v. Board of Education* ruled that racial segregation of children in public schools was unconstitutional, lawyers argued that Stephen Girard's original will and legacy were out of step with social change and effectively broke the law. The dispute dragged on through the courts, and by the sixties the NAACP had reached a point whereby the law had been exhausted. They decided to turn the Girard issue into a civil-rights matter. With Georgie Woods marshalling the support of his teenage audience via the airwaves, the dispute rose in both prominence and temperature.

Events like the Girard demonstration troubled Cassius. Enthused by the segregationist message of the Nation of Islam he believed that schools should be separated on racial lines and that black schools should teach African-American history. His own high school – Central High in Louisville – did not integrate white children until the seventies. But in the company of charismatic campaigners like Georgie Woods, he could be swayed. Woods always argued that it was not simply a matter of integration: it was about opening up the best possible opportunities to ghetto teenagers. Why should white kids alone benefit from Girard's fortunes?

The desegregation of Girard became a local cause célèbre that black teenagers and their parents could jointly support. The protests began in 1963 but gained momentum and become less easy to control right up until the summer of 1965 when the police department received word that protestors might attempt to scale the college's ten-foot-high walls, and promptly sent a thousand officers to patrol the area. The officers were originally met by a mere thirty-eight demonstrators, but each week the numbers grew, and at its height a ring of demonstrators around the campus numbered in the thousands and numerous arrests were made at the main gates. It was a rite of passage for many teenagers from the city's ghettos, one that directly coincided with the launch of an innovative new record label, Arctic Records, founded by another WDAS DJ, Jimmy Bishop (for a short spell the station's programme director and Georgie Woods' boss). Arctic showcased some of the area's most accomplished groups, notably The Volcanoes, Harold Melvin & The Blue Notes, The Tiffanys, Kenny Gamble, and The Temptones, a local mixed-race group which featured Daryl Hall and John Oates. Although the label was never officially tied to the Girard desegregation issue, its artists most definitely were.

Barbara Mason was only seventeen years old when the demonstrations flared up. She had been experimenting with songwriting since she was fourteen. A near neighbour of Weldon McDougal of The Larks, they periodically went along to the campus to picket, and as their friendship grew, McDougal brought her to Arctic, where her self-penned ballad 'Yes, I'm Ready' (1965) broke nationally and became the label's first hit.

Although Georgie Woods is now a footnote in the story of soul, who only fronted a couple of now obscure records, his influence within the evolution of music in Philadelphia is immense. One of those songs was 'Potato Salad', a primitive party rap credited to 'Broadway Eddie', a former bail bondsman turned record-store owner whose real name was Edward Warhoftig. An obscure novelty number, 'Potato Salad' was arranged by Vince Montana, who went on to be a founding figure in the disco movement, first with Philadelphia International and then in New York with Salsoul Records.

Woods stayed at WDAS until 1966, when yet another dispute about him using airtime to promote political causes led to his dismissal. He returned to his spiritual home with the Banks family at radio station WHAT and subsequently served as a vice-president of the Philadelphia NAACP chapter.

He was on air from six till nine on the night of 4 April 1968, when Martin Luther King was assassinated, and such was his status as a community broadcaster that, according to the editors of *The Broadcast Pioneers of Philadelphia*, he calmed the public mood. 'Many people in the city have credited Georgie Woods, Louise Williams and Jimmy Bishop . . . with directly being responsible for preventing rioting in the streets of Philadelphia after the assassination of Dr. Martin Luther King. WDAS suspended all regular programming in an unprecedented move by Bob Klein. [Gospel DJ] Louise Williams held down the first marathon shift while organizing her gospel library for use by all the other jocks. News people, civil-rights activists from Philadelphia and across the country appeared or phoned in constant reminders of Dr. King's teachings of non-violence. In 1969, George and WDAS urged the population of the area to turn in their guns. Many hundreds did so and Woods was credited with making Philadelphia a safer place to live.'

In later life Georgie Woods moved to the Sunshine State, commenting that 'I might be in Florida, but Philadelphia will always be my home'. He died there in 2005.

As far as Cassius and his law-abiding sponsors back in Louisville were concerned, Philadelphia had another notoriety. It had the misfortune to be one of the bloody arteries of illegal gambling and the Mafia's corrosive grip on boxing. Few fighters in the early sixties could escape the malign influence of organised crime. Cassius had in many ways broken the mould, seeking the backing of well-established local businessmen in his hometown, while the incumbent heavyweight champion Sonny Liston had become synonymous with crime, corruption and brooding violence. In a blistering obituary, *Village Voice* writer Joe Flaherty described Liston as 'a blatant *mother in a fucker's game*' and recounted the boxer's hatred of Philadelphia, where he encountered police harassment. When Liston was caught speeding in the city and fined, he told the judge, 'I'd rather be a lamppost in Denver than Mayor of Philadelphia.'

In March 1963, in contrast to Liston's crime-infested world, the respected magazine *Sports Illustrated* profiled the Louisville Sponsoring Group who had funded Cassius since his Olympic victory. The article spoke in disbelieving tones of how such a cast of honest and trustworthy men had found themselves in a world of gangsters:

> In the salt-and-pepper-carpeted, walnut-panelled, fibreglass-draped conference room of the law offices of Wyatt, Grafton & Sloss in Louisville, the meeting came to order – all business. Along the sides of the glossy, oblong table sat half a dozen captains of Kentucky industry – tobacco, whisky, horses, communications, transportation and banking – and at one end sat an attorney noted for his agility in the conundrums of tax law . . .
>
> In a time when prize fighting . . . is beclouded by underworld shenanigans, misappropriated funds, government investigation and a generally sorrowful malaise, Cassius Clay and his backers are a unique and uplifting sight. Clay's fists and his big mouth are making the gates, and the 11 men are making a kind of boxing history . . . Representative of an almost complete cross section of Louisville business, the backers are, with one exception, millionaires or heirs to family fortunes, and they are so innocent of any background in professional boxing that when you say 'uppercut' they think first of their income taxes. Yet they are giving boxing a fresh look. They have provided Clay an ideal, all-expenses-paid training program, they offer him the benefit of

all their experience and business acumen, and they surround him with a substantial moral and ethical environment, a rare commodity in professional boxing. And since they are independently wealthy Clay is assured that he will never end up exploited and broke through any fault of theirs.

Robert F. Kennedy, the president's brother, welcomed this good-citizen model and often talked of the group as the ideal blueprint for how boxers should be managed. He was determined to clean up boxing and Philadelphia was one of the cities where his staff focused their attention. Kennedy's career had begun in 1951 when he took up a role as a lawyer in the criminal division of the Justice Department. By 1957 he was chief counsel of the Senate Rackets Committee, the first staging post in what was to become a dramatic war with the Mafia. His first notable success came with corrupt labour unions, primarily in the Bakers and Confectioners Union, the Mechanics, the Carpenters, and the network of coin-machine operators who controlled pinball machines and the mob-infested jukebox industry, which gathered a tax on 45s from bar owners and teenage hangouts. When he became Attorney General in 1961, Kennedy intensified his fight against organised crime, targeting the gambling industry, prostitution, narcotics traffic and commercial pornography. Almost inevitably, boxing appeared on his radar. The once 'noble art' had become infested with rogue promoters, fraudulent bouts and betting scandals.

For a time it was a David v. Goliath operation. Organised crime had tentacles across America, from decrepit Mafia godfathers to smart suburban consigliore and street-level hustlers. Kennedy's operation was minuscule by comparison. In January 1961, the Crime and Rackets Section of the Justice Department employed fewer than twenty people and the better-resourced FBI under Hoover showed little interest in tackling the mob. The latter seemed disinclined to believe that organised crime even existed. In a series of barnstorming speeches, Kennedy raged against a 'private government of organized crime with an annual income of billions, resting on a base of human suffering and moral corrosion'. With the 1960 publication of his book *The Enemy Within*, Kennedy, now styled as RFK, saw the war on organised crime and corrupt boxing not merely as a matter of criminal activity but a matter of moral urgency. It became his cri de coeur.

By 1963, as Cassius built up his reputation as a heavyweight contender, RFK's team had grown to sixty, with officers across all the main urban centres, including Philadelphia. Under the watchful paranoid eye of Hoover, who interpreted the move as a threat to the FBI's power, RFK opened federal investigative bureaux in cities beyond Washington and tasked them with gathering information on racketeers. Congress approved a series of anti-crime laws, one of which sought to dismantle nationwide betting systems. In November 1962, a gambling and prostitution establishment in Detroit which had been turning over $20 million a year was raided and closed down, and in the first six months of 1963 over 150 racketeers were indicted. Then, in October of that year, RFK managed to persuade the gangster Joseph Valachi to testify against the mob. Valachi, an ex-getaway driver, thief and low-level soldier in the Luciano crime family, became the first member of the Cosa Nostra to reveal the activities of what RKF described as a 'cruel and calculating' organisation. The hearings in which he testified were broadcast live on television, fascinating a nation that was both appalled and intrigued by the fact that organised crime actually existed. It was against this backdrop that the business of boxing was put under the spotlight of criminal investigation.

Blinky Palermo and Frankie Carbo's vice-like grip on the middleweight boxing division dated back to 1949; their influence over middleweight champion Jake LaMotta, the notorious 'Raging Bull', had initially given them a pivotal hold over anyone and anywhere he might box. Their malevolence spread like a virus through the professional ranks, and at the height of their influence, Palermo and Carbo controlled the world welterweight champion Virgil 'Honeybear' Akins, the highly ranked heavyweight contender Clarence Henry, another welterweight champion Johnny Saxton, heavyweight contender Coley Wallace and the lightweight

Ike Williams. Their ambition was to move up the ranks to heavy-weight, where the real money was to be made.

Palermo had controlled boxing in Philadelphia for decades. He was a thorn in the side of Tom and Bob Montgomery, two brothers who were well known in the fight game there. Bob 'Bobcat' Montgomery was the former world lightweight champion, and his brother and manager Tom was Philadelphia's boxing commissioner. Keen to control all the major divisions, Palermo leaned on the Montgomerys, but he could not penetrate their close family ties or breach the racial divide that separated his largely Italian-American operation from the African-American fighters who gathered around the Montgomery clan. In 1963 Tom Montgomery's daughter left their Germantown home to carve out her own career. As a teenager, Tammi had sung and toured with the James Brown Revue. During that time, according to her family, she was sexually and physically abused by Brown. After a torrid affair with David Ruffin and failed attempts to build a career at Wand Records in New York and Chess in Chicago, Tammi agreed to a name change and signed for Detroit's Motown as Tammi Terrell, where she enjoyed brief but phenomenal success as a duet singer with Marvin Gaye.

In an interview with the *Observer* newspaper, sports columnist and screenplay writer Budd Schulberg remembered Palermo and Carbo's control of the welterweight division: 'Frankie Carbo, the mob's unofficial commissioner for boxing, controlled a lot of the welters and middles . . . Not every fight was fixed, of course, but from time to time Carbo and his lieutenants, like Blinky Palermo in Philadelphia, would put the fix in. When the Kid Gavilan–Johnny Saxton fight was won by Saxton on a decision in Philadelphia in 1954, I was covering it for *Sports Illustrated* and wrote a piece at that time saying boxing was a dirty business and must be cleaned up now. It was an open secret. All the press knew that one – and other fights – were fixed. Gavilan was a mob-controlled fighter, too, and when he fought Billy Graham it was clear Graham had been robbed of the title. The decision would be bought. If it was close, the judges would shade it the way they had been told.'

By the early sixties, Palermo and his partner not only controlled the Southside Philadelphia gyms, they owned a majority stake in the contract of the reigning heavyweight champion Sonny Liston and shared the winnings with the St Louis mobster John Vitale, who had been arrested on thirteen separate occasions on suspicion of murder, robbery and illegal gambling. RFK saw Palermo, Carbo and Vitale as legitimate targets in his campaign to clean up the sport, while they seized an opportunity to acquire a share of Liston's fights. Now living in Philadelphia, Liston was often spotted in the Sansom Deli conspiring with Palermo. The net was closing in on the gangsters, and a fascinating cat-and-mouse game was about to begin.

Cassius and his trainer saw Liston as the ultimate opponent, and they began a campaign of vilification to unsettle and enrage the brooding heavyweight champion. The scene was set for what was to become one of the most beguiling rivalries in modern sport.

In 1960, after serving short sentences for managing boxers without a licence, Palermo and Carbo were subpoenaed to appear before an investigation committee into mob control of boxing led by Senator Estes Kefauver of Tennessee. Kefauver's committee visited fourteen major cities in fifteen months at a time when everyday American consumers were buying their first television sets. When they reached New Orleans, a local television station requested permission to televise an hour of the proceedings. It was a surprise hit with audiences new to the rawness of live documentary testimony, and so by the time the committee hearings arrived in New York the stakes were raised and television companies were fighting over the transmission rights. Testifying before the committee in New York was Mafia boss Frank Costello, a razor-sharp gangster whose flashy style came to personify the Italian-American crime boss in the public imagination. When his legal counsel objected to the cameras, the operators directed their focus at Costello's hands, which twitched nervously; according to the pop psychology of the day, this confirmed his guilt to the nation. It was a hugely popular moment in early documentary television and fascinated older Americans just as powerfully as *American Bandstand* was engaging its teenage audience.

Palermo was summoned to appear but pleaded the Fifth Amendment, and then, in a frustrating testimony which enraged Senator Kefauver, Carbo pleaded the Fifth Amendment twenty-five times consecutively. As a consequence, the senator recommended that Palermo and Carbo be cited for Contempt of Congress. The following year, they were charged with conspiracy and extortion and found guilty of cheating the NBA welterweight champion Don Jordan out of his rightful earnings. After a three-month trial, in which Attorney General Senator Robert Kennedy served as prosecutor, Carbo and Palermo were each sentenced to a total of twenty-five years in prison.

But like so much of boxing chicanery at the time, a further twist was in store. Back in 1960, an NYPD undercover detective named Anthony Bernhard had appeared before the Kefauver Committee, where he described a private dinner attended by Blinky Palermo, Frankie Carbo and Sam Margolis, the Philadelphia vending-machine boss. The dinner had been held at Goldie Ahearn's Charcoal Pit Restaurant in Washington, DC – 'Where Champs Wine and Dine' – and on the guest list was one Angelo Dundee, who knew Margolis from their younger days around the gyms in South Philadelphia. Watching the proceedings from two other tables were undercover FBI agents. Restaurant owner turned boxing promoter Isidore Goldstein, aka Goldie Ahearn, was seen backslapping at least five members of the Mafia who individually and collectively had a trail of connections to the business end of professional boxing. It was a dinner that raised many suspicions, the most obvious being that Carbo was manoeuvring his way into two rival camps: the team that trained Cassius at the 5th Street Gym in Miami and Sonny Liston's already compromised management team. To the FBI officers, it confirmed their suspicions about boxing in the early sixties, a sport that even the eminent boxing correspondent Jimmy Cannon called 'the swill barrel of sports'. The forces of law and order were gradually tightening around Blinky Palermo; he had seen off various charges in the past, but the evidence was stacking up against him. As the guests laughed and drank, they seemed not only comfortable in each other's company but celebratory in their behaviour, as if a deal had been struck or arrangements were in place. What no one at the table was remotely aware of was the lengthy jail sentences that Carbo and Palermo were facing and how, in the years to come, the growing influence of Cassius X and the Nation of Islam would change the game.

A change is gonna come . . . A remarkable photograph of Sam Cooke and Cassius, taken the day after Cassius had become heavyweight champion of the world, during a photo shoot at the boxer's home in Miami. Cooke, who had thirty Top 40 hits between 1957 and 1964, had been Cassius's mentor in the world of entertainment. In 1963, he secured Cassius a recording contract with Columbia/CBS and collaborated with him on the song, 'The Gang's All Here'.

NEW YORK

The Winter of Boxing

On 3 February 1963, Cassius X had taken the Amtrak train north from Penn Station as it followed the Hudson River to Rensselaer, where he took a taxi to his hotel in Albany. The next day, he was due to appear before New York State's Joint Legislative Committee on Professional Boxing, which was contemplating a bill to abolish boxing. A series of troubling deaths in the ring had brought the sport from the back pages to the front, and three of them were linked to Cassius, although he was not on trial. A column in *The New York Times* entitled 'The Manly Art' thundered against boxing, questioning whether a sport that ends in fatal injuries should be tolerated in the state. Governor Nelson Rockefeller responded to widespread public disaffection with boxing after a dramatic night on Saturday, 24 March 1962, when the Cuban boxer Benny Paret was fatally injured during a televised bout from Madison Square Garden. Rockefeller launched an investigation into the managing and promotion of fights, heaping pressure on the members of the committee. 'The question everybody is asking is whether this fight was allowed to go on too long. A better question might be whether it, or any other professional prize-fight, should be allowed to start,' he declared. Boxing was in a perilous state and staring extinction in the face.

The Parlor Rooms in the New York State Capitol building had been ruined by modernity. Externally, the building had the same spectacular self-confidence of the White House, but inside it was a mess of chaotic compromise. The Westchester marble that adorned the exterior of the building had been carved by prisoners at Sing Sing Correctional Facility and pieced together into a stunning edifice of government power until progress took its cynical hold and twentieth-century business practice wrecked the building. False ceilings had been dropped beneath the original features to accommodate heating, ventilation and air-conditioning. Mezzanines had been jerry-built beneath the once soaring and magisterial vaults, the windows were fitted with milky glass, and the viewing galleries, originally built for the public to observe the Assembly's proceedings and marvel at democracy at work, were now walled off from the main chamber and used to house photocopiers and mountainous reams of paper. A once great building had been spoiled.

The politicians inside had much to reflect on. In 1962 there were 14 deaths in registered professional boxing; since 1945 a total of 216. In Los Angeles, on 21 September 1962, the Argentine heavyweight Alejandro Lavorante, a hard man who had once worked as a chauffeur cum hired muscle for Argentine dictator Juan Perón, failed to recover consciousness after being knocked out by the Detroit-born heavyweight Johnny Riggins. Once ranked number three in the world, Lavorante was plummeting down the rankings and told local sports journalists it would be 'back to the minors' if he didn't win. Mike Casey, editor of the All Time Boxing website, described Lavorante being carried from the ring on a stretcher. 'The pictures of him being helped onto his stool, his trunks a bloody mess, are still hard to look at. He looked as if he had been pulled from a mangled car.' Lavorante underwent extensive brain surgery and eventually returned home to Argentina, but he never recovered. He died in April 1964, only twenty-seven years old.

Cassius had fought Lavorante two months earlier, the latter succumbing to two knockdowns and a final count of ten. There was a cruel irony: the fight was a fundraiser for the boxing charity Fight For Lives, but Lavorante struggled to cope with Cassius's staggering pace and range of punches. The Argentinean had suffered so many knockouts in such a short period of time that he was probably carrying neurological damage with him to each new fight, and if his death was the result of cumulative beatings, then Cassius was one of several boxers who unintentionally contributed to it.

The spate of deaths had also claimed the life of the Detroit heavyweight Sonny Banks, the man who first knocked Cassius down. He died after a nine-bout round in May 1965 with Leotis Martin, a heavyweight from the Champs Gym in Philadelphia. Martin was a boxing enigma. Cursed by a debilitating stutter, he was painfully shy and withdrawn, and his reticence stood out in a sport more commonly associated with big mouths and braggadocio. For years Martin was overlooked, confined to an understudy role as his stablemate Joe Frazier rose up the heavyweight rankings. But Martin's shyness disguised a ferocious power. *Philadelphia Daily News* columnist Bill Conlin remembers the moment of contact. 'I can still hear the bass drum sound of Banks's head hitting the mat. And I can still see them, bearing him to the locker room on a stretcher, the fighter lapsing in and out of consciousness.' Curiously, those inside the dead boxer's camp were less sure that Martin had delivered the fatal blow. Banks' corner men claimed that he had been the victim of the dark arts, specifically an underhand practice common in many gyms at the time. The canvas had been torn, and rather than be replaced it was repaired with a coating of cement. Close witnesses claimed that Banks' head had struck a concrete patch, knocking him out cold. He fleetingly regained consciousness but lapsed back into a coma and died in hospital. Banks was the 65th professional boxer to die from ring-related injuries in a period of five years.

Anxiety about the death toll of boxing had been heightened by the rise of network television. On the evening of 24 March 1962, Madison Square Garden was circled with cameras for a live Friday night screening of the ABC show *Fight of the Week*. A prime-time audience of millions watched the Cuban Bernardo 'Benny the Kid' Paret fight the reigning welterweight champion Emile Griffith, a charismatic boxer who had many of the same flashy characteristics as Cassius. Paret was trapped in a corner and left hanging pathetically on the ropes. Ten days after the fight, he died of a brain haemorrhage in New York's Roosevelt Hospital. Millions had watched the gruesome scenes from the comfort of their homes. Cassius was back in Miami watching the fight on television. There was division in the ranks at the 5th Street Gym. Cassius's friend Luis Rodríguez was scheduled to fight Griffith in a double-header later in 1963, so the Cubans were vociferously backing his opponent, their friend and fellow exile Paret, while Cassius, hard-wired to support the African-American, was siding with Griffith, a popular figure on the streets of Harlem and, like Cassius, one of a new generation of boxers attuned to the soul music scene.

Emile Griffith was known in the ghetto for his ostentatious dress sense and openly gay lifestyle. Originally from the Virgin Islands, he had come to America as part of the great migration from the Caribbean in the fifties. He grew up in an overcrowded slum above a Chinese restaurant in central Harlem, where even from a young age he provided the main income for a sprawling family of brothers, sisters and cousins. A neighbour of the heroin-addicted doo-wop star Frankie Lymon, Griffith was driven by a youthful interest in fashion and would regularly walk the length of 125th Street, gazing at the hat shops, the fashion stores and the radiant 'clothes horses' that lit up Harlem street life. As a teenager, Griffith managed to secure a job at a milliners in Manhattan. It proved to be a transformative apprenticeship. Each day, he travelled downtown by subway to learn the techniques of hat design, working in a mainly female environment, surrounded by a riot of colours in a stuffy warehouse with no air-conditioning. In the summer, as New York broiled in claustrophobic heat, Griffith frequently stripped to the waist, happy to show off his muscular torso. By chance, his boss was an amateur boxing enthusiast and as a challenge, hatmaker Howard Albert joked that he could train Griffith to become a Golden Gloves champion. Egged on by the women he worked with, the workplace joke became a reality, and by 1958, with Albert as his co-manager, Griffith was regularly winning fights at the St Nicholas Arena, a training ground for Harlem's finest fighters. Griffith's celebrity grew like wildfire, and he was a regular at Harlem's early sixties soul haunts: the Hi-Hat, the Baby Grand, the Palm Café, Willie Abraham's Gold Lounge and the Shalimar. His fastidious fashion sense and soft-spoken manner cast him as one of the ghetto's most renowned 'sophisticated cissies', but his powerful fists, mechanical punching and physique earned him respect.

Then came the fateful night in 1962. As Griffith's career blossomed, he had been matched in a series of fights with Paret, who had moved to Spanish East Harlem as a teenager. *Sports Illustrated* described Paret as a man defined by arrogance. 'In his heyday, Benny (Kid) Paret was a cocky little man who favoured bright, heavy jewellery, but he once cut sugar cane for $2 a day in the fields of Santa Clara, Cuba, where he was born.' Initially, the two welterweights had considered themselves neighbourhood friends, but Paret's crude, impudent personality cast him as the polar opposite of the disarmingly elegant, charming Griffith.

Either instinctively, or at the behest of his management, Paret dropped the pretence of teenage friendship and began to target Griffith's sexuality. The rivalry tipped into open hatred. At the weigh-in, as they posed for the photographers at the scales, Paret cursed Griffith in Spanish calling him a *maricón*, gutter Spanish for homosexual. Later that day, he complained to his wife that his head hurt and he didn't want to fight, but he knew he couldn't back out. According to *Sports Illustrated*, the fight was marked with bad blood, and 'episodes of anger and resentment – butts, surly shoves, low blows and milling after the bell'. Then, in the tenth round, after persistent taunting, Griffith lost control. A contemporary report described the grotesque climax of the fight: 'Emile's hand banging against Benny's jaw as remorselessly as the clapper of a great, dark bell. Paret sagged back against the middle turnbuckle. Griffith's punches drove his head out between the top and middle strands. Benny was helpless, bleeding from his nose and a cut on his right cheek; his puffed eyes were closed. Still Griffith punched him, with mounting and maniacal rage, as though determined, literally, to wipe out both Paret and the memory of his taunt. There were, in all, about 15 uppercuts, followed by several hooks. Then Referee Goldstein was tugging at Griffith from behind, pulling him off. As Emile, berserk, struggling passionately in Goldstein's embrace, was dragged away, Paret, now obviously senseless, crumpled slowly and collapsed.'

The inquest into Paret's death pointed the finger not only at Griffith's untrammelled rage but at the New York Boxing Board which had allowed the fight to go ahead, despite three previous fights where suspicions that Paret was suffering from brain damage had been raised. It was the beginning of the long road of investigation that brought Cassius to Albany, to appear before the committee.

Boxing was on trial. On Monday, 4 February 1963, Cassius walked the short distance from his hotel, along State Street and up past the green lawns of east Capitol Park, and was then escorted through the lobbies of the State Capitol building and on to the stand. Giving evidence alongside him were Rocky Marciano, the retired lightweight Billy Graham, ex-New York Yankees infielder Gil McDougald and Edward 'Ned' Irish, basketball promoter and president of the New York Nicks. Sitting edgily throughout the proceedings was Harry Markson, the chief publicity officer of Madison Square Garden, who was perilously close to the mob but somehow managed to walk a virtuous path through tangled and poisonous terrain. For years now, he had been agonising over poor ticket revenue at the Garden and a fear that the halcyon days of boxing were in the past. But that was before Cassius came to town.

Cassius's next bout was with a local New Yorker, Doug Jones, then the third-ranked heavyweight in the division. The fight was scheduled for 13 March 1963, which would give Cassius a full month to train in New York and hone his phenomenal promotional skills in a city synonymous with hype. 'I'm gonna shake up this town,' he would tell *Time* magazine, inviting their photographer to follow him as he distributed free Florida oranges to passers-by in Times Square. It would be Cassius's first fight at Madison Square Garden and he was determined to squeeze every last drop of publicity out of the Jones bout. In a whirlwind of self-promotion Cassius toured New York, seeking out anyone who would listen. His assault on the Manhattan media was a master-class in self-promotion, including tours of network television shows, spontaneous stunts, back-page headlines and street-corner campaigning, and ignited a rush on ticket sales. The night before he travelled to attend the hearings, Cassius was a guest on *Ed Sullivan* where he joked about the forthcoming fight and performed one of his favourite magic tricks, in which he used sleight-of-hand to turn a blue chiffon handkerchief into a walking cane. He had been practising simple magic tricks since his childhood in Louisville, and although he was never a great talent, he was adept enough at deception and close-up magic to pull off uncomplicated tricks.

At the time of the Jones fight, New York's newspapers were on strike. The protracted dispute about low wages and resistance to new automated printing presses had negatively affected live theatre shows, new cinema releases and sporting events, so Cassius put his efforts into radio and television, appearing on the *Today* show live from RCA studios and later the same night with Johnny Carson on *The Tonight Show*, where he was a guest with Paul Anka's singing partner Micki Marlo. Ironically, it was a speculative live theatre appearance, squeezed in between the two television shows, that generated the most attention. Cassius travelled downtown to the Bitter End coffee-house on Bleecker Street, the heart of the beatnik Greenwich Village scene. Dressed in his trademark black suit and the tell-tale black bow tie, Cassius was escorted into the café by a small entourage of Harlem Muslims. On stage, standing with his back to the club's chipped and corroding brick wall, and in part shielded by a stand of microphones, he read from a sheet of white notepaper. As ever, his poems lacked subtlety or lyrical allusion but what they lacked in sophistication was made up for in the charming and clunky doggerel: 'My secret is self-confidence/A champion at birth/I'm

lyrical, I'm fresh, I'm smart/My fists have proved my worth.'
A crowd of up to 250 young and mostly white beatniks, many
bespectacled and wearing heavy duffel coats in the uniform of Left
Bank cool, cheered his verse, and as a finale four student girls took
to the stage, awkwardly raising his arms aloft in triumph.

(Later in life, the Bitter End evolved to become one of the great
spaces in the history of soul music's singer-songwriter era. Stevie
Wonder shed his Motown child-prodigy image and matured into
a substantial artist there, and it became the basement where Curtis
Mayfield recorded an album (*Curtis/Live!*, 1971) and rival Donny
Hathaway recorded side two of his New York album *Live* (1971),
which included a piano-led version of Marvin Gaye's historic
'What's Going On'.)

A few days before the fight, as momentum was gathering,
Cassius's opponent Doug Jones approached fight matchmaker
Teddy Brenner and demanded extra complimentary tickets for his
friends. There was a stand-off in Brenner's office when, according
to *Sports Illustrated*, Brenner stood up to Jones. 'Let me tell you
something, Doug, my boy,' he reportedly told the fighter. 'If you
don't show up, Clay can shadow-box three rounds, recite poetry
for ten minutes, and everybody will have a ball and go home happy.
But if Clay doesn't show up, we can announce that you're going to
fight a live gorilla and we'll have a riot from people demanding
their money back.'

Cassius was now the most talked-about boxer in the world
and, although not universally loved, he had generated so much
attention he could not be ignored. On 3 February 1963, he took
his place in the Albany legislature. Assembled before him in an
arch of sonorous concern were the members of the Joint Legislative
Committee on Professional Boxing – all men, all white, and all
drawn from the conservative mainstream. Their task: to get to
grips with boxing, its fatalities and its curious subcultures. High
on their agenda were deaths in the ring and rigged fights, which in
turn led the proceedings into the dark chicanery of betting
scandals and organised crime. Sitting opposite Cassius were: State
Senator William T. Conklin, a Brooklyn-based career politician
who, at the time, was a pioneering figure in the education of

children with special needs; State Senator Hunter Meighan, director of the Knickerbocker Federal Savings and Loan Company; the chairman of the Democratic Party in Queens, Assemblyman Moses M. Weinstein, distinguished by his pencil-thin moustache; the squat Assemblyman, Alexander Chananau; State Senator and lawyer Frank J. Pino; and Haywood J. Plumadore, the committee's bespectacled and owlish chairman. Plumadore began the proceedings and invited Cassius to make his own opening remarks. Something strange and possibly transformative happened. The boastful personality that had come to define the young boxer gave way to one of maturity, the joking rhyming couplets replaced with lyricism.

It is to Cassius's credit that he was confident in the face of white bureaucracy. Others before him had stumbled, evaded or simply run out of coherent words. As the committee probed him for his perspective on the malaise boxing had slumped into, Cassius gazed out the darkened windows to the snow-covered lawns outside, and spoke to the assembled room about changing times. Using the passage of the seasons to explain the state that the fight game had found itself in, he described boxing as living perilously in 'the winter of its life'. Cassius was now well versed in the ways of the media and frequently sat down with journalists and photographers to help them shape what their editors wanted. His words sounded as if they were aimed at *The New York Times* or the *Washington Post*. 'In winter, leaves are not on trees,' Cassius mused. 'The grass and flowers are dead; the mind is thinking of chilli and hot foods. Time is why. But the earth rotates around the sun . . . and in that time there are winter, spring, summer and fall . . . Time, it takes time. Time will tell. In boxing's winter, people lose interest, but I am here to liven things up. On March 13, I will be fighting at the Garden, and it will be a total sellout.'

It is not entirely clear where the metaphor of the 'winter of boxing' came from but it was at odds with the street-wise boxer's usual joking style. Some have since claimed it was borrowed from the assembled writers who crowded around him at the committee hearing. Among their number were Barney Nagler, boxing scribe at the *New York Post*, A.J. Liebling of *The New Yorker*, who famously described boxing as a 'sweet science', and the young *Sports Illustrated* journalist Frank Deford. Any one of the writers befriending the boxer might have used the seasons to lyricise the state that boxing was in. When Cassius stood down, he did so with an expression that several witnesses described variously as pride or contentedness. He seemed pleased with himself. 'When he stepped down, a faint odor of *hubris*, like Lilac Vegetal, lingered behind,' noted Liebling.

Cassius was an inveterate magpie, stealing phrases from radio DJs, R&B singers, rival boxers, famous magicians, journalists and, of course, the wrestler Gorgeous George, from whom he borrowed the catchphrase 'I am the greatest'. But one of his most audacious steals was channelling a speech by President Kennedy: 'Ask not what boxing can do for me, ask what I can do for boxing.' He had taken time to befriend the right people in the media, those who could promote his reputation. Despite the growing influence of the Nation of Islam's separatist creed, he had built up a close rapport with white sports writers and mainstream television commentators, among them the ABC sports journalist Howard Cosell and the BBC commentator Harry Carpenter. Cosell's expression – 'I'm just telling it like it is' – was often appropriated by Cassius when he passed remarks that were deemed hard-hitting or controversial. In 1966 Aaron Neville released his debut 'Tell It Like It Is', one of the seminal songs of the New Orleans soul scene and beyond. Telling it like it is became a slogan of the era, embedded in the mindset of the time.

On the journey back from Albany to Grand Central Station, Cassius found himself in the company of the sportswriter Frank Deford, who had been at the hearings. They were like mirror images – ambitious and self-confident, but from very different cultural backgrounds. It was a bizarre journey and one that Deford would come to regret. As the train rattled south towards New York City, Cassius borrowed the writer's notepad and pen, and began to sketch out a future vision of race relations in America. It was an odd and rambling exchange, in which Cassius improvised what appeared to be a map of an imaginary solar system, a planetary cosmos featuring a mothership descending to earth. Deford struggled to follow the wandering logic and scribbled cartography, as Cassius became ever more enthusiastic about his sketch. When the two men left each other, Deford claims to have felt he was in the company of 'a real fruitcake, endearing and very amusing but nutty'. What he had failed to pick up on was that Cassius was sketching out the cosmology of the Nation of Islam and the concept of the so-called Mother Plane or Wheel, as described in the visions of the prophet Ezekiel in the Hebrew Bible. It was a notion that was often described as the 'mothership' and implied a planetary escape from a white-dominated world, and one that has recurred on the outer fringes of African-American belief over decades and found its expression in various forms of music, including avant-garde jazz, particularly in the music of Sun Ra and his ever-changing Arkestra, and then within afro-futurist funk bands including Masterfleet (1974) and George Clinton and Parliament's seminal *Mothership Connection* (1975).

When the young journalist got home, he crumpled up Cassius's sketches and threw them away, not realising until many months later that he had bona fide proof of the boxer's growing closeness to the Nation of Islam. Until his death in 2017, by which time Deford was an institution within American sports broadcasting, he openly admitted that he missed his opportunity to break the biggest sporting story of the decade: Cassius Clay's impending conversion to Islam.

Later that night, Cassius arrived back in Miami where he began an intensive training regime to prepare for his forthcoming fight with Doug Jones, scheduled for 13 March. But by now, New York was becoming a second home of sorts. As a child, Cassius had fed off stories told to him by his father of Harlem nightlife and the political significance of the city within a city. His love affair with Dee Dee, which continued intermittently throughout the year, also brought him north to see her perform at the Apollo.

As Cassius shuttled between Miami and New York, talking up the Jones fight, Sharp was busy promoting her latest dance craze single 'Do The Bird' (Cameo, 1963), a pop song credited to the

Philadelphia-based Kal Mann and Dave Appell. She remained with Cameo-Parkway for another two unfruitful years, and hitched to the outdated image of the girl next door, her recording became more and more bland. As rival female soul vocalists such as Mary Wells at Motown, Barbara Lewis and Doris Troy at Atlantic, and Patti LaBelle and the Bluebelles rejected dance craze and began to record more challenging and emotionally complex material, Sharp struggled to shake off the straitjacket of lightweight pop. Restless about her future, she eventually took the decision to join a growing stable of artists at Atlantic's ATCO label, where she subsequently recorded a duet with Harlem's Ben E. King. But it seemed, in the spring of 1963, as her boyfriend's star was in the ascendancy, that her appeal was frozen in time.

Apart from his hometown of Louisville and the ghetto streets of Miami, New York had become the place that Cassius was most familiar with. He had first visited the city late in 1960, on his way to the Rome Olympics, where he was met by *Newsweek* journalist Dick Schaap, who had been commissioned to write features on potential gold medallists for *Sport* magazine. They spent a day and a night in each other's company. At the time Floyd Patterson was the reigning heavyweight champion, and Schaap remembers taking Cassius to Times Square, where he brandished a mocked-up newspaper with the headline 'Clay Signs Up To Fight Floyd Patterson'. They shared cheesecake at Jack Dempsey's, the boxing-themed bar located in the Brill Building on Broadway, which had just acted as a backdrop for the movie version of Rod Serling's *Requiem for a Heavyweight*, the story of a boxer brought down by dementia. They then crossed Broadway to the iconic jazz club Birdland, the spiritual home of saxophonist Charlie 'Yardbird' Parker. According to Cassius's frequently spun story, it was where he first drank alcohol, but his chaperone Dick Schaap claims that the young medallist, who wore his USA track top and gold medal throughout the night, asked for a fruit juice with one drop of bourbon, less than a spoonful, so that he could return home to Louisville and claim that he'd drunk hard liquor in Birdland. Cassius spoke repeatedly about wanting do things and go places that would impress his father back home. Short of cash, he made his way to Madison Square Garden, hoping that someone within the fight fraternity might recognise him. He found himself in the cramped and windowless offices of Teddy Brenner, at the time one of boxing's most renowned matchmakers and a man of significant influence, who organised fights at the venue. Brenner had come of age in the era of black-and-white television, where he came under pressure to provide well-matched fights to network bosses, who were petrified that a quick knockout would leave them short of a show. It is more than likely that Cassius simply wanted to meet Brenner and to jog him about his success at the Olympics. Young, black and penniless, he took the opportunity to borrow a $10 bill from Brenner, which he duly repaid, sending it by post from his home in Louisville. He used the cash to take the subway north to Harlem where he spent a day as any teenager would, marvelling at the capital of black America, walking along 125th Street, savouring every corner, gaping at the Apollo and ogling at the 'foxes' parading along the bustling streets. He even met Sugar Ray Robinson, but it was a short and brusque encounter that left Cassius deflated, a story he virtually rewrote when he told it back home.

Early in March 1963, Cassius checked in to the Plymouth Hotel, in a suite high above Central Park, which became his nerve centre for what was an extraordinary media blitz. On the afternoon of the fight, after a round of newspaper interviews, Cassius was resting in his hotel room when a visitor called. It was an unscheduled meeting, but the uninvited guest came with such memorable force that he became a fixture of the many dramatic moments to come.

Drew 'Bundini' Brown was first and foremost a character. A man of limitless self-invention, larger than life, who had all the guile and ebullience of a Harlem street hustler, he was in fact an ex-sailor. Born in Midway, Florida, he faked his age, at only thirteen years old, and ran away to sea as a mess boy, before joining the Merchant Marines and sailing the high seas for over twelve years. He wove these experiences of travelling the world and encountering different cultures into fantastical tales that he recounted brilliantly. He claimed variously to be an African prince or a wealthy businessman who had just arrived in town, but in truth his verbal skills were crafted in his adopted Harlem home, where he had the flashy style of a DJ or rapper. Later in life, he played an exaggerated version of himself as a gangster in the feature film *Shaft*. Ferdie Pacheco, the physician who joined Cassius's camp in the early days in Miami, described Bundini as 'a poet of the streets' and an incomparable 'source of energy' who could always raise Cassius's spirits when he was at a low ebb. It was Bundini, channelling street rap, who gave voice to the most memorable catchphrase in Cassius's armoury – 'float like a butterfly, sting like a bee'.

By the time Bundini had left Cassius's hotel room on the afternoon of the Doug Jones fight, he had secured a role as the cornerman for the boxer's forthcoming bouts. He became a familiar presence within the camp, a man whose bass voice hollered above even the noisiest crowds, and he added a new dimension to the blossoming personality of the young boxer, coaxing him to ever greater heights of entertainment. His most common cry from the sidelines was 'Dance, champ, dance' when he wanted Cassius to perform his trademark shuffle, and he would holler 'End the show' when Cassius was ahead on points and needed to bring the night to an end.

Bundini's love life was even more enthralling than his career at sea. He had a deep and real connection to soul music and, like Cassius, had a girlfriend in the industry. He'd seduced the great R&B star Ruth Brown, then one of the leading figures in the rise of Atlantic Records. It was no ordinary courtship. During a break in a week-long residence at the Apollo, where she was sharing the stage with ex-fighter Sugar Ray Robinson (then performing as a tap dancer), Ruth went for lunch to Ralph Bastone's Palm Café, two blocks from the Apollo on 125th Street. There, in a booth, some musical friends were holding court with a mysterious African. It was in fact Bundini speaking in an entirely made-up African tongue. He convinced Ruth that he was a wealthy African prince, but even when his ruse was exposed, the pair stayed in touch. Separated and perpetually at war with her husband – the saxophonist Willis 'Gator' Jackson, who had been born near Cassius's apartment in Miami's Overtown – Ruth enjoyed playing the field. She fell passionately in love with Bundini, whom she adored as a lovable rogue. On tour in Chattanooga, Ruth was rushed to hospital with a suspected tumour. X-rays revealed she was pregnant, and on her return to New York she gave birth to a son, Ronald David, in Mount Eden Hospital in the Bronx. Bundini was the father.

Ruth Brown was one of the great precursors of soul music. She grew up in Portsmouth, Virginia, the dock town that sat across the Elizabeth River from the burgeoning town of Norfolk, home to the so-called 'Tidewater Sound' and itself an oasis of independent soul music. She personified many of the stations on the journey to soul, rising as a child through gospel church and then crossing over to R&B. She signed for Atlantic Records in their infancy and, until the emergence of the self-styled 'King of Soul' Solomon Burke, she was one of their most successful artists.

Atlantic was an anomaly. While most independent labels were undercapitalised and barely surviving in ghettos across America, Atlantic was born into relative wealth, its unusual origins in the leafy neighbourhood of Embassy Row, Washington, DC, where the two sons of the Turkish ambassador Munir Ertegun moved in the most refined and privileged of social circles. Educated in London, where they saw Duke Ellington and Cab Calloway as children, and inspired by their mother Hayrünnisa's love of music, by 1935 brothers Ahmet and Nesuhi were already jazz fans and DC's thriving music scene was a seventh heaven. In their first tentative steps into music promotion, the brothers began organising concerts at home and then launched the first desegregated shows in the capital at the Jewish Community Center on 16th Street. The Ertegun brothers lived a young life like no other; in the early evenings they fulfilled their family duties at the embassy, circulating with visiting dignitaries and replenishing the glasses of the wives of European diplomats. Then by midnight they were gone, driving through the streets of Washington and heading for the noisy intersection corner of 7th and U Street, to hunt down jazz bars and after-hours clubs. When their father passed away and they were required to vacate the ambassadorial residence and return to Turkey, the brothers elected to stay in America. While studying at Georgetown University, Ahmet found work in a local record store where he began to learn about the music retail business. In 1946 he partnered with friends Herb and Mariam Abramson and the owner of the record store and founded two record labels specialising in jazz and gospel music. Both failed, but with financial backing from a long-time family friend, the society dentist Dr Vahdi Sabit, they started another independent label in 1947. It was called Atlantic Records, and with the Abramsons still in the frame, they all headed north to New York, where they set up in the Ritz Hotel before opening the first Atlantic offices on West 54th Street.

Ruth Brown was their first major signing, in memorable circumstances. She was scheduled to debut at the Apollo, but she fractured a leg in a car crash near Philadelphia and was rushed to hospital. Brown signed for Atlantic on 12 January 1949 while recuperating in her hospital bed in Chester, Pennsylvania. Propped up on crutches, she then recorded her first session. One of the songs, the blues-inspired ballad 'So Long' became a hit. Atlantic pushed her to try more upbeat songs, and in the next few years she became the best-selling black female performer of the early fifties. The car crash that nearly ended her career turned out to have a small but lasting influence. Brown took to wearing voluminous ball gowns on stage, to conceal her crippled leg and the cast she was forced to wear as she recovered. Unintentionally, it became her trademark, lending a glittering glamour to the toughness of R&B. Like the musical revolution underway at Motown in Detroit, a clash of opposites – the sophistication of fashion and raw vocal power – was kindling a new kind of music.

Atlantic was a label that across time would identify itself as 'the West Point of R&B' and come to shape soul music's universal popularity, showcasing LaVern Baker, Ray Charles, The Drifters, Otis Redding, Wilson Pickett, Aretha Franklin and Donny Hathaway. Ruth Brown's upbringing also reflected another of the key characteristics of early soul music. Like Aretha Franklin,

Backstage at the Apollo Theater in Harlem, December 1963, Cassius jokes around with the twelve-year-old Motown prodigy, Little Stevie Wonder, whose record 'Fingertips Parts 1 & 2' was a top-selling single at the time. Also featured in the photograph are Ronnie Spector of The Ronettes (second left), Cassius's girlfriend Dee Dee Sharp (in the white dress) and Dionne Warwick (seated beside Cassius, partially hidden behind Stevie Wonder). Almost fifty years later, in February 2012, Stevie Wonder, with Muhammad Ali seated beside him, played 'Happy Birthday' at a star-studded charity fundraiser to celebrate the sportsman's seventieth birthday.

Gladys Knight, David Ruffin of The Temptations, Stevie Wonder and latterly Michael Jackson, Brown was a child genius, whose precocious talent brought fame and financial reward to her family. She made her vocal debut aged four; her father, the choir director at the local Emmanuel African Methodist Episcopal Church in her native Portsmouth, had to lift her onto the church piano.

Cassius was by now the king of spin, responding to each and every promotional opportunity, no matter how small. In the twelve months between his appearance in front of the boxing committee in Albany and his title fight with Sonny Liston in February 1964, almost every reputable publication was pursuing him for an interview, and during those twelve hectic months, Cassius attracted the attention of the cream of new journalism: Tom Wolfe, Norman Mailer and Gay Talese, the *Esquire* writer whose essay 'Frank Sinatra Has A Cold' is still seen as one of the landmark essays on fame and celebrity.

Tom Wolfe spent a week with Cassius in New York in the run-up to the Jones fight, while the album *I Am The Greatest* was being recorded in Manhattan. What he wrote in his essay 'The Marvelous Mouth' was typical Wolfe: wandering, supercilious and fascinating. He met Cassius in a skyline suite at the Americana Hotel, where Cassius was holding court among a group of girlfriends collectively known as the 'foxes', who had been invited to the party by the Brooklyn soul singer Frankie Tucker. A one-time lead singer of a New York indie group called The Blazers, Tucker was performing later that night, and some of the party had been planning to go with him until Cassius secured group entry for a show at the Metropole Café on 7th Avenue, starring Lionel Hampton and the Harlem-born vocalist Leslie Uggams. As crowds swarmed around Cassius inside the Metropole, he admitted to Wolfe in an aside: 'I don't feel like I'm in boxing anymore. It's show business. Everything changes so fast.'

Cassius's fame had gripped New York. According to Wolfe, whose essay would be published in *Esquire* in October, 'His presence spread over the Metropole immediately. As I said, it is the perfect place for folk heroes, for there is no one in there who is not willing to be impressed. The management, a lot of guys in tuxedos with the kind of Hollywood black ties that tuck under the collars and are adorned with little pearl stickpins and such devices, was rushing up. A guy at the bar, conservatively dressed and about thirty, came up behind Cassius and touched him lightly at about the level of the sixth rib and went back to the bar and told his girl, "That's Cassius Clay. I just touched him, no kidding."'

The night ended in surreal fashion. A makeshift merengue band made up of immigrants from the Dominican Republic had assembled near their hotel. Rather than throw them some coins, Cassius took the band's corduroy-lined cardboard box, performed some of his own poems, fresh in his mind from the recording sessions, and drew a crowd. He then demanded that the crowd all contribute dollar bills to the band's takings. Wherever he went these days, there was a show.

Wolfe's most telling insight into the young boxer's life was his awareness of how the media and entertainment industries worked. It was one shared by Sugar Ray Robinson, who once said, 'His mouth makes more headlines than his fists.' For months, Cassius carried a roll of electricians' adhesive tape in his pocket, periodically taping over his own mouth to shut himself up, instinctively aware of the compelling photographic image it made.

This media awareness was not unique to Cassius and the world of boxing: it was a growing facet of the new soul entrepreneurs too. His friend Sam Cooke had set up his own publishing company. Berry Gordy had launched Motown and two publishing companies, Jobete and Stone Diamond. The former became the most successful publishing company in the history of soul music, controlling copyright in more than 15,000 songs from the classic Motown era, including 'My Girl' by The Temptations and 'I Heard It Through The Grapevine' by Marvin Gaye. And back in Miami, Clyde Killens had built a mini-empire of clubs, live venues and a booking agency that brought black music to Florida. It was an era when young African-Americans with ambition talked business, wealth and strategy, and when the power of black capitalism infiltrated music, Cassius listened and learned. He vowed to be living proof that the tired old victim stories of African-American talent being ripped off or duped out of money would not be his. Like the hip-hop stars he influenced, Cassius wanted to be paid in full. For their title-fight edition in 1964, *Sports Illustrated* photographed him sitting cheerfully on a mound of banknotes inside a New York bank vault as an armed guard looks on. Cassius had wanted the photo shoot to be done at the gold bullion reserves at Fort Knox, near his native Louisville, but time ruled that out.

As the two men shared a taxi ride uptown to the Graphics Group Studio, where the *Esquire* photo session was to be held, Wolfe was taken aback by how much Cassius had taught himself about real estate and the value of brownstone mansions in what was known as New York's Velvet Belt on the Upper East Side. Wolfe sensed that Cassius's simplistic poetry and superficial boasting disguised a deep understanding of business and finance. He seemed particularly attuned to his value in a marketplace increasingly shaped by commercial television. Their conversation even touched on an informed analysis of the money that would flow to him if he fought Sonny Liston and secured a deal for closed-circuit television coverage. On CBS, fights on Wednesday nights were sponsored by the brewing company Pabst Blue Ribbon, while on Friday nights Gillette was the sponsor. Both were top-performing shows in the Nielsen ratings, and despite the political anxiety about gangsters and deaths in the ring, big fights were still popular with armchair fight fans. Cassius used to joke that he was not a regular shaver and so he would be the first major fighter to win a title before he'd done a shaving commercial.

Cassius could recite from memory the revenues generated by Floyd Patterson's first title defence against Liston in Chicago. The fight grossed $4.8 million, the biggest amount in heavyweight history. A total of only $665,000 came from the live gate, the remainder from 260 theatre screenings which reached 600,000 fight fans. The Patterson v. Liston bout had been a game changer and attracted extensive publicity for television itself. Frank Sinatra had closed-circuit TV piped into his Los Angeles mansion and turned the fight into a charity fundraiser, charging friends $50 each to watch the bout and donating the proceeds to charity. The White House was wired for telecast too, and President Kennedy watched the fearless Liston destroy Patterson.

In the past, the big arguments in boxing had all been about the purse, the share of the gate after costs and promoters' fees, but new technology had brought network television into homes across America and a new revenue stream had opened up via Screen Theatre TV, the beam-backs of big fights to major cities. The Doug Jones fight had attracted local promoters in cities such as Miami and Denver to show the fight live in cinemas on 30-foot CinemaScope screens. Promoter Milt Willard scooped up the rights to beam the fight to the Denver Auditorium. He was a local hustler who had already promoted some of Liston's fights and he was keen to bring Cassius closer to his business. Cassius in turn was happy to receive his share of an entirely new market.

According to Wolfe, 'This demonstrates Cassius' chief mental asset, which is an unusual awareness, unusual for a fighter, at any rate. He is quite aware, even supersensitive at times, of other people's motives. He is aware of newspapermen's motives, his backers' motives, his trainers' motives, autograph hunters' motives and even the social motives of sophisticated white New Yorkers he has seen only at a glance.' It was a salient point that identified a major contradiction yet to come. Cassius was both informed about money and what it could buy, but his increasing closeness to the Nation of Islam posed a threat to his reputation and therefore his livelihood. For much of 1963 he decided that his faith had to be kept undercover, hidden from the marketplace. While he practised caution, his spiritual advisers, including Malcolm X, reminded him of the legacy of the 'white devils' and the Louisville businessmen who controlled his career.

Cassius had been offered a deal by the William Morris Agency, who had negotiated the contract for his album of poetry and music (won in a blind auction by Columbia Records) after Sam Cooke had tried to recommend Cassius to his partners at RCA. The album proved to be a minor hit and to this day remains a curiosity. But what is even more surprising is that Columbia chose the Greenwich Village poet Marianne Moore to write the sleeve notes. A more conventional choice, Milton Gross, the nationally syndicated sports columnist of *The New York Post*, also contributed. Moore was a friend of Ezra Pound and T.S. Eliot, a modernist with a substantial reputation in academic circles, and a fight fan. She paid warm homage to the young boxer's tongue-in-cheek posturing, describing him as a 'smiling pugilist' and writing: '*I Am The Greatest*, if meant seriously, is comic, and if meant comically, is comic. It is romantic comedy, it is poetic drama.' Channelling Shakespeare's great romantic comedy, Moore gave the album an alternative title, *Much Ado About Cassius*. Released in August 1963 and produced by comedy writer Gary Belkin, it consisted of a series of raps built around some of Cassius's most outrageous boasts, and rather than list tracks it was structured around a series of rounds preceded by the sound of a boxing bell. Songs included 'Will The Real Sonny Liston Please Fall Down', a passable cover version of Ben E. King's 'Stand By Me' and 'The Gang's All Here', featuring Sam Cooke. The album was nominated for a Best Comedy Performance Grammy, but was beaten by Allan Sherman's summer-camp parody song 'Hello Muddah, Hello Faddah (A Letter From Camp)'. It went on to sell around half a million copies in the US.

During his trip to London to fight Henry Cooper in June of 1963, Cassius met up with the British 'Voice of Boxing', Harry Carpenter. It was never a true friendship – more a calculated business relationship similar to the one he had with the American broadcaster Howard Cosell – but they did hit it off. Carpenter had already met Cassius a year before in Miami, where, incongruously, the two men played croquet against each other on a piece of spare ground near Overtown. This time, he invited Cassius to participate in a live link-up televised interview, with Carpenter in the BBC Studios in London and Cassius in the Columbia Recording Studios in New York. By sheer chance, the interview was scheduled during a break in a recording session with Sam Cooke, most likely at Columbia's old Studio A at 799 7th Avenue, where the two had come together to record their duet. With the cameras rolling and a live UK audience of millions watching, Cooke helps a clearly nervous Cassius through an a capella version of 'The Gang's All Here', which was a primitive party song like so many that were breaking out via R&B radio stations. The concept was simple: a relentless backing track, rhyming inanities and shout-outs to major cities around America. It was a template that in later years would produce Martha and the Vandellas' 'Dancing In The Street', The O'Jays' 'Love Train' and The Sugarhill Gang's 'Rapper's Delight'.

Emboldened by a round of high-value interviews, endless photo sessions, and his first meeting with Bundini on the afternoon of the fight, Cassius walked the few blocks from his hotel to Madison Square Garden. Back then, the Garden was located on 8th Avenue and 50th Street in what had once been a transport barn housing old trolley cars. Cassius paused outside the building to marvel at his own handiwork and admire a scene unusual in the embattled world of boxing. 'House Full' signs were being erected around the box office and a strict ticket-only entry system had been put in place. It was a symbolic moment, one that seemed single-handedly to have reversed the fortunes of boxing, showing that an exciting heavyweight bristling with charisma and attitude could attract people away from their television sets to soak up the atmosphere of a live fight.

For all the hype and the excited run on ticket sales, Doug Jones proved to be a more formidable opponent than Cassius and his corner had anticipated. The fight lasted the distance (ten rounds) and eventually, after noisy derisive shouts from the crowd who favoured Jones, Cassius was given the verdict. Not everyone was convinced. Jones was adamant that he was cheated out of what would have been a significant victory. 'Clay ran like a thief,' he said. 'I carried the fight to him. Suppose I went the other way, what kind of fight would it have been? Clay didn't hit me with any solid punches. There wasn't any real power in his punches.' The fight was something of a setback for Cassius, although he would never admit it in public. Mike Casey, the revered boxing writer, saw the fight from Jones's perspective and described the ex-Air Force heavyweight as a constant threat throughout the proceedings. 'Tough, stolid and unimpressed by other men's reputations,' Casey wrote, 'Doug slammed a big right into Clay's jaw that shook him down to his feet. It wasn't the only uncomfortable moment for Cassius. Jones also rocked him in the fourth and seventh rounds as

Clay struggled to cope with Doug's no-nonsense pressure. Doug was exposing Cassius as a work still very much in progress. Already accustomed to dominating his opponents, the young ace wasn't happy with being harried and pushed back.'

When Mike Silver later interviewed Jones for *The Ring*, the fighter insisted that for all the noisy publicity that was by then surrounding Cassius, he was never intimidated. 'I treated all my opponents the same,' he told Silver. 'I set out to do what I had to do. To me, he was just another fighter. In fact I was bigger than him. Then I didn't even consider him as good as the others I fought. Clay's people thought they were getting a soft touch. But when I was coming up I didn't fight guys from the graveyard. In other words, I didn't fight stiffs. I fought guys that I really had to produce. Because if you didn't you got your brains knocked out.'

When the narrow verdict was announced (the two judges both gave it to Clay 5-4-1 and the referee gave him 8-1-1), *Sports Illustrated* described the 'unbridled outrage of the crowd, which, hearing the unanimous decision, screamed it was a fix and littered the ring with trash, whiskey bottles and at least one switchblade knife'. The Jones fight stirred doubts within Cassius's camp, and raised hopes across the conservative world of boxing that the publicity-hungry Cassius Clay was outreaching himself. There was growing resentment towards the young contender who was seen by many as flighty, opinionated and insubstantial, and in the eyes of the majority of fight fans was wholly unprepared to fight Sonny Liston for the heavyweight championship of the world. Mike Casey summarised the prospect as one of a flake versus a real fighter. 'During his magnificent pomp, Clay's speed, skill and reflexes allowed him to rip up the textbook of boxing and get away with moves that stunned and horrified the traditionalists. He shunned a traditional high guard, he leaned back to avoid punches, he danced and bounced and threw his own punches from all sorts of funky angles. In the parlance of the day, he wasn't a "proper fighter". Liston was a proper fighter. Clay was a flake whose unique formula surely couldn't work over the long haul. In the hugely unlikely event of Liston not nailing him to the floor, somebody else would.' Liston had watched the fight on telecast, back in Cassius's adopted hometown of Miami, and come to the same conclusion.

After the Jones fight, Cassius decided to stay on in New York. He relocated to the famous Hotel Theresa in Harlem. With an album to promote and invitations to appear on network television, he remained there on and off until early summer.

It was another experience to impress his father. The towering white terracotta building sat at the vibrant heart of Harlem life on 7th Avenue. For the first time in his life, Cassius broke with protocol and checked into the hotel as 'Cassius X', either to test the name out or, more likely, confident that in Harlem it would seem neither strange nor out of place. It proved to be a near-perfect location, in close proximity to the Manhattan media but immersed in folklore, a place he had longed to visit since adolescence. Cassius strode along 125th Street with all the self-confidence of a superstar, but dangling from his wrist was a camera, which he took with him wherever he went in Harlem, still an out-of-town tourist at heart. He rested up after the Jones fight and trained infrequently, once entertaining the local boxing fraternity at the famous Gleason's Gym used by Miles Davis, which was then located in the meat-packing district of the Bronx.

Although Cassius rarely drank alcohol and was a disciplined trainer, he immersed himself in the nightlife, visiting all the bars and venues, including the Apollo, which at the time was an unrivalled showcase for the next generation of black music artists, many of them signed to the new independent labels. Soul was flourishing here. James Brown's residency at the Apollo was a show that was revered as a triumph of high-energy showmanship and came to define soul music at its most ferocious. His ground-breaking album *Live At The Apollo* was recorded on a Wednesday night in October 1962 and became something of a phenomenon, spending sixty-six consecutive weeks in the *Billboard* charts. At the time, Brown was signed to King Records of Cincinnati, and had a catalogue of best-selling R&B records to his name, including his growling answer-record to Dee Dee Sharp's dance craze hit, 'Mashed Potatoes USA' (1962), the tear-drenched ballad 'Prisoner Of Love' (1963) and 'Night Train' (1962), which was to become the menacing theme tune of Cassius's nemesis – Sonny Liston.

Meanwhile, Cassius's relationship with Malcolm X was deepening. He visited his mentor at Mosque No. 7, the Shabazz Restaurant and the Hotel Theresa, soliciting his advice about all things spiritual and professional. Although it was never acrimonious or divisive, Cassius felt torn between his growing closeness to Malcolm X and his main link to the world of black entertainment, Sam Cooke. By coincidence, the singer was also staying at the Theresa, while appearing at his annual show at the Apollo in late June. He was backed by the Detroit singer Mary Wells, who was on the road promoting her eighth Motown single, 'Your Old Stand By'/'What Love Has Joined Together' (1963). At the time, Wells was dating Cooke's acolyte Cecil Womack, brother of Bobby, and her career had been a phenomenal breakthrough. Her next two singles – the jaunty 'What's Easy For Two Is So Hard For One' (1963) and the global hit 'My Guy' (1964) – became era-defining singles of sixties soul, but her reign as Motown's first superstar was short-lived and her career suffered a shattering setback; she left the label after a brutal dispute over royalties, and while bedridden with tuberculosis, her career lost its momentum.

Sam Cooke and Cassius X's overlapping stay in Harlem was a chance to deepen their friendship, but it never quite happened. An initial energy had brought them together, but in truth it was based on opportunism on both sides, rather than any deep or lasting filial bond. Religion was one barrier. Throughout his journey from the gospel choirs of Chicago to the bars of Harlem, Cooke remained a Christian and did not share Cassius's deepening interest in Islam. Cooke was by now a deeply troubled man, questioning the very meaning of his existence. His marriage was a mess, he and his wife Barbara were sleeping around, barely disguising their infidelity, and he chose to be on the road, appearing in venues that his talent had long outgrown and agreeing to business meetings in New York that would take him away from his family in Los Angeles.

In early June 1963, Cooke returned home and agreed with his wife that they would attend the opening of Smalls Paradise West, the Los Angeles branch of Harlem's famous basement soul club Smalls Paradise, then co-owned by basketball star Wilt Chamberlain. Opening the venue was Decca recording star and organist Earl Grant, and according to witnesses, Sam and his wife were among a group of West Coast music celebrities who were drinking with wild abandon. The following morning, hungover, Sam made his way to the offices of his indie label SAR Records while Barbara stayed at home to look after their children. During the day, as the SAR team worked on a recording of Mel Carter's 'Time Of Young Love' – a dated lover's ballad scheduled for release on SAR's sister label Derby Records – Cooke took a phone call from home. His infant son Vincent had fallen in the family swimming pool. By the time he arrived home, delayed by the congested traffic, the boy was dead. The death widened the rift that had already built up between husband and wife, and recriminations followed. When Sam met up with Cassius later that month, he was a changed man: quieter, melancholic and disenchanted with fame. The joking, the rhyming, the boisterous showiness were gone for good.

Vincent Cooke was buried on 19 June 1963, a significant date in the story of civil rights. That same day, the body of the assassinated civil-rights activist Medgar Evers was interned at Arlington Cemetery. Evers, the field secretary of the NAACP, had been shot in the back, in the driveway of his home in Jackson, Mississippi, by the white supremacist and Klansman Byron De La Beckwith. Evers, a Second World War army veteran was buried with full military honours at a funeral attended by more than 3,000 people. The temperature of civil rights was soaring. Eight days earlier, President Kennedy, energised by the scenes in Birmingham, had given a televised speech outlining the civil-rights legislation he planned to submit to Congress, telling the audience: 'The fires of frustration and discord are burning in every city, North and South, where legal remedies are not at hand. Redress is sought in the streets, in demonstrations, parades, and protests which create tensions and threaten violence and threaten lives.

'We face, therefore, a moral crisis as a country and as a people. It cannot be met by repressive police action. It cannot be left to increased demonstrations in the streets. It cannot be quieted by token moves or talk. It is time to act in the Congress, in your State and local legislative body and, above all, in all of our daily lives. It is not enough to pin the blame on others, to say this is a problem of one section of the country or another, or deplore the fact that we face. A great change is at hand, and our task, our obligation, is to make that revolution, that change, peaceful and constructive for all.'

The politics of race was being played out in nearly every arena of American life, not least in boxing, where the heavyweight rankings were increasingly written about as a battle of perceived racial typologies. Cassius's contentious victory over Doug Jones in the Garden took him to third in the rankings behind Floyd Patterson and Sonny Liston. The first match between the two champions had dramatically brought racial differentiation to the surface; the winner of the rematch was destined to meet Cassius.

Boxing has always been used to characterise the wider society, and sports writers had identified the personality traits of the top three fighters and ascribed to them stereotypes of African-American experience. Floyd Patterson was the personification of a fighter loved by the establishment. Gifted yet modest, he was often seen as the archetypal sportsman. When he defeated the injured Swedish heavyweight Ingemar Johansson, Patterson helped carry him back to his corner and generously offered him a return match on the spot. The boxing historian Bert Sugar saw it as an unusual act of kindness in a sport mired by hatred. 'You try to tell people how kind Patterson was and how difficult it was to reconcile that with boxing. I've never seen anything like that in the world of sports.' In another fight Patterson reputedly picked up his opponent's dislodged mouthpiece and handed it back to him. When ahead on points or having cut open his opponent's face he was known to redirect his blows to the body to avoid injuring his opponent. *The New York Times* described Patterson as the great anomaly: 'He was a good guy in the bad world of boxing. He was sweet-tempered and reclusive. He spoke softly and never lost his boyhood shyness.' His trainer Cus D'Amato called Patterson 'a kind of a stranger', and Red Smith, the *New York Times* sports columnist, called him 'the man of peace who loves to fight'.

For a time in the early sixties Floyd Patterson was the favoured fighter of the NAACP and he was famously discouraged from fighting Sonny Liston by none other than President Kennedy. Both feared that Liston's darkly criminal image would be a reversal for civil rights. Patterson was a product of Brooklyn's sprawling Bedford-Stuyvesant projects and became a poster boy for rehabilitation. He had been a frequent truant who fell behind in school. At eleven, he could neither read nor write, and his mother had him committed to a school for emotionally disturbed boys. His new teachers helped him learn to read and encouraged him to take up boxing. His life turned around and he discovered training, discipline and a politeness that endeared him to many. Dave Anderson, the Pulitzer Prize-winning sports writer, praised him as 'a gentle gladiator, a martyr persecuted by the demons of his profession'.

Patterson had become a reassuring figure for the civil-rights movement; he was a boxer who could represent his community with dignity and decorum but who had experienced first-hand the corrosive impact of ghetto deprivation. His image was far removed from that of his contemporary, Sonny Liston, who had been imprisoned for armed robbery and learned to box in the Missouri State Penitentiary. A chaplain introduced him to the sport, and for the first time in his life, Liston was an achiever. His strength marked him out as a natural heavyweight and he excelled in the boxing regime. A ferocious puncher with an intimidating presence, he was barred from boxing in New York State due to alleged gangster connections and never successfully shook off the image of being the mob's hired hard man. Columnist Dan Parker described him as 'a sinister creature, full of hatred for the world' and argued that America did not want a convict as champion. The former boxing promoter turned Hollywood scriptwriter Harold Conrad was even more blunt. 'Sonny Liston was a mean fucker. I mean, he had everybody scared stiff . . .

When Sonny gave you the evil eye,' he told Thomas Hauser, 'you shrunk to two feet tall.'

In August 1963, with the clock ticking on their editorial plans for Christmas, *Esquire* magazine commissioned the celebrated art director George Lois to design an eye-catching, festive cover that would reflect the growing interest in heavyweight boxing. Lois had an idea that took him to Las Vegas and a suite at the Thunderbird Hotel, where Liston trained. Photographer Carl Fischer and Lois lugged their equipment through the lobbies and converted the hotel room into a makeshift studio. In a suitcase was a carefully folded Santa costume, an elf's hat and an acrylic white beard. Their plan was to put the most notorious boxer on the planet on *Esquire*'s Christmas cover. At first Liston refused to don the costume, anxious that he was being set up or mocked, but Fischer managed to persuade him that it would be a positive way to soften his image. The photograph was unusually powerful and disrupted the image of a white and rosy-cheeked Father Christmas of old. Liston stared blankly into the camera, the hat framing his head, with a white pom-pom trailing down to his earlobe. It was sinister, haunting and spectacular. But the American public were not ready for such radical re-invention: they wanted Liston to remain the bad guy. At the time, *Esquire* was the Hearst Corporation's top-grossing magazine and regularly earned twice as much revenue for full-colour ads than any other magazine. But on this occasion their creative boldness proved too much, and complaints and cancelled subscriptions flooded into the editor's office. The magazine lost an estimated $750,000 in lost revenues as agencies pulled their slots. Despite winning numerous awards for its audacity, the consensus was that Middle America was not ready for a black Santa, especially if that Santa was Sonny Liston. When Cassius was shown the cover, he allegedly told George Lois, 'That's the last black motherfucker anyone wants to see coming down their chimney.'

The writer LeRoi Jones, later to become Amiri Baraka, believed this was all racial stereotyping and that Liston had become 'the big black negro in every white man's hallway, waiting to do him in, deal him under, for all the hurts white men have been able to inflict on his world'. The author Mark Karm wrote that 'the white public saw him as evil, a naked example of inconsolable black hostility.' Joe Flaherty of the *Village Voice* was more sympathetic. He saw a world stacked up against Liston. 'He arrived at a time when hopes of integration were high in the air . . . and Patterson and Ralph Bunche were everybody's prototypical black men. I can't recall anyone I know . . . who publicly wanted Liston to beat Patterson for the heavyweight championship. In Patterson's corner were clustered Jimmy Baldwin, Norman Mailer, Pete Hamill, and the NAACP (which didn't even want Patterson to give Liston the fight, because of what Liston would do to the "Negro image").'

Into this exaggerated melodrama came Cassius Clay, witty, confident and, for some, 'uppity', who personified a new generation of African-Americans. Patterson once claimed that Cassius complicated what for many was a simple narrative of good and evil. 'The prize-fighter is considered by most people to be merely a tough, insensitive man, a dumb half-naked entertainer wearing a muzzled mouthpiece. He is supposed to stick to his trade – fighting and keeping his mouth shut and pretending that he hates his opponent.' Black journalist Alex Poinsett, a gifted tennis player whose sporting career was cut short by racial bias in the sport, wrote extensively for *Ebony* magazine and was probably the first journalist to detect a more complex side to Cassius. 'When he says, "I am the greatest," he is not just thinking about boxing . . .' Poinsett wrote knowingly, 'lingering behind his words is the bitter sarcasm of Dick Gregory, the shrill defiance of Miles Davis, the utter contempt of Malcolm X. He smiles easily, but, behind it all, behind the publicity gimmicks and boyish buffoonery, behind the brashness, Cassius Marcellus Clay – and this fact has evaded the sports writing fraternity – is a blast furnace of racial pride.'

In the immediate aftermath of the Doug Jones bout, Cassius had become obsessed with fighting Liston, the champion he feared but in an act of typical bravado dubbed 'the ugly bear'. What was not yet part of the narrative of types was the spiritual journey that Cassius was undertaking.

When Cassius reconnected with Malcolm X in New York and began to meet him alone to test his beliefs in private, he was still apprehensive about his journey to full conversion and his two visits to high-profile Nation rallies in Detroit and Philadelphia were noticed only by the minority press. Only his most trusted inner circle knew him as Cassius X, and those who saw him sporting black bow ties saw it as a mark of sophistication rather than a statement of faith. The vast majority of boxing fans around the world considered the new challenger to be eccentric, knew him by his growing list of nicknames – 'The Louisville Lip', 'Cassius the Gaseous' or simply 'Cass the Gas' – and were oblivious of his new allegiances.

One person close to Cassius who had picked up on it was Bill Faversham. He had received letters – some of which may have originated in the Kentucky field offices of the FBI – describing how the boxer had befriended Malcolm X and was at risk of being exploited by the Nation of Islam.

When Angelo Dundee and Bill Faversham met to discuss Cassius's next fight, they discussed the pros and cons of travelling to London to fight Henry Cooper in a series of 'title elimination bouts' which would ultimately determine who would go on to fight Liston. Cassius's fear of flying would almost certainly be an issue, and they thought he might turn down the opportunity. Nor was it guaranteed box office in America: Cooper was largely unknown beyond Europe. Set against that, he was eminently beatable and the protective trainer reckoned he would be unlikely to threaten Cassius the way Jones had done. Neither man was wholly convinced that, even if Cassius fought Cooper, a win would actually secure a title fight. Liston's management were a reptilian lot and unlikely to stick to any agreement that was not etched in blood; a title eliminator was fine in words but ultimately meaningless unless it suited the Mafia. Another factor was marketability. Cassius was box-office gold, and a victory would open up Europe to him like never before. When the fight against Cooper was green-lit, Faversham, concerned about outside influence, elected to fly to London too. Faversham usually flew on his company's Brown-Forman DC-3 private jet, but this time he planned an overnight transatlantic flight to London which, for the avoidance of doubt, he paid for with his own money. Throughout his period as a part-owner of Cassius's fight contracts he was frugal with expenses and refuted any suggestions that as a white businessman he was exploiting a black fighter.

Faversham was a lanky giant of a man who walked uncomfortably in an ill-fitting suit and towered over Cassius. He had other motives for wishing to visit London. His father William Faversham Sr had been born there, where he had risen through the ranks of the theatre profession to become a very successful Shakespearean actor before moving to Broadway and finally retiring in Louisville. Faversham had been raised on tales of London and its bewitching theatre district and was keen to walk in his old man's shoes. Deep down, he also relished the razzmatazz that had built up around Cassius and enjoyed being a ringside VIP. But Faversham also had a third motive. He suspected that the influence of the Nation of Islam, while only a rumour for now, was a real and present threat to his consortium's control over the career of their prize asset, the boy he called Cassius Clay. Faversham had already called into the Clays' family home to share his concerns and discovered that they shared some of them. Before they left for Europe, he began to sense a chilling in his once congenial relationship with Cassius. He sensed that Cassius was only half-listening to his advice and the enthusiastic bond they had shared in the early days was evaporating.

Things were troubling Cassius too. He had had long conversations with Malcolm X and Jeremiah Shabazz but was struggling to fully comprehend the theology of Yakub of the Tribe of Shabazz, the black scientist whose experiments led to the creation of an evil white race and the nemesis of the Nation's followers: the character of the 'white devil'. Cassius had deep respect for Angelo Dundee and he had always found Bill Faversham amiable. Both were men he struggled to cast as 'white devils', but it was clear that he was learning to live with the contradictions of his new faith and was no longer comfortable about being guided by rich white men.

As *Sports Illustrated* described in June 1963: 'England never did nor never shall lie at the proud foot of a conqueror, Shakespeare says, and, sure enough, she has endured plague, blitzkrieg, treacle pudding and Gauls. But then one day last week came the biggest gall of all. A TWA jet shrieked into London and discharged bumptious Cassius Clay. Instinctively, Britain braced . . .'

Cassius arrived in London to fight British heavyweight Henry Cooper at the height of the Profumo affair. In the bottom left corner of the *Daily Mirror*, in a type size he can't have been too happy about: CASSIUS CLAY: FIGHT SENSATION. Press coverage of the political scandal overshadowed his bout with Cooper, who he beat in five rounds, as predicted.

LONDON

Scandal in Soho

When slum landlord and sometime boxing promoter Peter Rachman died of a massive heart attack on a dank November night in 1962, it unlocked a scandal that gripped British society for decades to come and cast a shadow over Cassius's fight in London, almost seven months later. Most British people knew Cassius from a television appearance, when he was interviewed by the BBC's Harry Carpenter at the top of the Empire State Building in advance of his trip to London. Rachman's knowledge of the fighter went much further back, to the time he took bets from London's stridently patriotic Polish community backing their countryman, the outstanding light heavyweight, Zbigniew 'Ziggy' Pietrzykowski. Cassius was unknown to them, but Ziggy was an eleven-times Polish champion, and one of the very few boxers who had fought in three successive Olympic Games, winning a medal in each. Like many fight fans, Rachman was fascinated by Cassius's predictions; for example, 'Archie Moore will fall in four' came true when Cassius won by a TKO in the fourth round at the Los Angeles Arena. It was his self-confidence and uncanny predictions that alerted fight fans to the emergence of a bright new star in the seemingly inexhaustible conveyor belt of African-American boxing talent. But for Rachman it was his victory over Pietrzykowski that brought him to mind. Rachman was a pimp and a racketeer, but he was a true Polish patriot, whose family had died in the Holocaust and who could never forgive or forget what Germany and Russia had done to his homeland during the Second World War.

He was born in the border town of Lwów in 1919, the son of a Jewish dentist, and after the invasion of Poland, he joined the Resistance. He was interned first by the Nazis and then in a Soviet labour camp where he endured unimaginable hardship. After escaping and serving in the Middle East and Italy, he was demobilised and moved to England in 1948, where he built up a huge property portfolio in West London and drove around with a gun in his Rolls-Royce. A gold bracelet engraved with serial numbers was found on his wrist when he died, leading to speculation that his fortune was stashed away in Swiss bank accounts, never to be found. According to the underground newspaper the *International Times*, 'his property dealings began when he started finding rooms for prostitutes', and by 1954, 'initially using a Bayswater Road phone-box as an "office", he ran a letting agency in Notting Hill. Like Harlem in New York and Overtown in Miami, Notting Hill was by then the gathering place of Britain's West Indian immigrant community; it had dominated the news in 1958 when street riots broke out between gangs of white Teddy Boys and West Indian families who had recently arrived on board the SS *Windrush*, seeking citizenship and employment. Racism was rife and blatant. The windows of letting houses in the area carried the signs 'No Blacks, No Dogs, No Irish', and it was in this racially divided hotbed that Rachman developed his property empire, opening his decrepit houses to multiple occupancy and exploiting the needs of the poorest, most desperate immigrants. At the time of his death, the *Sunday People* newspaper condemned his world of 'vice and drugs, violence and blackmail, extortion and slum landlordism the like of which this country has never seen and let us hope never will again'.

According to dancer and model Mandy Rice-Davies, who was cohabiting with Rachman at the time of his death and occasionally slept with him for cash and access to his luxury cars, he was an approachable, even likable man, who resembled a shy bespectacled businessman rather than a violent enforcer and pimp. But behind the front of back-slapping bonhomie, he was a ruthless manipulator who used low-level henchmen to do his bidding, forcing up rents and evicting indebted clients. His enforcers were initially drawn from his Polish partisan pals and then, as his houses filled up with immigrants from the Caribbean, he began to hire a generation of West Indian street hustlers. Among their number was Michael de Freitas, a Trinidadian immigrant who rented one of Rachman's flats. He was an early convert to Black Power and followed in the footsteps of Malcolm X when he eliminated his Portuguese surname and became known as Michael X. In his new guise, de Freitas became one of the faces of radical black Britain and was involved in the first Notting Hill Carnival in 1967. Two years later, he became the self-appointed leader of a Black Power commune called the Black House, modelled on the community outreach work of America's Black Panthers. To raise funds for the commune, Michael X (now going under the name of Abdul Malik) convinced John Lennon and Yoko Ono to donate locks of their hair to be sold to raise funds. But in 1971 he skipped bail after being charged with extortion and returned to Trinidad to set up an agricultural commune. When two dead bodies were found on his land – one of them Gale Benson, the white socialite daughter of a Conservative MP – he was charged with murder and hanged in Port of Spain's Royal Jail.

A contemporary of de Freitas and another of Rachman's henchmen was Aloysius 'Lucky' Gordon. Born in Kingston, Jamaica, he arrived in London in 1947 to join his brother Wilfred, a jazz musician known as 'Syco'. Gordon, a drug dealer and street pimp who hung out in the shebeens and drug dens of Notting Hill, was to become one of the dramatic cast of characters that eclipsed Cassius's fight in London, as the popular press gorged on stories about his teenage girlfriend Christine Keeler, who was attracting press attention for her sexual liaisons with powerful men.

Keeler was a friend of Rice-Davies (they were both hostesses in Murray's Cabaret Club in Soho) and had also encountered Rachman, memorably telling one newspaper that 'sex to Rachman was like cleaning his teeth and I was his toothbrush'. Freed from the constraints of libel, the tabloids began to dig into the complicated life of Peter Rachman, untangling his bizarre love affair with the younger and significantly more glamorous Rice-Davies, thus igniting a long fuse of connections that led them to Christine Keeler and her trysts with John Profumo, the Secretary of State for War in the Conservative government of the day.

At his death, Rachman's property empire was worth millions, but he himself died homeless and without citizenship – a Polish partisan to the bitter end. He kept a detailed albeit barely legible notebook which was annotated with arcane scribbles and numbers that seemed to be paramilitary code. Some claimed at the time that he was close to outliers within the Polish émigré community who bore deep grudges about the war and were plotting retaliation on German and Russian targets. Dotted among the code names and addresses of partisans across the UK were the phone numbers of several prostitutes. Some were hopeless drug addicts, others sophisticated escorts; many of them were used and abused by Rachman himself. Curiously, among the jumbled names of sex workers and Polish partisans, he had also jotted down the names of people whom he aspired to meet, among them Cassius Clay, the film star Elizabeth Taylor and the pop singer Dusty Springfield.

It was not to be. By the time Cassius touched down in Britain, Rachman was dead and his legacy of exploitation and sleazy sexual profiteering had ignited the mother of all scandals. His closeness to Christine Keeler had set the gossip columns alight.

On the night of 26 May 1963, Cassius walked briskly through the terminal building at Idlewild, the New York airport that in a matter of months would become known as JFK International. He periodically broke into a run, his brother Rudy, his school friend Jimmy Ellis and the Philadelphia boxer Don Warner close behind as they hurried to catch the TWA overnight flight to London. His luggage had seen marked improvements since he'd left the family home as a kid. The old gym bags of the past had been dumped in favour of a Royal Stewart tartan suitcase full of freshly laundered shirts, a herring-bone jacket and a black bow tie. A matching carrier held a dress suit, his favourite white frilled shirt and a satin hooded dressing gown with the words 'The Greatest' embroidered on the back.

By prior arrangement, the young boxers met Sugar Ray Robinson at the departure gate and they were still back-slapping as their tickets were checked. Rudy and Jimmy had been hired as Cassius's travelling sparring partners; Warner was on his way to fight Henry Cooper's twin brother George. He had made the first tentative steps on his journey to join the Nation of Islam and was regularly attending Mosque No. 12 in Philadelphia, then under the ministerial leadership of Malcolm X, who counted Philadelphia and Harlem among his biggest territories. Warner eventually changed his name to Hasan Muhammad and Rudy became Rahman Ali. Only Jimmy resisted the appeal of the Nation. He was a devout Christian who had protected status within Cassius's travelling entourage. Cassius had warned all his contacts in the Nation that Jimmy was a good guy and his faith had to be respected.

Coincidentally, Sugar Ray was on his way to England to be guest of honour at a British title fight between middleweight champion George Aldridge and the Irish challenger, Mick Leahy, at Nottingham Ice Stadium to be held on 28 May. An impromptu party in the skies broke out as the plane rose over Queens. Cassius had not quite overcome his fear of flying and nervously joked louder than the rest of the guys, resisting the temptation to have a whisky to calm his nerves, and reminding the others that Allah and not Johnnie Walker would guide his path.

The London that Cassius landed in was gripped by the sex scandal that the press were now calling 'The Profumo Affair'. The intertwined lives of two glamorous young women, a high-ranking politician and a Russian spy had been exposed as a consequence of a knife fight in the Flamingo, one of London's underground soul clubs, and the repercussions would disrupt the unwritten rules of the British class system and eventually bring down the ruling Conservative government.

When Cassius arrived at Heathrow he was all but ignored. He signed autographs at immigration, and a fleet of courtesy cars took the boxers to their hotel, the Piccadilly on Shaftesbury Avenue, in the heart of London's theatre land. The men checked into their rooms, signed a promoter's chit for expenses and spending money, and planned their assault on London. Cassius had already agreed to a series of public appearances that he hoped would put him on the front pages of the British newspapers, and had secured a training gym in a Territorial Army drill hall opposite White City underground station. It was an open house with next to no security; journalists were welcomed and given permission to come and go as they pleased as Cassius held impromptu press conferences and posed for photographs between training sessions. Before he set off from New York, he had been kitted out in the garb of a natty London city gent: pin-stripe trousers, waistcoat, suede spats, rolled umbrella, carnation and bowler hat. Always conscious of the need for a striking image, he kept the clothing at the drill hall in case he had to quickly change for a photographer bereft of an idea.

The Cooper fight was scheduled for 18 June 1963, and the promoter was one of the doyens of British boxing, Israel Jacob Solomons, the self-styled 'Man from Petticoat Lane' better known as 'Jack'. Solomons was an archetypal Jewish impresario, frequently chomping a huge cigar as he roared down the phone to conclude a deal. The young Peter Rachman had once worked as the in-house scorer in Solomons' billiard hall on Great Windmill Street, and the two men had continued to trade with each other, finding profit in gambling, boxing and property deals. When Cassius touched down in London, Solomons allocated one of his most trusted lieutenants, a tiny, balding and ill-at-ease man named Dave Edgar, to escort the fighter around London's major tourist spots. Wherever they went – Buckingham Palace, Piccadilly Circus or Trafalgar Square – crowds gathered and London bobbies in their trademark helmets turned up to keep order. The cover of that month's *Sports Illustrated* had

Cassius stripped to the waist and sporting Lonsdale boxing shorts with an image of Big Ben and the River Thames as a backdrop. One photograph shows Cassius eating a banana surrounded by police and well-wishers outside the Raymond Revue Bar, then Soho's most famous strip club. Edgar was given the unenviable job of making sure Cassius was catered for, but he wasn't quite sure how to go about it and offered the boxers female company, alcohol and cigarettes. These distractions were brushed away, and Cassius and his pals asked Edgar where they could listen to the latest black music – 'where the brothers hang out?' Edgar, clueless and out of his depth, asked the hotel concierge, who provided the address of a jazz club in Soho at 37 Wardour Street – the Flamingo.

The Flamingo was a subterranean den with a heavy reputation. Associated in the minds of the police with drug dealing, petty criminality and knife crime, it was also a key staging post in the development of black music in Europe and undoubtedly one of the most important venues in the evolution of British pop music. On the first day of June 1963, photographs of Cassius waiting outside the club show him dressed in a check jacket, white shirt and black bow tie, backed by a club bouncer. The club's signage above him reads: 'Open Tonight Britain's Finest Modern Jazz Rendezvous'. Hidden behind Cassius is a poster for that weekend's all-night soul club. Regrettably, there are no photographs of Cassius, Rudy or Jimmy inside the club; it was pitch-black and lit only by dim sidelights and flickering candle bulbs.

It is likely that the artist on the night was the diminutive, energetic R&B singer Sugar Pie DeSanto, a veteran of the James Brown Revue, who was in London at the time to promote her single 'Crazy Lovin'' (Checker, 1963) and contracted to play the Flamingo. The 'Mingo', as it was known, was not the only pioneering black music club in England. A new generation of underground venues had sprung up: the Mojo Club was further north in Sheffield; the Twisted Wheel, a one-time left-wing coffee bar in Manchester had transformed into one of the country's top R&B all-nighters; and elsewhere in London there was the Scene in

'Where do the brothers hang out?' Cassius pays a visit to 'Britain's Finest Modern Jazz Rendezvous' in Soho, 21 May 1963. The Flamingo Club on Wardour Street was a focal point for soul fans, young Mods, American GIs and small-time gangsters. Blues musician John Mayall once described it as 'a very dark and evil-smelling basement . . . It had that seedy sort of atmosphere and there was a lot of pill-popping. You usually had to scrape a couple of people off the floor when you emerged into Soho at dawn.'

Ham Yard (deeper into Soho), Tiles on Oxford Street, the Cue Club in Paddington and the Ram Jam Club in Brixton. The Flamingo was operated by the music impresario, record-label owner and jazz fanatic Jeffrey Kruger. It probably had the edgiest clientele of any club in the city. There were young West Indians from the *Windrush* generation who had come to Britain with their parents on Commonwealth passports; there were Soho sex workers who flocked there when the strip clubs and brothels closed for the night; there were Greek, Maltese and Jamaican gangsters; there were working musicians like Rod Stewart and Alexis Korner, who congregated there after their London shows were finished; and there were black American service personnel on weekend leave from USAF military bases across the UK, many travelling from Cambridgeshire and some from as far away as the Holy Loch submarine base in the west of Scotland. The club's music policy of jazz, R&B, ska and the emergent sounds of soul music drew a regular underage audience, and the venue was a breeding ground for the Mod movement.

Britain was undergoing a racial transformation of its own. Until Mod clubs sprang up across the UK from 1963 onwards, black music was confined to a small number of mostly Caribbean performers re-enacting traditional forms. Winifred Atwell, a Trinidadian pianist, had hits with soft piano reworkings of ragtime; Shirley Bassey from Cardiff's multicultural Tiger Bay enjoyed huge success with her cover version of the old Jamaican folk song, 'The Banana Boat Song', and others; and the Guyanese actor Cy Grant became a regular feature on national television with his charming calypso songs. It was the calm before an almighty storm. The Mods wanted edgier, more contemporary music, and records from black America began to flood into the UK via the port towns and specialist import shops.

If there was such a thing as a house band at the Flamingo, it was Georgie Fame and the Blue Flames. In March 1962, a year before Cassius landed in London, and a month after the pop singer Billy Fury had sacked them as his backing band for being 'too jazzy', the Blue Flames started a three-year residency at the club. Their style, which ranged from jazz to R&B, was hardwired to developments in the music of the American ghettos and was pitch-perfect for the acoustics of a smoky basement. Georgie Fame had joined the management group run by the quixotic Larry Parnes, a failed jazz pianist who owned a part-share in a Soho bar near the Flamingo and was at the time London's major pop svengali. Parnes had an instinctive understanding of the sixties teenage market and scoured pubs and social clubs for new talent, ruthlessly shaping their image into something more dynamic and marketable. One of Parnes's many ploys was the old Hollywood trope of changing the names of his artists – so guitarist Tommy Hicks became Tommy Steele, vocalist Reg Patterson became Marty Wilde, Ron Wycherley became Billy Fury, and Clive Powell, a working-class prodigy from the Lancashire cotton mills, became Georgie Fame. Having moved to London as a wide-eyed teenager, Fame became obsessed with the great American jazz and R&B keyboard artists, among them Willie Mabon and Jimmy Smith. He fell under Parnes's influence but was relegated to the fringes of his organisation and had to make his own way in the business, working tirelessly in jazz and Mod clubs, and on the lucrative GI circuit, performing for the American military in camps across the UK, crouched determinedly over his fashionable Hammond organ. The Blue Flames' set included versions of songs by Rufus Thomas, Jimmy Witherspoon, Booker T. and the M.G.s, and Motown's Berry Gordy and Smokey Robinson. But the cover version most adored by the dancers was Fame's energetic cover of the Phil Upchurch instrumental 'Can't Sit Down', a hyperactive classic in the first generation of soul all-nighters. According to *Queen* magazine, Fame later remembered: 'We'd be coming in from playing an American air force base somewhere in Suffolk and we'd throw the gear back in the wagon and drive back to London and get back to the all-nighter in time for our set. We did the 1 a.m. and the 4.30 a.m. set. The guys would open the way through the crowd for us and help us carry the shit on to the stage.'

In the mid-sixties the Flamingo was the testing ground for

UK-based soul groups that included serving GIs in their ranks – Ronnie Jones and the Knight-Timers, vocalist Herbie Goins, who had served in the US Army medical corps with Motown's Edwin Starr, and Geno Washington, who was stationed in East Anglia and later had chart success with the Ram Jam Band. In the book *Beautiful Idiots and Brilliant Lunatics*, Fame told the author Rob Baker that the Flamingo stood out from the crowd. 'It was the only place where black American GIs could hang out, dance and get out of it. By midnight, when the club opened, most of them were out of it. They would have left the base late afternoon, got on the train with a bottle of something and by the time they came into the club they would be raving.' Fame recalled seeing Cassius on the dance floor on several occasions, but that may have been exaggerated over time: there is only evidence that he visited once.

In the summer of 1963, Georgie Fame and the Blue Flames were preparing to record a live album entitled *Rhythm And Blues At The Flamingo*. The opening track was well known within boxing subculture as the song synonymous with the reigning heavyweight champion Sonny Liston – Jimmy Forrest's relentless R&B and jazz classic 'Night Train'. 'Night Train' haunted Cassius, reminding him of Liston and his fearsome reputation. He always shrugged it off in company but he once told his brother in confidence that there was something 'scary and weird' about the tune, as if it carried the power of the devil.

Periodically, Fame would extend the range of his band's output by inviting guest musicians to join him on stage. In the months running up to Cassius's arrival in London, Fame had collaborated with several Jamaican musicians, among them Millie Small, the ska star Prince Buster and the Jamaican-British soul band Jimmy James and the Vagabonds. It was through his relationships with exiled Jamaicans that he befriended Wilfred 'Syco' Gordon, who had emigrated to West London in the late forties. Syco was a Flamingo regular, and the lead vocalist with his own ska group, Syco & the Caribs, who recorded on the pioneering Blue Beat label, a mainstay of Jamaican music. Often misspelt as Syko, his most successful record was a rock-steady cover version of the Rufus

Thomas funk tune 'The Dog'. He once described the Flamingo as a place where young black men were welcome in a city that could seem cold and unwelcoming. 'We'd walk in smoking ganja, taking pills and all these beautiful girls were so nice. We'd start making friends with them and start dancing. White and black would mix together. Like brother and sister . . . All the pimps and the gangsters used to hang out down there, and we had a good time. They used to have all the prostitutes, you know. When they finished work they'd come down there and pick up the black guys. They just liked the black guys, the way we used to dress nice; they used to pay us, to go with them, you know.' Syco was a prominent and well-liked character among a gang of young Jamaican hustlers, which included his brother, the Rachman enforcer Aloysius 'Lucky' Gordon. Lucky styled himself like a Black Power radical: leather jacket, roll-neck jumper and beret, all black. He had earned his nickname when his impoverished parents won $6,000 in a lottery in Kingston, immediately after his birth. But in the dark nightlife of sixties London, his luck had already run out.

Throughout the final week of May 1963, when Cassius arrived in London, the press were chasing down stories about Lucky, variously describing him as a jazz promoter, a soul singer and a drug peddler. He was in every respect a complex character in a complex story. Lucky was one of four men romantically linked to Christine Keeler, the showgirl who moved among the British elite. Keeler was a friend of the society osteopath Dr Stephen Ward, who frequently fixed up lucrative dates with his rich friends for Keeler. The two of them first met Lucky in the spring of 1962 when they bought grass from him at the El Rio café, a hangout for artists and street-smart teenagers on Westbourne Park Road near Notting Hill. Throughout the early sixties El Rio was Peter Rachman's back office and a magnet for writers, musicians and intellectuals. Gordon and Keeler became lovers, and she frequently accompanied him to the Flamingo, to shebeens in Notting Hill and to Syco's ska and blue beat shows. Meanwhile, at the opposite end of the social spectrum, she was having an affair with the British Secretary of State for War, John Profumo, whom she had met at a pool party at Lord Astor's Italianate mansion, Cliveden House, in Berkshire. On the same occasion, Keeler had met the Russian Embassy's naval attaché, Yevgeni Ivanov, believed to be a high-ranking Soviet spy, and it was her meetings with Ivanov that brought fears of spying and surveillance into her convoluted sex life. It was the era of Cold War paranoia, and this apparent connection between a senior government minister and a Russian diplomat caused the greatest unease. The British intelligence service, MI5, for whom Stephen Ward had occasionally worked, turned on their own contact and began investigating the rumours of Keeler's intimacies. By now, she was struggling to juggle her various lovers and living in mortal fear of Lucky's violent possessiveness. As her life spun out of control, Keeler sought the support of another Flamingo regular and sometime jazz promoter named Johnny Edgecombe, in the hope that he would protect her from Lucky's threats. Edgecombe had been a teenage stowaway from a sailing family in Antigua who moved to London in 1947, and he operated in the city's underworld as a jazz singer and amateur boxer. He had a string of petty crime convictions, including unlawful possession of drugs, theft and living off immoral earnings, for which he was jailed in 1959.

Keeler's scatty life reached up through the class system from the illegal house parties of Notting Hill and the all-night soul clubs of Soho to the privileged London elite whom she met through her friend and confidant Stephen Ward. As well as being an osteopath to the upper class, Ward was a gifted portrait artist whose address book contained the numbers of beautiful young life-drawing models. As the hedonism of sixties London intensified, Ward was perfectly placed to fix dates, arrange parties and connect people from radically different walks of life. Between 1961 and1963, two of his closest female friends were Keeler and Rice-Davies. They lived with him, listened to his advice, enjoyed his company and earned cash by befriending richer, older men, many of whom were Ward's clientele.

Keeler was a regular visitor to the Flamingo's soul all-nighters

Sex, spies and showgirls. Christine Keeler was the woman at the heart of the Profumo affair, and one of the few to upstage Cassius in the media. Pictured here on 6 June 1963, Keeler leaves her friend's flat in Marylebone after death threats.

too. She had been working since the age of seventeen at the famous Murray's Cabaret Club on Beak Street, a mainstay of the Soho sex industry that had been around 1913. Keeler was hired to perform two shows a night, during which she walked around topless, wearing not much more than a pair of stilettos, a jewelled headdress and cape. She chatted with the customers between shows and enticed them to buy overpriced drinks. To avoid being caught out by London's strict licensing laws, which prohibited drinking after 11 p.m., the club was run on a 'bottle-party system'. This was a contrivance that allowed patrons to sign a voucher which enabled them to drink alcohol that they had previously 'ordered' but not yet paid for. After they ended their shifts at Murray's, Keeler and Rice-Davies would meet up with their boyfriends and head for the Flamingo.

Although the story of Keeler and Profumo had been well-known gossip for months, it was on the dance floor of the Flamingo that the scandal finally exploded. Edgecombe was seeing Keeler on a regular basis and arrived at the club with the intention of warning Gordon to stay away from her. The two men squared up to each other amidst the sweaty crowd. Although many have claimed that Georgie Fame was on stage at the time, it was in fact Tubby Hayes, the British saxophonist, who had recently returned from recording an album in New York. Edgecombe flung a chair at Gordon, the commotion forced Hayes and his band to stop playing, and the dancers parted as the two men scuffled on the floor. Edgecombe pulled out a flick-knife – a weapon that had been banned in Britain since 1959, on the back of public anxiety about youth gangs and the rise of the Teddy Boys – and slashed Gordon's face. Blood spurted onto the club's walls, and Keeler later described the incident: 'the knife flashed . . . Lucky had his hands to his face. He screamed with rage and pain. The cut ran from his forehead to his chin down the side of his face, and the blood poured into his eyes, blinding him. "You'll go inside for this!" he screamed. "I'll get the law, you'll go inside."'

With American GIs being summoned as witnesses to the fight, the FBI now became embroiled. Tip-offs from the British Secret

Service and unsubstantiated accusations of espionage and Russian involvement had dramatically raised the stakes. J. Edgar Hoover was briefed daily about the unfolding story, and when it was discovered that Keeler and her friend Mandy had spent time in America trying to secure modelling work, the agency went into overdrive, trying to track their movements and ascertain whom they had met in New York. Two FBI agents were dispatched to London and three black American servicemen, presumed to be based at the USAF base in Ruislip, West London, were secretly flown back to America to be interrogated. Caroline Kennedy, author of *How the English Establishment Framed Stephen Ward*, claims that, according to FBI files, the three GIs were interrogated at Bolling Air Force base in Washington, DC, and subjected to lie-detector tests. It was established that 'the three negroes had met Keeler in low class nightclubs, generally frequented by non-Caucasian elements in London'. The description, dripping with racism, almost certainly referred to the Flamingo all-nighters and other R&B clubs in the red-light district of Soho.

The story was far from over, though. Two weeks later, when Gordon's stitches were removed at hospital, he gathered up the fragments of thread and made his way to Keeler's flat. He handed the bloodied remnants of the seventeen stitches to Rice-Davies as a threatening token. Then, in December 1962, Keeler ended her love affair with Edgecombe after catching him with another girl. In a fit of pique, she decided to inform the police that it was Edgecombe who had attacked Lucky at the Flamingo two months previously and she was now willing to testify against him. Gordon and Edgecombe continued to pursue each other, and the threats escalated. When Keeler refused to speak to Edgecombe, he showed up with a gun and angrily shot seven bullets at the door of her flat. Fearing for her life, Keeler called Stephen Ward, and he rang the police. It proved to be a catastrophic decision. Edgecombe was arrested and charges were lodged.

The London newspapers were delirious. The law of the land allowed newspapers to report verbatim the evidence or exchanges that surfaced in court proceedings, and now that a court case was

At the height of press interest in the Profumo-Keeler sex scandal, on 11 July 1963, two regulars at the Flamingo Club – John Edgecombe (pictured left) and Aloysius 'Lucky' Gordon (right) – are taken from Wandsworth Prison for interviews with Lord Denning, who is investigating the affair. Edgecombe was serving a seven-year sentence for possessing a firearm with intent to endanger life, Gordon three years for assaulting Christine Keeler. In 2009, Edgecombe said of Keeler: 'She was so naïve. She wasn't evil. She liked having a good time.'

imminent and the threat of libel gone, newspapers could now print incriminating evidence without fear of prosecution. An opportunity had arisen for questions to be asked under oath, and so a low-level assault in a soul nightclub had escalated into a vendetta that brought both men to court. The extraordinary life of Christine Keeler was unravelling, and her friends in high places were about to face the cold wind of public exposure. For many journalists in the popular press, the only story in town was Keeler and Cassius Clay was a back-page sideshow.

There was a further twist in this slow-burning tale. Edgecombe was tried at the Old Bailey and given a seven-year jail sentence for possessing a firearm. 'I suppose I was in love with her,' he told the court. Keeler, however, was conspicuous by her absence. To avoid appearing in the witness box, probably pressurised by acquaintances of Profumo, she had fled to Spain and was subsequently fined for her non-appearance. The following day, *The Daily Express* cunningly led with two apparently unconnected stories: one was headlined 'War Minister Shock'; the other, beside a prominent photograph of Keeler, bore one word, 'Vanished'. It was a piece of editorial chicanery that further stoked the rumour mill.

Despite numerous attempts to quash the story and find solutions backstage in the smoky gentlemen's clubs of Mayfair, Profumo was compelled to deliver a personal statement to a rapt House of Commons. He vehemently denied any wrongdoing. 'I have not seen her since December 1961. It is wholly and completely untrue that I am in any way connected with or responsible for her absence from the trial.' Profumo then uttered the fateful words: 'There has been no impropriety whatsoever in my acquaintance with Miss Keeler.' He left the chamber to the cheers of the Conservative MPs; Prime Minister Harold Macmillan demonstrated his support by walking alongside him with his hand firmly on the Secretary of State's shoulder.

His words were, of course, lies. Later that evening, confident that everything would now blow over, Profumo went to a dinner dance at Quaglino's brasserie with his wife, the former actress Valerie Hobson, in what the newspapers described as 'a show of togetherness'. A few days later, during a lunch with Chapman Pincher, the *Daily Express*'s defence correspondent, Profumo said: 'Look, I love my wife, and she loves me, and that's all that matters. Anyway, who's going to believe the word of this whore against the word of a man who has been in Government for ten years?' It was a cruel remark that revealed the snobbery that persisted in post-war Britain.

Cassius was, by his own admission, baffled by the significance of the Profumo affair. Several photographers took the opportunity to link the scandal to the forthcoming big fight and snapped Cassius reading newspapers emblazoned with blaring headlines about it. Others tried to get him to comment about a story he knew next to nothing about, asking him which woman he found the prettiest, Christine or Mandy. He seemed to side with the blonde but, as ever, joked his way out of commitment. None of his London stunts made anything like the impact he had hoped for, and while the forthcoming fight with local hero Henry Cooper had sporting intrigue, the Profumo affair had it all – sex, spying, race and social class – and, most dramatically of all, a knife fight on the dancefloor of the Flamingo Club.

On 27 May 1963, with the Edgecombe court case fresh in the public mind, Cassius travelled north in a Rolls-Royce and checked into the Victoria Hotel in Nottingham. He had agreed to accompany Sugar Ray Robinson as a guest of honour at a British title fight between middleweights George Aldridge and Mick Leahy. At the end of the contest, Cassius, Sugar Ray and the black British boxer Randy Turpin jumped into the ring to embrace the victorious Leahy. Back at the hotel, Cassius told fans and local journalists that he would not be photographed drinking a traditional pint of beer as it was against his religion to drink alcohol. Instead he agreed to be photographed holding a pint tumbler full of limeade.

Although he co-operated with daft stunts and photo opportunities, Cassius had not wholly endeared himself to the British press. He had called Cooper 'a tramp, a bum, and a cripple not worth training for', a remark that had gone down like a ton of bricks. Cassius then exacerbated the insult by repeating a slur he had made before he left Miami. 'I'm tired of training to fight stiffs,' he grumbled to one journalist. 'All I want is a crack at Liston.' Those watching stateside had seen it all before. In their June 1963 issue, *Sports Illustrated* wrote, 'Cassius in England applied the economic theory he has found so workable in the U.S.: to sweeten the gate you must first sour the people.'

On 5 June 1963, less than a fortnight before the fight with Cooper, John Profumo resigned from office after admitting he had misled parliament. A few days later, the *Daily Mirror* ran with a sports picture on its inside pages: Cassius reading the paper with the headline 'The Profumos Head Home: My Profound Remorse'. It showed a grim-faced Profumo in the driving seat beside his wife, partly concealed by a head scarf. She had suffered excruciating indignities throughout the scandal and was returning home in the certain knowledge that her partner had been conducting a secret affair. Her face hid a hundred angry questions.

Henry Cooper was never the greatest boxer but nor was he a stiff. For reasons deeply ingrained in the British psyche, Cooper had become a hugely popular sporting institution. He was an honourable opponent, but the patriotism surrounding his fight against Cassius obfuscated his many weaknesses. He was a reasonably good fighter, strong but ponderous; however, he had paper-thin skin stretched over swollen eyebrows and so was vulnerable to cuts and heavy bleeding. By far his greatest asset was his image and personality – he epitomised the post-war values of honesty and stoicism that working-class London admired.

Henry was born the elder of twin boys, in Southwark. He described himself as an 'Elephant' boy, meaning he grew up near Elephant and Castle, an area famous for horse trading and street markets. He spent part of his childhood as an evacuee in Lancing, West Sussex, far from the bombs that were destroying huge swathes of London during the Blitz. After the war, the boys returned to Athelney Road School, queued for rations, chopped wood, did paper rounds and generally lived off their wits. In every respect they lived an archetypal Cockney life, shaped by the war's deprivations and dogged self-reliance.

As an amateur, Cooper won seventy-three of his eighty-four bouts and represented Great Britain at the 1952 Olympic Games in Helsinki; he then joined the Royal Army Ordnance Corps, the so-called 'boxer's regiment', where he trained in ammunition boots, a habit that he persisted with into his professional career. The boots were something more than a gimmick. They were a symbol of Cooper's working-class authenticity and national service in pursuit of the war effort.

In February 1953, Cooper became an Army champion, winning the UK light heavyweight championship. On the brink of being despatched to fight a British colonial war against the Mau Mau in Kenya, Henry and George returned to their pre-war trade as plasterers and plotted their entry into professional boxing. It was in the jungle of council housing estates in South London where Cooper lived and trained that he cultivated the persona of a decent and approachable man. He trained at the Fellowship Inn on the Bellingham 'Homes for Heroes' estate in Lewisham, built to ease inner-city crowding and provide homes for returning soldiers and their families. For weeks prior to his fight with Cassius, he set up camp at the Fellowship, taking his meals there, training in the back room, and only stopping if a wedding reception had hired the space.

Cooper possessed none of Cassius's flashy self-confidence. He was too polite, too self-effacing or too limited in his vocabulary to engage in a flamboyant war of words with the young American. The only thing he said by way of a pre-fight analysis was that he had watched the Doug Jones fight in a cinema in London's East End and had been unimpressed. He felt Jones had deserved to win, and in that opinion he was not alone.

Cooper's thick Thames Estuary accent often dropped or suffocated the 'H' sound, which led to him inheriting the nickname 'Our 'Enry'. His rise, like his conversational style, was plodding but persistent. Early promise had stuttered in 1956 when he lost four consecutive fights, the most notable being against the Swede Ingemar Johansson, who had all but ended his aspirations of becoming European heavyweight champion. It was a sequence of defeats that was not easy to explain and it ate away at Cooper's

The Kentucky Three, 28 May 1963. Cassius, brother Rudy (left) and sparring partner and gospel singer Jimmy Ellis would rise at six to jog in the streets of central London, often ending their training session shadow boxing in The Mall for half an hour.

confidence for years to come. Yet, set against that were exceptional, unexpected victories, not least against the second-ranked heavyweight in the world, Zora Folley, in 1958. Rejuvenated by beating Folley, Cooper went on to win the British and Empire heavyweight title, beating his Cockney rival Brian London. He would remain British champion for twelve undefeated years, amiable and unspectacular, and later forge a successful career in television and advertising.

Back in London from his short trip to Nottingham, Cassius re-established his routines. He was woken each morning at 5 a.m. by his Westclox alarm clock and began to prepare for his first training session of the day. Unlike his solo runs across Biscayne Bay as the Miami sun rose, his early morning run took him through the silent streets of central London, along Piccadilly, through the fringes of Mayfair, down to The Mall and into Hyde Park. He never ran alone; he was always in a hooded triumvirate with Rudy and Jimmy. They must have made an intimidating sight – like a gangster rap posse out of their time – young, intense, and in matching white sportswear, black gloves and hiking boots. Even before the day had started in earnest, Cassius and his crew posed for photographs, often framed by the terrace of trees on the Mall. By 9 a.m. at the latest, Cassius was back at the hotel hoovering up the breakfast buffet until a limousine took him to his training gym in West London.

Something odd and entirely accidental was unfolding which played to Britain's obsession about social class. While Henry Cooper stuck loyally to his working-class roots, Cassius assumed the unlikely role of the aristocracy. He posed for the cameras outside Buckingham Palace and made a heavily publicised visit to the Duke of Edinburgh's tailor, Gieves & Hawkes, at No. 1 Savile Row. He frequently took to the streets of London sporting the bowler hat and umbrella he'd purchased in New York. The hatter at Gieves & Hawkes on Savile Row was concerned that Cassius's bowler appeared lopsided, and although he tried to tutor him to look less jaunty, Cassius took it all as a joke. As the hours ticked down on the fight, it became clear that there was a genuine gulf in class, one that would inevitably favour Cassius. The pre-fight publicity underlined the differences: Cassius was his usual outrageous self, while Cooper modestly parried away any invitation to boast back. 'After five rounds,' Cassius predicted, 'Henry Cooper will think his name is Gordon Cooper: he'll be in orbit.' (It was a topical joke. Astronaut Gordon Cooper had been launched into space only a few weeks earlier on 15 May 1963, aboard the *Faith 7* spacecraft and became renowned as the first American to spend an entire day in space.)

One London newspaper, in part to mock Cassius, assigned its drama critic to cover the event. The American press flew in for the occasion, and there was a stand-off between international columnists and the local media who were whipping up sentiment and patriotism. In their issue of 10 June 1963, *Sports Illustrated* wrote that 'columnists gruffed about [Cassius's] rudeness, his immodesty and his big mouth. Did he really mind? Hardly. His critics had fallen into the baited trap, his philosophy of sweet-and-sour ham was working like a charm, and tickets were selling like fish and chips.' Cassius jokingly threatened to retire if Cooper beat him.

On the day of the fight, the heavens opened. There were fears that torrential rain would chase away the crowds, but despite the grim weather, almost 2,000 people queued up to see the weigh-in at the Palladium Theatre. Cassius had the star's dressing room, which had recently been vacated by the pop singer Susan Maughan, who had some success with two crushingly awful dance records, 'Mama Do The Twist' (Phillips, 1962) and 'Baby Doll Twist' (Phillips, 1962), before having a chart smash with the effervescent 'Bobby's Girl' (Phillips, 1962). At the weigh-in, Cassius was resplendent in a head-to-toe red satin gown; Cooper, dressed in shorts and an unflattering cardigan, looked like an East End granddad rather than a prize fighter. Never a true heavyweight, Cooper confessed later that he had loaded his shorts with lead piping to give a false impression of his size and had entered the ring at no more than 78 kilos, substantially lighter than his opponent.

The fight was broadcast live across the world and relayed into cinemas in every major American city. It was an A-list celebrity event that attracted the cream of cinema and sport: Elizabeth Taylor and Richard Burton were there; so were actors George Raft and Stanley Baker, and retired heavyweight champion Rocky Marciano. *Ring* magazine reported on Cassius's orchestrated entrance, in which he wore a fake crown (it then sat throughout the fight on an ornamental cushion). 'In the best tradition of English evenings, it was cold and rainy. Half a dozen red-tunicked gentlemen in the ring heralded his approach with a fanfare played on three-foot, flag-draped trumpets, and a spotlight glinted off his purple-and-gold crown. While hoots of derision followed his steps, a seething BBC announcer snapped that Clay was "ridiculous" and he "cheapened the fight game". But Cassius was smiling. The noise he heard was in direct proportion to the number of tickets sold (35,000) and his cut of the gate (about $60,000).'

The fight was London's first open-air boxing match in many years, held in a centre-piece ring surrounded on all sides by fight fans at Wembley's Empire Stadium, in North London, an arena more synonymous with football and greyhound racing. Cooper had one weapon in his artillery – a thumping left hook frequently referred to as ''Enry's 'Ammer'. If he were to win the fight he would have to catch Cassius off guard and connect with a left uppercut. As chance would have it, he had one golden opportunity to deliver the hammer blow, and ever since, in the myopic eyes of English sports journalism, the fight will always hinge on one remarkable moment in the dying moments of the fourth round when Cooper unleashed his celebrated left hook on his unsuspecting opponent.

For a few moments, the so-called 'punch of the century' threatened to knock Cassius out. He slid down against the ropes, and his ambition to fight Sonny Liston for the heavyweight championship of the world looked doomed. Huddled with his cornermen, Angelo Dundee panicked and appeared to be shouting orders. The referee was called, and eventually commentator Harry Carpenter revealed to the audience at home that Cassius had a torn glove and there would have to be a break.

Meanwhile, Cassius's cut man, Chickie Ferrara, broke vials of smelling salts under his nose and dropped ice cubes down his shorts, an old trick to help revive a stunned boxer. It was not a huge delay but it was enough for Cassius to regroup.

The next day, the *Sun* newspaper called foul under the headline 'Cheat Fury At Cassius Trainer'. It was a mystery that has never been satisfactorily resolved and has irked British fight fans for decades since: did Cassius damage his glove earlier in the fight? Or did the cunning trainer tamper with the glove to buy Cassius precious time? The length of the recovery time has increased over the years. 'Minutes, they said. An age, they said,' ringside time-keeper Stan Courtney recalls. 'At no time was I instructed to stop my watch to allow for the refitting of the gloves. Therefore, I waited until I got the signal . . . to ring the bell. When I did so, my watch showed that the interval between rounds had in fact been 1:40.' It had only been forty seconds more than the regulation break time between rounds, but for many who have hitched their wagon to Cooper it was an eternity.

Whatever the truth, the fight recommenced and quality inevit-ably triumphed. According to one critic, Cassius responded by 'taking lacerating advantage of Cooper's curse, those protuberant eyebrows across which his skin is stretched so thinly'. Cassius woke up and proceeded to pulverise Cooper, opening up a hideous gash above his left eye, winning on a TKO in the following round, when the referee stopped the fight, in his own words to 'prevent an annihilation'. Cooper's vulnerable eyebrows were shredded and blood streamed down his face as if he had been in a car crash. 'In 2 minutes 15 seconds, he nearly tore Cooper's head off his shoulders,' *The New York Times* reported. 'Few men have absorbed such a beating in so short a time.'

The following month, the fallout from the Profumo affair contin-ued. Amidst an atmosphere of bitter revenge, the press and the politicians were demanding that heads roll. Stephen Ward was brought to trial for 'living off immoral earnings'. Despite his eloquent defence, the jury doubted that the pittance in rent he had once received from Mandy Rice-Davies and Christine Keeler for allowing them to stay at his apartment had not come from the proceedings of prostitution. They found him guilty. (In reality, the two women contributed what they could to Ward's perfectly moral earnings from his osteopathy business and portrait painting and periodically repaid small loans.)

In 2014, Geoffrey Robinson QC, author of *Stephen Ward Was Innocent, OK*, wrote: 'The criminal charges were a nonsense and the truth about the trial is still being covered up [the files will not be made public until 2046] . . . At a time of moral panic, after John Profumo's lies, it was possible for a prosecutor to condemn him as "a thoroughly filthy fellow" . . . The judge told the jury it could convict Ward because none of his friends had come forward to support him – a preposterous direction, because his friends were afraid of reputational ruin.'

Abandoned and publicly shamed, on 30 July 1963, Ward wrote several moving, and witty, letters to those who had stuck by him, before taking an overdose of Nembutal. He was rushed to hospital and sentencing was delayed, but he never recovered. On 3 August, Stephen Ward died without regaining consciousness, a scapegoat for the whole toxic affair.

Four months later, in December, after a drunken tape-recorded confession, Christine Keeler admitted that she had lied about Lucky assaulting her and pleaded guilty to perjury and conspiracy to obstruct justice. Her barrister made a plea to the judge before sentencing: 'Ward is dead, Profumo is disgraced. And now I know your lordship will resist the temptation to take what I might call society's pound of flesh.' It was to no avail. Keeler was sentenced to nine months in jail, which ended what her barrister referred to as 'the last chapter in this long saga that has been called the Keeler affair'. Individual tragedy and criminal injustice aside, the Profumo affair had profound repercussions for British democracy: in October, Prime Minister MacMillan resigned on health grounds, the Conservative Party's reputation was in tatters, and in the subsequent general election, Harold Wilson's Labour Party swept to power.

By the time of Ward's death, Cassius was back in Miami, with Sonny Liston preying on his mind. The boxing press were still fascinated by Cassius's personality, but the contests with Doug Jones in New York and Henry Cooper in London had exposed weaknesses in the young boxer. Doubt was creeping in. Many thought Cassius had been outclassed by Jones, and the dramatic punch which floored him in Wembley Stadium was still fresh in the memory. Maybe Cassius was all style and no substance. Cassius once said, 'I've received more publicity than any fighter in history. I talk to reporters till their fingers are sore.' He wasn't aware quite how sore those fingers had become. Earlier in 1963, *New York Post* columnist Pete Hamill had described Cassius as 'a young man with a lot of charm who is in danger of becoming a dreadful bore'. And in the run-up to the Cooper fight, Hamill's counterpart at *The New York Times*, the Pulitzer Prize-winning Arthur Daley, scythed into Cassius too. 'The time has come,' he wrote, 'for the precious Cassius Marcellus to modify his public image. He's a handsome kid with so engaging a personality that he instantly attracts and wins everyone he meets. This amusing charmer uses the device of constant braggadocio to gain attention. However, his boasting now begins to irritate. What began as an amusing byplay has started to pall. The exceedingly likeable Clay is lousing up his public relations by his boasting and it's high time he eased off.'

It was as if Cassius had heard Daley whispering in his ear. His prediction that he would end the Cooper bout in the fifth round had come true, and it was clear to even the most zealous of British fight fans that he was easily the better boxer, but after the fight, he refused to wear the pantomime crown that he had had specially made with red-and-gold cardboard and adorned with cosmetic jewellery. Cassius had said he would leave the stadium as the King of England but he had the good grace to reel in the clowning. He congratulated his opponent, offered up a few self-deprecating quotes to the British press, and admitted that Cooper's punch had rattled him. 'That punch was felt by my ancestors in Africa,' he quipped.

Back in America, the vast majority of the sport's experts were now siding with the seemingly indestructible Sonny Liston. According to a growing army of critics, the Louisville Lip was staring annihilation in the face and about to get the mightiest comeuppance of his young life.

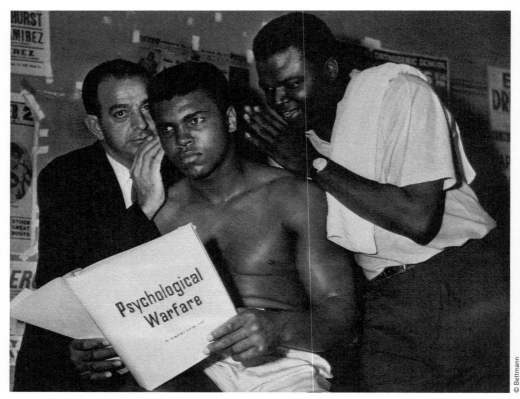

In the 5th Street Gym, Angelo Dundee, Cassius and Bundini ham it up for the press in advance of the Liston bout. Their strategy of psychological warfare stemmed from a conviction that the only way to defeat Liston was to play with his mind. They subjected him to a relentless campaign of gibes and bragging – anything to upset and enrage, and detract from his ferocious ability.

MIAMI

The Fight That Changed America

Cassius was in light training back in Miami on 22 November 1963, when President John F. Kennedy was assassinated in Dallas. Unlike many celebrities of the time, he rarely talked about Kennedy's death: there was no reflection on the day or anything etched in his memory to be returned to in later years. His sometime driver Gene Kilroy has admitted that when they returned to their car once, on a visit to a southern college, they found it riddled with bullet holes. 'Ali believed that anybody could be assassinated at any time and that there was always that crazy person out there who could come up and shoot you,' he once told the *Daily Telegraph*. But he was convinced that Allah would always protect him and showed none of the outpouring of anxiety that supposedly gripped America. What he did not know was that the assassination of the president would only exacerbate tensions within the leadership of the Nation of Islam.

When Malcolm X travelled to Queens on 1 December, to address a meeting about racism within the New York schools system, hundreds came to hear him speak. The police turned up in force.

Tension crackled. He was circumspect on stage but off stage he talked angrily about the problems at the Nation of Islam headquarters in Chicago and levelled accusations about the promiscuity of its ageing leader. According to his biographer Manning Marable, 'as late as November 1963, Malcolm X did not recognize that the political path he had deliberately chosen would quickly lead to his expulsion from the Nation'. On 2 December, he flew to Chicago for his routine monthly meeting with Elijah Muhammad. It turned out to be a disciplinary hearing more akin to a kangaroo court than a business discussion. Malcolm X was told that he was suspended from the organisation for ninety days and banned from preaching or even entering his power base at Harlem's Mosque No. 7.

For all his newfound zeal and closeness to the Nation, Cassius knew nothing about the disputes at the highest echelons, that Muhammad and Malcolm X were at daggers drawn, and that a power struggle – fuelled by the black ops of the FBI – was threatening to tear the Nation apart. Malcolm X had discovered that Muhammad had fathered children out of wedlock and was a serial womaniser, while Muhammad was jealous of Malcolm X's celebrity and paranoid that it foreshadowed an attempt to depose him. Such was the depth of Muhammad's resentment, he determined to reduce Malcolm X's visibility and forbade him from talking to the press. Chance then took a hold. On 1 December, Muhammad was forced to backtrack when he had to cancel a long-planned speaking engagement at the Manhattan Center in New York due to travel difficulties. An audience of about 700 was anticipated, many of them congregants of Mosque No. 7, and a minority black non-Muslims. Malcolm X was the obvious substitute. Throughout his speech, he was careful to avoid references to the late president, but he let his guard drop in the Q&A session that followed. When asked about the assassination, he improvised a clumsy response, saying that Kennedy had been 'twiddling his thumbs' when the South Vietnamese president Ngo Dinh Diem was murdered. (Diem had been killed in a coup twenty days before Kennedy's death.) He then went on to say that it was an instance of 'the chickens coming home to roost'. Had he stopped there, he might have avoided an almighty hailstorm of controversy but he elaborated: 'Being an old farm boy myself, chickens coming home to roost never did make me sad; they've always made me glad.' It was interpreted as evidence that he was glad about the president's assassination, which not only contravened the published opinion of the Nation of Islam but was in direct violation of his promise to Muhammad that he would simply deliver the speech and not court trouble. It sparked a press reaction that brought the dispute between Muhammad and Malcolm X to an irreversible point of crisis.

An army of FBI agents were now encircling all their lives. The prurient FBI director, J. Edgar Hoover, pored over reports of Muhammad's sex life, which detailed how he had pursued and impregnated several young secretaries working in the Nation's Chicago offices, Malcolm X was being tracked daily, and a deep undercover officer of the New York Bureau of Special Services (BOSS) named Eugene Roberts had managed to secure a job on Malcolm X's security detail. Cassius was under their scrutiny too. A file had been opened at the Louisville field office, which was benign at first and listed his various boxing triumphs, but later recounted his meetings with the Nation of Islam, his presence at the rally in Detroit and his visits to mosques in Miami and Philadelphia. The file had been shared with the Miami field office, and while Cassius was not followed every day, his movements were being logged and his more outlandish comments recorded.

In mid-November 1963 federal agents had tracked Malcolm X on a long drive to Kalamazoo in Michigan, where he met his mother. He had recently secured her release from the state mental hospital. 'It may shock you to learn that two weeks ago I had dinner with my mother for the first time in 25 years,' he wrote in a letter to his biographer Alex Haley. 'She is now residing with my brother Philbert in Lansing.' Haley replied that he was delighted and moved by the news and that it had what he described as the calibre of a 'happy ending'. But the idea of a happy ending in the now compromised life of Malcolm X proved to be wishful thinking. Kennedy's assassination had distorted the public mood and a fatalistic pessimism had gripped whole sectors of society. It was as if America had lost its capacity to smile. Several critics, admittedly those who least liked Cassius, claimed that his clowning was inappropriate to the times and his boasting disrespectful. A new judgemental tone crept into pop music too. One of the greatest pop albums of the era – Phil Spector's *A Christmas Gift For You* featuring Darlene Love and The Ronettes – was temporarily withdrawn from the market because it sounded too cheerful in the immediate aftermath of the president's death. Vaughn Meader's comedy album *The First Family*, aimed at the same laugh-at-home market as Cassius's album *I Am The Greatest*, was removed from sale and pulped, and the chirpy dance craze records of acts like Chubby Checker and Dee Dee Sharp seemed to vanish overnight. One of Dee Dee Sharp's last recordings for Cameo-Parkway, before the big fight, was a teen-girl double-sider, 'Never Pick A Pretty Boy'/He's No Ordinary Guy' (Cameo, 1963). It spoke to a relationship that was already fading: her relationship with Cassius was often lived out at a distance, they were on different trajectories of fame, and her pop success was on the wane. But most of all, their religious beliefs were at odds as she remained faithful to her gospel childhood and Cassius moved inexorably towards Islam.

The winter storms in the north created a cash-rich bonanza for the southern beach resorts of Florida. Always wise to an opportunity, Angelo Dundee's brother, boxing promoter Chris, opened up his 5th Street Gym to visitors. Beneath the sign reading 'Stop and Pay Fifty Cents. No Dead Beats', an elderly Jewish woman named Hattie Ambush collected the admission money at the door and offered a friendly face to the tourists. The gym was wallowing in its reputation as 'The Sorbonne of Boxing', an academy where only the most talented came to train, and the public queued up for two separate sessions, morning and evening, to catch a glimpse of the famous. Luis Rodríguez and Rudy Clay were on daily duty along with a flock of sparring partners and emergent fighters. The lucky ones got to see Cassius himself in full flow, part-training and part-theatre, as he weaved and danced his way through a session, commenting about the world and the dopes he was planning to rope. It was three years since Cassius had arrived at the gym as a novice, and since then he had stormed the heavyweight rankings, disposing of nineteen rival professionals and abandoning his slave name. Now he walked the streets of Overtown as Cassius X, the most controversial and self-assured boxer on the planet. Only one obstacle stood in the way, the most daunting barrier to the world heavyweight title that any boxer could contemplate – Charles 'Sonny' Liston.

More myths have congregated around Sonny Liston than any boxer before or since. He was born in St Francis County, Arkansas, on 8 May 1932, although there has always been doubt about his real age as he had no birth certificate and may have faked his age as a teenager. He was the twenty-fourth child of twenty-five, the son of a dirt-poor sharecropper Tobe Liston and his second wife, Helen. It was a chaotic upbringing in circumstances close to slavery, working a hand-to-mouth existence in cotton fields. After years of savage beatings from her violent, alcoholic husband, his mother left home and the family disintegrated. Liston took to the road as a teenage runaway and headed north to the blues bars and juke joints of post-war St Louis. A giant of a boy, illiterate but streetwise, he spent a wayward adolescence around the notorious DeBaliviere Strip, a mini-Harlem and an unsung milestone in the evolution of soul music. St Louis was nicknamed the 'City of Gabriels', a biblical nod to the wealth of horn players who populated the burgeoning music scene, and was known as a stronghold of rhythm and blues.

By 1946, Sonny Liston was a violent delinquent. Employing his immense strength, he carried out a series of muggings and armed robberies and was arrested more than twenty times. In 1950, he was convicted of two counts of larceny and first-degree robbery and spent more than two years as Prisoner 63723 in the Missouri State Penitentiary in Jefferson City.

Prison was a turning point in his life. Father Alois Stevens, the chaplain who introduced him to boxing, saw something click. He described Liston as 'the most perfect specimen of manhood I had ever seen. Powerful arms, big shoulders. Pretty soon he was knocking out everybody in the gym. His hands were so large! I couldn't believe it. They always had trouble with his gloves, trouble getting them on when his hands were wrapped.'

Although he was illiterate, Liston proved to be a fast learner. Success in the prison boxing programme led to his early release. In 1952, the parole board agreed that he would be better off fighting in the National Golden Gloves tournament than festering in jail. Progress was instant. He became a professional on September 1953, knocking out Don Smith in a single round in the local St Louis Arena.

It was in his final days banged up in Jeff City jail that he first heard Jimmy Forrest's 'Night Train' on an All American Five radio, the centrepiece of his cell block. Forrest had been a tenor-saxophonist with the Duke Ellington Band from 1948 although Liston knew him from his days as the house saxophonist at Club Bolo on Easton Avenue, one of Sonny's criminal hotspots. In 1952, for two full months, 'Night Train' topped the *Billboard* R&B charts and the song became embedded in Liston's psyche. Some have called it his signature tune but it was much more than that – it was his electroconvulsive therapy. He skipped to it, he sparred to it, and before he left his dressing room to enter the ring, he listened to it one more time. When James Brown released his version in 1962, Liston embraced it again although he always claimed to prefer Forrest's original. He thought of it as his song: the shuddering image of a relentless train rumbling in the black of night epitomised his menacing persona. When a fight with Cassius had first been mooted and before their rivalry intensified, Liston liked to hear people talk about the chills of fear that Cassius felt when 'Night Train' came on the radio.

It's alleged that he trained held back by chains, as if he were part of a prison chain-gang, although the rumour has never been veri-fied. Coincidence certainly helped this myth; as Liston rampaged through the heavyweight rankings from 1960 onwards, Sam Cooke's 'Chain Gang' was an international hit.

In 1961, Liston had gone twenty-one fights undefeated, seeing off credible challengers like Cleveland Williams, Eddie Machen and Zora Folley, as he punched his way towards Floyd Patterson's title. It was then that James Brown, the leading male artist on the roster of King Records in Cincinnati, recorded a new version of 'Night Train'. Brown and his Famous Flames stripped away its jazz resonance and rebuilt the tune as an aggressive, no-holds-barred R&B stomper. As soul music matured it followed many paths but two of the most distinctive were already visible in the charts of 1962. The Miracles' 'Shop Around' and The Marvelettes' 'Please Mr Postman' signified the group-harmony music that would dominate the music of Detroit, Chicago and Philadelphia for years to come, while the raw energy of James Brown's 'Night Train' blew them away and set the tone for funk and hip-hop.

'Night Train' was a song of such powerful force that it never left the catalogue of soul and funk for long. Brown's backing band, the J.B.'s, incorporated the saxophone break of 'Night Train' in their single 'All Aboard The Soul Funky Train' in 1975, and from there it was subsequently sampled by Jay-Z and British hip-hop group Outlaw Posse. It also hinted at the dynamics of the fight to come and two parallel success stories: Cassius's smooth syncopated elegance and Liston's destructive power. Quite apart from its significance to Sonny Liston's reputation, the night train became a recurring metaphor in soul music: the train of emancipation and civil rights in James Carr's 'Freedom Train' (Goldwax, 1968); the name of the most famous syndicated television show in the history of black music, *Soul Train*; the train of hope and thwarted ambition in Don Thomas's song 'Come On Train' (NUVJ, 1973); and the regretful love song of a prodigal son returning home to the old town, in Gladys Knight's epic 'Midnight Train To Georgia' (Buddha, 1973).

On his release from jail, Liston was desperate for work. He befriended John Joseph Vitale, the sometime head of the St Louis Mafia. Vitale secured Liston a union card with Local 110 and found him a job for $25 a week working as a labourer. Vitale exploited Liston's brute strength by using him as a strike breaker to terrorise union men who were challenging pay grades in the concrete industry. Sonny then became a debt collector for the Syrian mobster Ray Sarkis, and Vitale tightened his grip on the boxer by investing in Liston's contracts, eventually partnering him with Blinky Palermo and Frankie Carbo.

Liston's visibility on the streets of St Louis and his transparent associations with local crime figures made him an easy target for the police. His fledgling boxing career was interrupted in the winter of 1956, this time for nine months, when he was sent to the St Louis workhouse for assaulting a policeman and stealing his gun. In those early, desperate days as he tried to build a life after jail, he became beholden to the mob. He was arrested on five separate occasions on suspicion of larceny, gambling and strong-arm violence, his reputation worsening with every arrest. To the loose talkers in the world of boxing, of which there were many, his work in the concrete industry and his nefarious bosses led them to speculate that Liston had peppered the bridges of America's expanding highway system with bodies. It was an old Mafia legend for which there is scant evidence, but in some corners of the boxing world, Liston was reputed to be a stone-cold killer.

To avoid further police harassment in St Louis and to be closer to his new owner, Blinky Palermo, Liston relocated to Philadelphia, where his career ignited. Then, after yet another altercation with local police he moved on again to a quiet neighbourhood in Denver. Liston won twenty-six consecutive bouts over five years, and his title-winning victory on 25 September 1962 broke the record for consecutive heavyweight victories. After a mere two minutes, he knocked out Floyd Patterson, the first time that a reigning heavyweight champion had been counted out in the first round. With his intimidating demeanour, unrelenting fury in the ring, his background as a convict and his associations with organised crime, Sonny Liston rapidly became the most feared boxer in heavyweight history: the man America loved to hate.

Journalists were enthralled by the rivalry that was building up between Liston and Cassius. Neither were particularly liked by the press and so stereotyping came to the fore. One fighter took you on a rollercoaster of boastful, brilliant innovation and the other to the very heart of darkness. Liston's many redeeming factors were eclipsed by his criminal past. He was an intensely shy man trying to rehabilitate, at ease with his own company, but even his quiet diffidence was held against him. Joe Flaherty of the *Village Voice* remembered a personal audience with Liston at a time when debates about his actual age had reached the press. 'Was Sonny Satan?' he asked. 'Not really, but he'd make a helluva understudy . . . He sat in a small cubicle, naked and sweating after a workout. He just stared at me, not speaking while I waited to be assigned a furnace in his kingdom. In a booming castrato voice I finally asked: "Is 36 really your age?" Slowly, he looked up, and I looked down, hoping the Divine Editor would cancel that question. He boomed: "My mammy says I'm 36. Are you calling my mammy a liar?"'

These stories pursued Liston wherever he went. But those close to him saw an entirely different character. W.P. Steinhauser, one of the wardens who knew Liston from his time in Jefferson City Penitentiary, noted his shyness. 'He was the sort of fellow you almost had to draw a conversation out of.' Others, like the broadcaster Jack McKinney, who befriended Liston during his days in Philadelphia, and once sparred in the ring with him for a local television feature, considered him 'a deeply sensitive guy, with an I.Q. that was probably higher than any boxer I've ever known before or since'. It was a fact that Liston's IQ was far higher than that of Cassius, but the poet and proselytiser was a much better communicator, and so on the surface seemed smarter and more self-confident. Another friend, Tommy Manning, claimed that Liston had a photographic memory and an uncanny ability to mimic the mannerisms of the top black comedians of the day – Dick Gregory, Moms Mabley and Stepin Fetchit – although it was something he did only in the company of those he liked. His gentleness with children was also well known. He was clearly a man of much greater depth than the profiles permitted. But these positive voices were lost in the clamour, and few listened to a story that America did not want to hear.

Of course Liston didn't exactly help himself. He frequently played up the image of the battle-hardened bad boy, and to avoid the hell of speaking to strangers he simply stared them out. In his award-winning short story, 'Sonny Liston Was a Friend of Mine', the writer Thom Jones, the son of a damaged and schizophrenic boxer, followed the fortunes of his central character, an aspiring fighter called Kid Dynamite, on a visit to Liston's training camp in Aurora, Illinois. The story, loosely based on fact, is set in August 1962, as Liston prepares for his first title fight with Floyd Patterson.

Jones describes the ease with which Liston disposes of a queue of carefully selected sparring partners and gives a rope-skipping exhibition on the floor of the dance hall. 'The record player continued to blare Night-Train as Kid Dynamite looked up at the sparse crowd, most of them reporters jotting notes on their press pads. Kid Dynamite heard one of the trainers tell a *Life* magazine reporter that during training Liston ate nothing but rare steak, carrot juice, goat's milk and vegetables. He said Sonny Liston was the only private citizen in America to own a carrot juicer.'

Liston destroyed Patterson over two humiliating title fights, one in Comiskey Park, Chicago, in September 1962, and the other originally planned for Miami in the spring of 1963. For a tense few months Liston and Cassius actually trained alongside each other at the 5th Street Gym, but they were never close. For his return fight with Patterson, Liston was so confident of victory he used Miami as a playground, basking poolside by day and showing up at soul shows in the Knight Beat and the Fiesta Playhouse late into the night. Then, unexpectedly, he tore knee ligaments while fooling around on a golf course and the second title fight was postponed to July. Held at the Convention Center in Las Vegas, 109 cities took live television coverage. Patterson was floored three times and the fight was over after little more than two minutes, confirming Liston's supremacy and all but ending Patterson's credibility as a champion.

Cassius had travelled to Las Vegas to jump on the bandwagon and seize an opportunity to force himself into contention as Liston's next challenger. He reckoned that the only way he could beat Liston was to get inside his mind and unsettle him temperamentally, and on that day he embarked on an unprecedented and highly risky strategy.

Cassius decided to gatecrash Liston's victory party in the Thunderbird Hotel casino, an outrageous act of one-upmanship from a challenger. He approached Liston's table and interrupted a game of craps, calling the heavyweight champion a 'big ugly bear' – the insult he had used repeatedly to belittle Liston. Their confrontation has gone down in boxing folklore. Liston apologised to his table of fellow gamblers and said, 'Come on over and sit on my knee and finish your orange juice.' He waved his championship belt over his head and continued: 'Listen, kid. You'd better fight my trainer instead of me. You'd still lose, but at least you won't get killed.' Cassius refused to leave and continued to pester Liston, then suddenly something in Liston snapped and he stood up. 'Listen, you nigger faggot. If you don't get out of here in ten seconds I'm gonna pull that big tongue out of your mouth and stick it up your ass.' It was not an idle threat. Liston began to insult Cassius with homophobic taunts, drawing on his first-hand experience of prison subculture. His biographer Paul Gallender describes the stand-off as unheard-of even in the world of boxing hype. According to boxing folklore, probably grossly exaggerated, Liston then threw down a copy of the March 1963 edition of *Time* magazine, the cover of which featured Cassius with two crimson boxing gloves, holding a book of poetry, and pissed on the cover.

A marker had been put down. Cassius relied on his insolence, but few gave fast-talking much hope in the face of Liston's brutal reputation. If Las Vegas was where it all kicked off, then Miami was the place where Cassius's campaign of 'psychological warfare' was hatched. As Angelo Dundee worked on tactics to neutralise Liston's ferocious jabbing, Cassius and his gang conjured up stunts to get inside Liston's head. Howard Bingham later claimed that 'I guess what he tried to do was drive Sonny Liston crazy' and boxing promoter Harold Conrad praised the campaign as 'genius'. It was a bold and at times brilliant piece of manipulation designed to enrage and unsettle the champion.

There was a geographic irony in Cassius's scheming. Only a few miles from the 5th Street Gym on the University of Miami's campus was the CIA's centre for intelligence gathering and covert operations: codename JMWAVE, the Central Intelligence Agency station in Florida. JMWAVE was located south of Miami in a heavily wooded 1,571-acre tract that was once the property of the University of Miami. In a carefully staged disguise, the numerous buildings and staff members were said to belong to a company called Zenith Technological Enterprises. JMWAVE pioneered psychological operations and served as the headquarters for Operation Mongoose, the Kennedy-authorised project to overthrow Castro's regime in Cuba. In the leaky days of the early sixties, the top secret JMWAVE campus was well known as a centre of the CIA's more sinister operations. A photograph of the time, taken on 6 February 1964, at the 5th Street Gym, shows Dundee and Bundini pretending to whisper conspiratorially in Cassius's ears as he reads from a manila folder with the words 'Psychological Warfare' on the cover.

It is not entirely clear why Cassius took the decision to play with Liston's mind. Some say it was a reaction to the fear he felt, others that it was a more cruel expression of the put-downs he'd used against other opponents, and still others claim that it was taking the old ghetto game of 'the dozens' – bragging and trading insults – to an extreme. Mark Kram of *Sports Illustrated* remembers their very first encounter, in November 1962. Cassius had just defeated the ageing wise man Archie Moore, and was standing in front of a mirror applying rouge to his face. 'I keep lookin' like an angel 'stead of a fighter,' Cassius joked to the gathering behind him. One of the onlookers was Liston, who had come into the dressing room to congratulate the young fighter. Liston placed a heavy hand on Cassius's shoulder and said, 'Take care, kid. I'm going to need you. But I'm going to have to beat you like I'm your daddy.' It was typical of the jail talk that Liston deployed to unsettle his opponents and, according to Kram, it sent shivers down Cassius's spine.

From that moment on, those closest to Cassius sensed a fear of Liston that not even his most flamboyant boasting could disguise. It had taken him three years as a professional to cultivate a personality that could survive at the top of the heavyweight rankings, but for many it reeked of fakery and showmanship rather than the rigours of the fight game.

'The public personalities of Liston and Clay appeared to be polar opposites,' wrote Liston biographer Paul Gallender. 'Liston's had been cultivated over a lifetime of hard knocks and he shunned the spotlight because being the centre of attention had brought him only bad things. He let his silence speak for him whenever possible . . . As good looking and likeable as Clay was, he had to make people pay attention to him.' Betty Shabazz, the wife of Malcolm X, had yet another perspective on their relationship: she pointed out that in Cassius's spiritual meetings with Malcolm X 'they talked continuously about how David slew Goliath, and that God would not allow someone who believed in him to fail, regardless of how powerful the opponent was'.

In the early days of November 1963, three months before the fight, Cassius was being pursued by journalists from the *Courier-Journal*, his hometown newspaper. Word had leaked from military sources that Draft Board 47 had sent papers to his parents' home instructing him to attend a Selective Services physical examination as part of his induction into military service. Bill Faversham thought he could manage the issue and at first proposed a deferment. When that was waved away, he enquired if Cassius could be drafted into the Louisville National Guard or a local reserve unit. Liston, smelling cowardice, seized on the news and told journalists: 'If they take Cassius into the army I want to go too, so I can protect him. If he gets a deferment and we fight, the army won't want him – there won't be anything left of him.' These were the early days of a dramatic and pivotal chapter in Cassius X's life that would eventually escalate into a major legal battle, in which Cassius – by then Muhammad Ali – would declare himself a conscientious objector and be stripped of his right to box professionally.

Meanwhile Liston cut a solitary and forlorn figure as he trained underneath the Silver Bismarck palm trees of Key Biscayne, shrouded in a black hooded sweatshirt, shadow-punching his way through the dawn and gazing out towards Stiltsville, the scattered community of offshore stilt houses in the bay. One of these, Crawfish Eddie's, had once been a speakeasy and illegal gambling den in the Prohibition era but had long since been wrecked by a hurricane. Another stilt house, the Quarterdeck Club, had been destroyed by fire in 1961 but a grounded yacht, *The Bikini Club*, was still visible in the distance, rammed into the mudflats. It was a vista with an air of decadence, of unsavoury business and past crimes, a world that Liston knew only too well.

Miami traditionally came alive after Thanksgiving. As ice-cold weather threatened Canada and the northern industrial cities, hundreds of thousands of snowbirds headed south to Florida, the

22 February 1964, days before the big fight. According to *Sports Illustrated*: 'Sonny Liston was one bad dude. Yet there were flaws in Liston's armor . . . he had fought less than nine minutes in thirty-five months. He was ill equipped for a long bout. Clay and trainer Angelo Dundee carefully studied films of Liston's fights, searching for signs of telegraphed punches. There were also reports of Liston having missed training sessions due to an unspecified injury. Many suspected his official age of thirty-one might be a few years short.'

wealthiest staying on until the Jewish feast of Passover in April. They came in trains, planes and automobiles, and prominent among their numbers were rich executives from the entertainment industry, attracted to Miami by the chance to relax and strike deals in the sun. In December, Morris Levy, his sidekick Dominic Ciaffone, the Mafia's place man on the board of Roulette Records, and Big Nat McCalla, a vice president at Roulette who was Levy's right-hand man, descended on Florida with their hired muscle. McCalla was a bear of a man, feared by many, with a reputation not unlike that of Sonny Liston. With soul music on the cusp of breaking nationwide, he was seen to have the right credentials to operate in the ghetto communities of New York and to bring undiscovered talent to market. McCalla was the owner of a tiny R&B music label, Calla Records, home to Betty Lavette, Jerry Williams and Cecil and the Fascinations, which was poised to become one of the Big Apple's leading soul indies. Levy's success was based on the worst kind of sharp practice. A Sephardic Jew from Harlem whose real name was Moishe, Levy owned the famous Birdland jazz club in Manhattan and had invested in his own snowbird nest, a luxury villa on Miami Beach. He spent the winter there, running his portfolio of businesses, protected by high white walls, security alarms and a platoon of house servants, most of them cheap labour from the Cuban community. In the last months of 1963, his flagship label Roulette Records was releasing singles by Lou Christie, Sam and Dave, Dinah Washington and the Peppermint Lounge twist star Joey Dee. None of them had much positive to say about their experience working for Levy.

The new independent labels – Chess, Motown, King and Stax – were fighting to get noticed in an unfair market. They were by far the best hope for young singers, but they came with built-in risk and the fallout rate was high. Careers were made and crushed, opportunities were promised and then snatched away, luck was either in or out, and the pecking order for financial reward was often baffling and corrupt.

Sam and Dave had just returned to Miami with their tails between their legs. They had left two years ago with high hopes but now they were back to square one. They had failed to make an impact in New York, while Cassius, the young boxer they had befriended at the King of Hearts Club in Liberty City, was now a national celebrity. Sam and Dave were labouring away in obscurity at the coal face of black music, facing all the indignities and exploitation that new talent underwent. Between 1962 and 1963, as Cassius soared up the heavyweight rankings, Sam and Dave released six singles, all of which tanked: 'Keep A Walkin', 'No More Pain' and 'She's Alright' were released in 1962 and 'You Ain't No Big Thing Baby', 'I Got A Thing Going On' and 'If She'll Still Have Me' were poorly distributed in 1963. Nothing about their plodding and mediocre style hinted at the stellar success that lay just around the corner. Beaten and ready to retire from the recording industry, they returned to their old haunts in Overtown, cursing Morris Levy for cheating them out of the small amount of money they were due from their dismal record sales.

In the late summer of 1963, Sam and Dave reconnected with local producer and distributor Henry Stone. He had tried to discourage them from becoming too embroiled with Levy and his henchmen, but now, after much resistance, he passed on the address of Levy's luxury villa complex on Miami Beach. Low on cash and high on grievance, the singers headed for the villa to demand a showdown with Levy. A Cuban housemaid answered the door and informed the residents they had visitors. Not recognising them, Levy assumed they were burglars and the police were called, at which point the duo left the premises with a vague promise that he would look into their claim for royalties when he was back in New York. 'Morris Levy didn't even know who we were,' Sam Moore said despondently. 'We're signed to your label, sir.' It was a humiliating end to Sam and Dave's dalliance with the big time. Desperate for cash, they returned yet again to the King of Hearts club. According to Miami singer and producer Steve Alaimo, who also performed there, they were back at the bottom of the ladder. 'The door of the dressing room had bullet holes in it and people would watch you through them while you were in there getting ready,' he recalled.

By November 1963, Liston was warming to the idea of silencing the mouthy Cassius and the soul singers Sam and Dave were back on the carousel again, this time recording where they started, with Henry Stone's local label Alston Records. They released 'Never, Never' with a blistering B-side written by Stone called 'Lotta Lovin'' (Alston, 1964). It was a song that captured the 'double-dynamite' energy for which they were soon to became widely known and reignited the hope that there was life in the duo yet. In a chance conversation with his colleague Jerry Wexler of Atlantic Records, Stone tipped him off that Sam and Dave were free from their obligations to Roulette and that he should come south to see them live in Miami. Like Wexler, with whom he built up a distribution agreement, Stone had been born and raised in a middle-class Jewish home (with the family name of Epstein) in the Bronx. With the winter snow already threatening to isolate Manhattan, it was an attractive offer. Within a matter of weeks Wexler was a VIP guest at the King of Hearts, and witnessed Sam and Dave tearing up the room.

The duo's career was saved on that hot, sticky night. Wexler was blown away by their performance and assigned them to Atlantic's Memphis subsidiary Stax Records, where they were taken under the wings of the writer/producer team of David Porter and Isaac Hayes. It was in this new and more creative environment that they shook off their dismal days of exploitation at Roulette to record some of the greatest raw soul records of the era, including the rousing, gospel-tinged 'You Don't Know Like I Know' (Stax, 1966), a song that was tailor-made for the urban R&B charts and for the influential Mod clubs emerging across Europe. The next single – the unequivocally sexual 'Hold On, I'm Comin'' (Stax, 1966) – was a global hit. According to Stax mythology, it was rush-recorded after a throwaway line that lyricist David Porter shouted when he was delayed in the studio toilets. The song effortlessly climbed to the summit of the R&B charts and carried the imprimatur of Stax around the world. It has since been covered by a galaxy of stars, including Aretha Franklin, Tom Jones, Solomon Burke, Bryan Ferry, Eric Clapton, B.B. King and Bruce Springsteen.

However, bound together and only ever finding a true partnership on stage, success amplified Sam and Dave's differences. Photo shoots, travel plans and radio interviews became a battlefield, and what began as petty bickering grew into full-blown stand-offs. They ignored each other as they travelled from city to city, often insisting on different dressing rooms and travelling in separate cars. By February 1968, their epic signature song 'Soul Man' (Stax, 1967) had reached the pinnacle of the charts and was spreading like wildfire around the world. The concept for the song had come from Isaac Hayes, who had seen television coverage of the riots in Newark and Detroit in the summer of 1967 and noticed the word 'soul' daubed on windows and walls. Hayes told a *Washington Post* journalist: 'If you put soul on your door, looters and arsonists would bypass it, like with the blood of the lamb during the days of Passover. And so we extrapolated that as pride – I'm a soul brother, I'm a soul man.'

Sam and Dave eventually separated in 1970. Performing the same hit songs time and again took its toll, but they had precious few options as drug addiction had destroyed their reputations. Their pathetic, soul-destroying feud worsened when they were performing in Europe as part of the Stax/Volt tour, losing them their credibility with promoters and impeding recording opportunities. When Stax and Atlantic parted company acrimoniously in the spring of 1968, it was the beginning of a long and humiliating decline for Sam and Dave. Both men brought out solo records, but their failure to chart only increased the bitterness. Sam Moore claims that they did not speak for over twelve years, they did not even have each other's phone number, and when they did communicate it was through intermediaries, often lawyers. The pair's last performance together was at an oldies concert on New Year's Eve, 1981, at the Old Waldorf on San Francisco's Battery Street. They could barely look at each other. Older and heavier by now, the Sultans of Sweat still persisted with their signature routine, in which they danced face to face reverberating like pneumatic drills. The show ended on an exaggerated hand shake – one of the most phoney acts in the history of soul music. They walked off stage and never spoke to each other again. When Dave Prater died in a car crash in Sycamore, Georgia, in 1988, journalists struggled to get a word of condolence from Sam Moore, who had fought a long battle with drug addiction. By then, soul music had amassed its own catalogue of tragedies: the death of Otis Redding in a plane crash, Tammi Terrell's collapse with a brain haemorrhage and Florence Ballard's tragic decline into alcoholism and poverty. But one of the most understated tragedies of all were the last days of Sam and Dave, two warring men inextricably bound together by necessity.

In November 1963, one of the most damaging disputes in the history of African-American politics was festering within the Nation of Islam. On 4 November, Cassius travelled from his Miami base to Chicago, where he spent a day in and around Muhammad's Temple of Islam No. 2, then the Nation's headquarters, an old yellow-brick building on South Greenwood Avenue. It was a detour on his way to sign a contract that would commit him to fighting Liston for the heavyweight championship of the world. Cassius was charmed by Muhammad, who praised him for his dedication to the storefront Miami mosque, and although the details of their meeting are sketchy and speculative, whatever they discussed that day seems to have strengthened and possibly sealed Cassius's relationship with the Nation's leadership.

Cassius and his entourage chartered a bus in Chicago and his signwriter father had joined them to paint it with provocative slogans: THE WORLD'S MOST COLORFUL FIGHTER: CASSIUS CLAY on one side and SONNY LISTON WILL GO IN EIGHT on the other. The bus, nicknamed 'Big Red', was decorated in the same flamboyant style as the travelling jazz and soul buses that transported Duke Ellington and his orchestra and the Motown stars on their southern tours. With Cassius, Rudy, Howard Bingham and Bundini on board, the bus headed for Denver, by now Liston's base and the city chosen by his management as the most convenient for a contract-signing press conference. According to the *Denver Post*, Cassius's entourage arrived in the Five Points neighbourhood, then a decaying local ghetto nicknamed the 'Harlem of the West'. They were looking for Liston, and there was logic in their choice of location. This was a majority African-American district with a phenomenal legacy in jazz and R&B. At the five-way intersection on the corner of 27th and Welton Street was the centre-piece Rossonian Hotel Lounge, the most important jazz club on the trail between Kansas City and Los Angeles. Duke Ellington, Count Basie, Nat King Cole, Billie Holiday and Ella Fitzgerald had all played there in the days of segregation, but by the early sixties, the area had lost its glamour and was crumbling under the weight of crime and poverty, now populated with dive bars, late-night soul clubs and sex shops.

Into the darkness came Cassius and his followers, dressed like The Temptations in dark sunglasses, pork-pie hats, and cool overcoats. They emerged from the bus screaming at the top of their voices. 'I'm bear hunting. Liston's too ugly to be champ,' Cassius yelled. 'The champ should be pretty like me.' Street kids crowded around and customers flooded out of the bars. Eventually, when the commotion died down, an onlooker explained that Liston had never lived in Five Points. He directed the bus to Liston's home on Monaco Parkway, among the landscaped gardens of Denver's salubrious Park Hill, which, apart from Liston and his wife Geraldine, was an all-white enclave.

Long after midnight, now with a convoy of journalists and photographers from the local press, Cassius's noisy caravan drove towards Park Hill. Around 3 a.m., the bus pulled up outside Liston's home. Cassius ran onto the front lawn shouting like a man possessed. He sent Howard Bingham to knock on Liston's door, while another friend honked the bus horn. The entire neighbourhood was woken by the noise. Liston opened the door wearing his pyjamas and brandishing a poker to ward off the intruders.

The incident became big news beyond Denver and something strange crept into the narrative. Howard described seeing a brooding eye staring through the security peephole and then Liston emerging in a bathrobe. Biographer Jonathan Eig described him sporting a gold smoking jacket and carrying a gold-encrusted cane. Some testified that he was dressed in polka-dot pyjamas, others a silk kimono. With each new invented detail, it was clear that some journalists were playing along with Cassius's game, portraying Liston in a ludicrous and far from fearful light.

Eventually, five police cruisers arrived on the scene. Cassius and his friends were sent packing. It was a triumph for the challenger, though. He had encouraged the media to depict the battle-hardened ex-con as ridiculous and, far from living with his own people, enjoying the good life in a whites-only suburb in silky nightwear. For Liston the episode was deeply hurtful. He was ashamed that his neighbours had been disturbed and that many of their worst fears about his presence had come to pass. Despite being the boxer America loved to hate, Liston had racked up enough cash to buy a house in a peaceful, crime-free neighbourhood. He was apoplectic that his right to a quiet life had been undermined by the man he saw as an attention-seeking scumbag.

The following day, at the Denver Hilton, Liston and Clay signed the title-fight contract and a date was pencilled for two months away, sometime in February 1964. The bookies made Liston the clear favourite and the purse reflected his status as champion. Liston was to receive 40 per cent of the live gate and ancillary rights including TV, radio and movie revenue. Cassius, the challenger and a distant outsider, was on 22½ per cent.

That night, Cassius reacquainted himself with Denver's soul clubs. He had agreed with a local promoter and R&B DJ, Leroy Smith, to make a guest appearance as a singer and comedian at the Colorado Negro Voters Club, where he sang several cover versions, including the ubiquitous Ben E. King hit 'Stand By Me'. The Voters Club was a remarkable place in its own right, a centre for voter registration, a meeting hall for the Pullman's union and a cutting-edge soul venue which regularly staged shows by James Brown and, soon, Sam and Dave and Otis Redding. It was the brainchild of Leroy Smith, who in the late forties had become Denver's first black disc jockey when KFEL-AM launched a midnight R&B show, *Rocking with Leroy*. Smith was a record-shop owner who was a prominent arms dealer in Denver, and his Rhythm Records and Sporting Goods shop at 2619 Welton Street stocked Motown records and Remington rifles side by side.

No definitive announcement had yet been made about the date or location of the fight as Liston's management juggled with the headache of different permutations. Los Angeles offered the advantage of a favourable February climate and large-scale arenas, but there was a drawback: the promoters wanted to close down live screenings in the lucrative closed-circuit TV market, virtually 'blacking out' one of the nation's largest consumer markets. Detroit was a serious possibility. The Motor City left the East and West Coast markets open to closed-circuit TV, but Detroit would limit live gate takings, as the only suitable venue was Olympia Stadium, where Berry Gordy had once fought on the undercard of a Joe Louis bout. Another possibility was Chicago, the scene of the first Liston v. Patterson title fight. The Chicago Stadium could host upwards of 20,000 for an indoor fight but the loss of TV across the Midwest proved prohibitive when the numbers were crunched, Then there was Las Vegas, where no substantial TV markets would need to be blacked out, but the Convention Center would mean a small crowd, and a substantial under-performance on live gate revenue.

As the likely cities came and went and the calculations became increasingly tricky, Liston's management made the fatal error of putting profit before prospects and started to think seriously about Miami. They reasoned that Liston was such a surefire favourite that taking the fight to Cassius's adopted hometown was no great risk. So the fight was finally set for 25 February 1964 and the agreed venue was the Miami Beach Convention Center, a few miles from Overtown and within jogging distance of the 5th Street Gym where Cassius had been training for years. By a bizarre set of largely financial calculations, Cassius had gained the home advantage and the 'Fight of the Century' was heading south.

In December 1963, with the title fight date now set, Cassius made contact with the mosque in Harlem and invited Malcolm X and his family on an all-expenses-paid trip to his training camp on Miami Beach. He was now aware of the disagreements at the heart of the Nation of Islam but did not grasp just how deep and drastic they had become. On 15 January 1964, Malcolm X, his wife Betty and their two young daughters Attalah and Qubilah flew south. Cassius met them at the airport, where he was tailed through the arrivals hall by FBI agents from the North Beach field office. Using his own charge card, Cassius booked the family into a room at the Hampton House Motel, a famous black-owned residence in Brownsville where the

Congress of Racial Equality (CORE) held their weekly meetings. For black customers, the Hampton was the jewel in the crown of segregated hotels, offering valet parking, 24-hour food service, a banquet hall and a jazz club. It had status too. The Hampton had regularly played home not only to Martin Luther King but also to the great Christian gospel stars Mahalia Jackson, Clara Ward and the Reverend C.L. Franklin. By the winter of 1963/4, the clientele was increasingly drawn from businessmen or the ranks of northern-based soul music. Vocalists Chuck Jackson, Jackie Wilson and Smokey Robinson, although visiting the city to perform in the affluent hotels on Miami Beach could not actually stay in them.

Malcolm X's arrival in Miami sent shockwaves through Cassius's camp. Bill Faversham's worst fear had come home to roost. He had long suspected Cassius's religious choice, but now it was on flagrant display, and the risk to the Louisville Sponsoring Group was becoming more apparent. The fight promoters were nervous too: the presence of the most notorious Muslim firebrand was at best a distraction and at worst a threat to ticket sales. The press were now piling into the debate, dragging up Malcolm's most rabid comments and playing up the Nation of Islam's resentment of white authority.

On 19 January, Betty Shabazz and their daughters flew back to New York, but Malcolm stayed on, ostensibly to spend time with Cassius and mentally prepare him for the fight. Sam Saxon, loyal to the Chicago leadership, tried to minimise the effect of Malcolm X's presence and advised him to return to New York, but to no avail. 'At the time we were getting ready to fight Sonny Liston,' he told Hauser, 'Malcolm came down and asked would it be okay if he went over to the gym. I said, "You know everybody knows who you are, and it's better if you don't go," because it wasn't acceptable in those days. But Malcolm didn't listen to me. He went over to the gym, trying to get publicity for himself, and the promoters threatened to call off the fight.'

A few days later, on 21 January, Malcolm did return to New York. Without consulting his trainer, Cassius travelled with him, and they spent the next few days together in Harlem. Their connection was now attracting attention in many different circles: in the deeply conservative world of America's boxing commissions where a barely disguised racism still held court; in Cassius's family home where his parents were troubled by the friendship; at the sports desks of newspapers across New York; and, most bitterly, in Elijah Muhammad's headquarters.

Malcolm was suspended from attending Nation events, so Cassius travelled alone to a rally at the Rockland Palace on the corner of 155th Street. There was a deep irony in the choice of venue. During the Harlem Renaissance in the twenties, the Rockland was home to outrageous 'faggot balls' which attracted thousands, including the curious such as Tallulah Bankhead, scandalised the press, and set the scene for the eighties vogue scene. Cassius was tracked to the Rockland by FBI agents who, along with local police, were now keeping a 24-hour watch on Malcolm X's home on 97th Street, in East Elmhurst, Queens, in part to protect the vulnerable family.

The Nation of Islam were suing Malcolm for reclamation of his house, which they claimed they owned, and he had already received informal notice to leave. He stayed put and doggedly fought the instructions in court. In February 1964, Malcolm X's car was blown up, and after that attempt on his life, he rarely travelled anywhere without bodyguards. The FBI intercepted several death threats and logged one phone call taken by Betty warning that her husband was 'as good as dead'. In the end, his dispute with the Nation would intensify to such an extent that the house was firebombed a year later, on 14 February 1965, the night before the eviction notice was due to be postponed. The family were fast asleep when Molotov cocktails crashed through the living-room windows in the early hours. The house was engulfed in flames and few of the family's possessions survived. Malcolm X was assassinated a week later, on 21 February.

As the FBI increased their surveillance of American radicals, they also devoted an astonishing number of wasted hours to pop music. Strange things were afoot. The top-selling R&B record of January 1964 was 'Louie Louie' by The Kingsmen. The song had been written ten years earlier by Richard Perry, a singer from the Los Angeles doo-wop scene and reflected a now common trend – a white group re-recording an underground R&B record and gaining chart success. The widespread popularity of the song and difficulty in discerning the lyrics led anxious parents to suspect the song was obscene. A complaint originating from a head teacher at Sarasota High School, south of Tampa, triggered the Governor of Indiana, Matthew E. Welsh, to employ state law to ban radio stations from playing the record. The FBI was tasked with deciding whether or not those involved with the song violated laws against the interstate transportation of obscene material. They also focused on a bizarre trope of the day – teenagers playing the 45rpm single at 33rpm to detect profane lyrics – but that investigation fizzled out too. Many pop musicians including The Beatles, the Rolling Stones and Bob Dylan were watched by FBI agents. While Cassius trained for the Liston fight, Dylan was being tracked on a daily basis, in part because of his romance with Suze Rotolo, the girl who appears with him on the cover of *The Freewheelin' Bob Dylan* (Columbia, 1963). At the time, Rotolo, the daughter of Communist party members, was referred to as a 'red-diaper' baby and so was distrusted by the FBI. The indigenous Canadian-American folk singer Buffy Saint-Marie had only just signed a deal to record her debut album *It's My Way* (Vanguard, 1964) when the FBI first showed interest in her life too. Interest in her intensified with the war in Vietnam and a surge of interest in Native American rights. She claimed the FBI intrusion into her daily life 'affected her career but it didn't affect my life. It was all done in total secrecy. It's not like they tell you they're gonna deny your rights or trample your freedom or gag you – they just do it.' And they continued to do so for years to come, trailing John Lennon and amassing more than 300 pieces of intelligence information on the former Beatle.

Liston returned to Miami four weeks before the fight. When his plane from Denver touched down, an airport VIP ambassador drove to the runway to meet him. Out of nowhere, Cassius appeared with journalists in tow and chased Liston's vehicle across the asphalt. It was a surreal moment that had the unintended consequence of tipping into farce. Some doubted whether this was a serious fight or just another contrivance in a sport riddled with fixes and fakery. On 8 February *The New York Times* reported on another antic in the campaign of psychological warfare when Cassius and his entourage tried to gatecrash Liston's camp:

'Clay and nine muscular members of his entourage attracted a crowd of more than 500 in front of the suburban Surfside Auditorium where Liston, the heavyweight champion, was upstairs training for their Feb. 25 title bout. One member of the group [Howard Bingham] did get upstairs, but was quickly ousted. "I'm ready to go to jail if I'm breaking the law, but I'm not doing a thing," Clay told the Surfside police chief, Wiley B. Barefoot. "This is a public place and I have a right to go inside."'

Boxer Willie Pastrano, who was part of Angelo Dundee's camp and had trained alongside Cassius for years, summed it up: 'It's his show. Cassius has trouble getting off the stage.'

As if the dramatic temperature in Miami wasn't high enough, The Beatles then flew in five days later, bringing another level of glamour to the city and causing even more commotion. Five thousand screaming fans swarmed the Fab Four on the tarmac outside Concourse 3. A local newspaper described the scene: 'Outshrieking a jet, Miami teenagers smashed a plate glass door, broke 23 jalousies and tore up 12 chairs at the airport Thursday to greet England's cultural gift to America, the Beatles.' The band's stay in Miami was a circus of stunts echoing those surrounding the Big Fight. The *Miami Herald* had instructed two copy boys, a reporter and a photographer to dress up in mop-top wigs and dark suits and ride around in an airport cart clutching guitar cases before the real Beatles arrived to whip up interest and secure zany photos for the next day's newspaper. Flanked by thirty bodyguards, the real John, Paul, George and Ringo waved to the crowd for ten seconds, then jumped into two waiting limousines which took them at high speed to their hotel, the Deauville. McCartney described their arrival as an awakening. 'Miami was like paradise,' he reflected later. 'We had never been anywhere where there were palm trees. We were real tourists; we had our Pentax cameras and took a lot of pictures. I've still got a lot of photos of motorcycle cops with their guns. We'd never seen a policeman with a gun . . .'

According to *Time* magazine, 'The next morning, Feb. 14, the

Beatles were set to have a *Life* magazine photo shoot in the hotel pool. For practical purposes, though, the Deauville couldn't seal off the area from its other guests. Thus, the place was a mob scene, impossible to navigate. At the last minute the comedian Myron Cohen, who was on the same Ed Sullivan bill as the Beatles, phoned a friend who lived nearby and asked if some people could use her pool. A short time later, two convertibles pulled up to a nearby bungalow with the entire entourage spilling out of the seats. Despite a sudden cold snap that blanketed the city, the Beatles' manager Brian Epstein ordered them right into the pool.'

The Dade County School Superintendent Joe Hall reminded schools of their duty to warn pupils about truancy or what became known in the local vernacular as 'Beatling', as thousands of teenagers tracked the band throughout the city. Crowds poured onto the wharfs at Coral Gables to watch them trying to water-ski from the back of a 23-foot Formula race boat in the bay. The band then hit the clubs, including the Peppermint Lounge where they watched Hank Ballard & The Midnighters and house band The B.G. Ramblers, and Club Mau Mau, where The Coasters were the live act. At first The Beatles were hesitant about dancing in front of a group, but as crowds flocked to the floor they eventually joined in when The Coasters covered Dee Dee Sharp's 'Mashed Potato Time'.

The Beatles had already appeared on *Ed Sullivan*, which reached 73 million people live from New York. Such was the impact that they agreed to appear for a second time on the show, this time live from the Deauville, the luxury 540-room beach resort on Collins Avenue. Only when The Supremes did a series of shows at the hotel five years later was its segregation policy finally consigned to history.

Beatlemania was at its ecstatic height and broadcasters CBS had given out 3,500 passes, but the concert hall in the Deauville could only hold 2,600, and police were forced to block the road and calm angry ticketholders. According to Nielsen ratings released the morning after their Miami show, the previous viewing figures were trumped: this time more than 74 million people tuned in, setting a record for the largest-ever audience for an entertainment programme. (It wouldn't be matched until 1980 when over 80 million watched the 'Who Shot J.R.?' episode of *Dallas*.)

Looking awkwardly conspicuous in the teenage audience were Joe Louis and his friend Sonny Liston. They watched with curiosity as The Beatles performed six songs in their current playlist: 'She Loves You', 'This Boy', 'All My Loving', 'I Saw Her Standing There', 'From Me To You' and 'I Want To Hold Your Hand'. Missing from the set was 'Twist And Shout', the song The Beatles had become synonymous with. They had first heard the Isley Brothers single back in 1962 on a Wand Records import which had been released in the slipstream of the dance craze. Its powerful R&B vocals and chugging beat had struck a chord with the Mod clubs in Europe. By the time The Beatles' version was available in the US, they had fallen victim to the sharp practices of the record industry. Brian Epstein had agreed a deal with the famous R&B label Vee-Jay, and so for a few brief months The Beatles were destined to become label mates with Betty Everett, The Impressions and the Staple Singers. But distrust undermined the deal and relationships with Vee-Jay soured. In July 1963 Vee-Jay planned to release 'Please, Please Me' but the label's crippling cashflow problems meant that the release date was postponed and Vee-Jay quickly folded. The Beatles' London-based management cited non-payment of royalties and tore up the original contract, and as a consequence, Epstein considered that the release of The Beatles version of 'Twist And Shout', which briefly appeared in record shops on the Vee-Jay subsidiary Tollie Records, to be little better than a bootleg.

An obsession had been gathering momentum in British teenage culture. It had begun in the beatnik coffee bars, then gathered momentum in Mod clubs like the Flamingo and eventually the northern soul scene in the industrial north. Obscure imported music from the ghettos of America had become the driving beat of night clubs, and many of the new groups formed in the UK between 1958 and 1964 were in awe of the sounds of black America. The raw rock 'n' roll, the restless R&B and the smoother sounds of Detroit soul became their reference points. Some were simply cover bands paying homage, but others like The Beatles used these influences to craft their own identity. When a wave of UK beat bands washed up on the shores of America, the recording industry called it the 'British Invasion', but that was always a misnomer – it was closer to a reverberation, the music of black America returning in new forms.

On their 1965 tour, which included the record-breaking Shea Stadium performance, The Beatles took their homage to a new level, inviting the Motown singer Brenda Holloway to become their first female support. Marvin Gaye was introduced to the crowd but the unpredictable and often shy singer did not perform, despite the offer of soul music's most disciplined show band, King Curtis and the Kingpins, the house band at the Apollo. Walking off the plane on arrival in New York, Paul McCartney was carrying a US copy of *Um, Um, Um, Um, Um, Um – The Best Of Major Lance* (OKeh, 1964). By this time The Beatles had recorded three records from the fledgling Motown organisation in Detroit: cover versions of The Marvelettes' debut, 'Please Mr Postman', Barrett Strong's 'Money (That's What I Want)' and The Miracles' 'You Really Got A Hold On Me', songs that had been the backbone of some of their early live performances at the Star Club in Hamburg's Reeperbahn and back home at the Cavern in Liverpool.

The Beatles were not alone. Other bands associated with the British Invasion dug deep into the wealth of black music for inspiration. Excello, the Nashville label, shipped blues and R&B recordings by Slim Harpo, Earl Gaines, Lightnin' Slim and Roscoe Shelton across the Atlantic and had somehow secured distribution in import shops in London, where Mick Jagger and Keith Richards were among the avid collectors. The Yardbirds' debut single was a cover of Billy Boy Arnold's 'I Wish You Would' (Vee-Jay, 1955); Wayne Fontana and the Mindbenders had a transatlantic hit covering the record of the moment, Major Lance's 'Um, Um, Um, Um, Um, Um' (OKeh, 1963); Nina Simone's blistering 'Please Don't Let Me Be Misunderstood' (Philips, 1964) was a hit for The Animals; and the Rolling Stones recorded Arthur Alexander's love-wars single 'You Better Move On' (Dot, 1961) and The Valentinos' 'It's All Over Now' (SAR, 1964), a hugely profitable global success which, perhaps understandably, irked The Valentinos' lead singer Bobby Womack for the rest of his days.

Bluesman Willie Dixon's songs were hugely popular within the early sixties British underground scene. The debut albums of the

Rolling Stones, Cream and Led Zeppelin all featured his songs and, driven by Jagger's obsessive collecting of imported American vinyl, the Stones took his 'Little Red Rooster' to the top of the UK charts in 1964. It was one of the few times that an authentic blues record fought off pop to climb to number one. Dixon was in many respects the archetypal victim of the traffic of music. One landmark case, which only came to court when he was semi-retired and laid low by diabetes and an amputated leg, established that Led Zeppelin's 'Whole Lotta Love' leaned far too heavily on 'You Need Love', a song written by Dixon and sung by Muddy Waters in 1962. Dixon sued the group in 1985 and won, provoking guitarist Jimmy Page to tell one journalist, 'You only get caught when you're successful. That's the game.' It was the game that Sam Cooke had taught Cassius – the cynical ploys of the recording industry and how they were stacked against African-American artists. He stressed the importance of three things: protect your copyright, protect your image rights, and make sure you get paid.

For some singers in the first days of soul it proved to be an era of rip-off; for a much smaller number it brought a visibility that allowed them to shape a profitable career against the backdrop of racial inequality. One of the greatest records of the British Invasion was a cover of Bessie Banks' 'Go Now' (Tiger, 1964) by The Moody Blues. It was a depressing example of how power and access to success were still stacked against African-American talent, as it tried to break out of small indie-label music. Bessie Banks had arranged to record the original, but the plans were scuppered. 'I remember 1963 Kennedy was assassinated,' Banks told the soul music executive Ady Croasdell. 'It was announced over the radio. At the time, I was rehearsing in the office of Leiber and Stoller. We called it a day. Everyone was in tears. "Come back next week and we will be ready to record 'Go Now'," and we did so. I was happy and excited that maybe this time I'll make it. "Go Now" was released and right away it was chosen Pick Hit of the Week on W.I.N.S. Radio. That means your record is played for seven days. Four days went by, I was so thrilled. On day five, when I heard the first line, I thought it was me, but all of a sudden, I realized it wasn't. At the end of the song it was announced, "The Moody Blues singing

'Go Now'." I was too out-done.' This was the time of the end of Bessie Banks' career, so I thought. America's DJs had stopped promoting American artists.'

With the heavyweight title fight fast approaching and the British Invasion in fifth gear, *Life* magazine photographer Harry Benson decided to bring the participants together. He convinced The Beatles to leave their beach hotel for an impromptu photo session at Cassius's training camp. He had already taken the now iconic photograph of the group having a pillow fight in their room at the George V Hotel near the Arc de Triomphe in Paris, on the night they discovered 'I Wanna Hold Your Hand' had gone to number one in the USA.

Inside the 5th Street Gym, there was an awkward introduction. Neither The Beatles nor Cassius knew of each other, and there was a moment when Lennon thought they were wasting their time and wanted to leave. Egged on by Benson, The Beatles entered the ring and pretended to fight Cassius four on one, and then, in a choreographed line-up, Cassius posed, arm outstretched, appearing to knock them all down domino-style. The photographs have since entered the gallery of sixties iconography, a meeting of stars who went on to shape perceptions of the decade. In his book *Ali: A Life*, Jonathan Eig described the mood in the gym as 'a compelling hybrid – rebel-clowns' – absolutely attuned to the era.

The Beatles had only been in Miami for a couple of days, but the impression they left behind was indelible, even therapeutic. Phillip Norman, author of *Shout: The True Story of The Beatles*, a study of how they changed the face of pop culture, believes that their appearances on *The Ed Sullivan Show* – broadcast ten weeks after the death of John F. Kennedy – 'met America's need for a new idol, a new toy, a painkilling drug and a laugh'.

Others were less kind. The hard-boiled New York columnist Jimmy Cannon, who loathed Cassius and once described boxing as the 'red light district of sport', erupted when he learned second-hand about The Beatles meeting Cassius in Miami. What he saw was the desecration of sixties pop culture. 'Clay is part of the Beatle Movement,' Cannon fumed. 'He fits in with the famous singers no

'Hello there, Beatles,' said Cassius when he first met the four Liverpudlians at his training camp in Miami, on the afternoon of 18 February 1964. 'We should do some roadshows together. We'll get rich.'

one can hear and the punks riding motorcycles with iron crosses pinned to their leather jackets and Batman and the boys with their long dirty hair and the girls with the unwashed look and the college kids dancing naked at secret proms held in apartments and the revolt of students who get a check from Dad every first of the month and the painters who copy the labels off soup cans and the surf bums who refuse to work and the whole pampered style-making cult of the bored young.' Cannon was a man profoundly uncomfortable with the changes that were ripping up American life and one who could never quite accept that Cassius was something much more than a showman.

Just when everyone most needed a period of calm, Malcolm X decided to return to Miami – this time alone. Cassius's closeness to the Nation of Islam was now an open secret and, according to the promoters, beginning to have a negative impact on ticket sales. Fight promoter Bill McDonald had estimated that he would have to take in $800,000 from the box office just to break even, and stories linking the fight to black radicalism were apparently scaring off older white fans. The Miami Convention Hall was a 15,744-seater venue and, with three days to go, only half the tickets had been sold. On hearing that Malcolm X was back in town, McDonald threatened to pull the plug and cancel the fight. But a compromise was reached: Malcolm agreed to stay in Overtown and keep a low profile until the night of the fight. In return he was given a VIP package and his preferred seat – number 7. The number seven is significant in Islamic numerology – 'The one who eats seven dates of al-'Aaliyah in the morning will not be harmed that day by poison or witchcraft.'

As the big fight drew closer, the boxing press began to heap doubt on Cassius's chances. Arthur Daley of *The New York Times* claimed that an 'aura of artificiality' surrounded the fight: 'it doesn't even rate being called a match made by popular demand. The only one who demanded it was Cassius, a precocious master of ballyhoo, who lulls himself to sleep at night not by counting sheep but by counting money. He'll be seeing stars when Sonny hits him . . .' Milton Gross of the *New York Post* saw a fighter whose hype disguised his mediocrity. 'Cassius the fighter, like Cassius the recording star, is a figment of somebody else's imagination,' he wrote. 'Only in this day of mediocrity could he be fighting for the world heavyweight championship.'

Meanwhile, the reigning champion was training in the most unorthodox way. It was hardcore vaudeville, so full of power that it attracted a paying audience. Promoter Chris Dundee set up a stall to bring tourists into the gym, each paying 99 cents to watch Liston work out. He opened the show in a conventional way with four rounds of shadow-boxing with 175-pounder Allan Thomas, an orthodox light heavyweight from Chicago. Next came three rounds on the heavy bag, three rounds on the speed bag, and then the pièce de résistance – rapid rope-skipping to the pumping strains of James Brown's 'Night Train'. Brown was virtually the only entertainer who supported Liston, commenting that 'Sonny Liston isn't the worst person in the . . . world and should not be treated like he's the world's first public figure to have a record of being in trouble.' The remark demonstrated empathy; he had his own record of being in trouble, as a boxer and criminal. Liston's cornermen, huddled around a box record player, returned the needle to the start. The record played for 3 minutes and 35 seconds, and was played six times. Then, to end the show, Liston got a medicine ball hurled at his stomach a number of times, and performed sixty-four jerking sit-ups on a specially designed back-board. When the show was over, he, unsurprisingly, would return to his villa to sleep.

As the clock ticked down on the fight, Liston intervened in a dispute about screenings. He refused to agree that it could be shown in New Orleans, because the cinema that had been chosen by local operators was segregated. The civil-rights organisation CORE was active in New Orleans and had successfully picketed a segregated Woolworths store on Canal Street, but the pace of change within the city's segregated school system was glacial. CORE got in touch with Liston, who stood up to his management team and insisted that if the seating in New Orleans was segregated the plugs would be pulled. 'I feel that the colour of my people's money is the same as anyone else's,' Liston told the press. 'They should get the same seats. If not, I don't want those places to get the fight.' He succeeded, and the local restrictions were lifted.

The weigh-in was chaotic. Jim Murray of the *Los Angeles Times*, a sportswriter whose columns sparkled with one-liners, wrote at the time that 'the weigh-in . . . should have been painted by Hogarth'. He saw in the eighteenth-century satirist's work a similar mood of sharp humour and conceit. Cassius strutted into the room, brandishing a cane that Malcolm X had given him for spiritual sustenance and chanting, 'I was born for this day. I am the champ, he is a chump, I am the greatest.' According to BBC reports, he taunted Liston: 'You're a tramp. I am going to eat you up. Somebody's going to die at the ringside tonight. Are you scared?' He was subsequently fined $2,500 for 'disgraceful conduct'. Liston, who the BBC described as 'The Dark Destroyer', was wearing a silk hooded robe, and motioned to swat his opponent away, as if he was an irritating fly. Cassius erupted in a volley of threats and boasts; even when the fight doctor was examining his heart with a stethoscope, he refused to shut up. Miami police officers, loaded down with guns and handcuffs, circled the boxers, fearful that the fight might erupt prematurely.

On the night, in a moment of touching fraternity, Cassius left his dressing room early to show support for Rudy, who was fighting on the undercard against local debutant, Matthew 'Chip' Johnson. He sat impassively far from the ringside, dressed in a dark suit with his customary black bow tie, urging his brother to victory at a time when most boxers would be in their dressing room focusing on their fight plan. Rudy was never as good a boxer as his brother, nor did he share Cassius's vivacious personality, but they had a deep and unshakable love for each other. They were rarely apart and often leant on each other for reassurance as they made the journey from high school to the temples of the Nation of Islam. After taking a pounding from Johnson, Rudy's superior technique triumphed and he was given the fight on a split decision.

Cassius returned to his dressing room to change, then came into the ring – long before Liston – dancing with unbridled joy and relishing the limelight. David Remnick, the Pulitzer Prize-winning writer, set up the fight with his characteristic attention to detail. 'On the night of February 25, 1964, Cassius Clay entered the ring in Miami Beach wearing a short white robe, "The Lip" stitched on the back,' he wrote in *The Atlantic* magazine. 'He was fast, sleek, and twenty-two. But, for the first time in his life, and the last, he was afraid. The ring was crowded with has-beens and would-be's, liege men and pugs. Clay ignored them. He began bouncing on the balls of his feet, shuffling joylessly at first, like a marathon dancer at ten to midnight, but then with more speed, more pleasure. After a few minutes, Sonny Liston, the heavyweight champion of the world, stepped through the ropes and onto the canvas, gingerly, like a man easing himself into a canoe. He wore a hooded robe. His eyes were unworried, and they were blank, the dead eyes of a man who'd never got a favour out of life and never given one out. He was not likely to give one to Cassius Clay.'

Rain pelted down on the Miami Beach Convention Center as fight fans scurried to shelter in the auditorium. A stream of people headed for Hall C, where the ring had been secured to the concrete floor. The seventh row was peppered with big names. Jerry Brandt from the William Morris Agency, who was negotiating to bring the Rolling Stones to America, had bought a batch of tickets in the best seats. He had invited Allen Klein, Sam Cooke's manager and the business partner of the Apollo's in-house R&B DJ Jocko Henderson. At the time, Klein was negotiating to buy a stake in the ailing Philadelphia label Cameo-Parkway and had become an adviser to Chubby Checker and Dee Dee Sharp. Klein was soon to become the financial sorcerer of the British Invasion and the US manager of both The Beatles and the Stones. His wife Betty was with him, and Cooke was accompanied by his wife Barbara. Cooke's mentor and collaborator J.W. Alexander, who co-owned SAR and Derby Records and showcased the early careers of Johnnie Taylor, Billy Preston and The Valentinos starring Bobby Womack, also joined the party. Further along row 7 was Malcolm X. Cameras were trained on him not just by news photographers but also by a detail of FBI agents scattered around the hall. Sitting with Malcolm X was his friend Osman Karriem, who had recently been hired as Cassius's road manager. Prior to his conversion to Islam, he'd been known as Archie Robinson, manager of The Platters, and had come to prominence back in 1959 when he defended four members of the group who had been accused of consorting with white prostitutes in a Cincinnati hotel bedroom. The Platters were associated with sweet, romantic harmonies like 'Smoke Gets In Your Eyes' (Mercury, 1958), 'Harbour Lights' (Mercury, 1960) and 'Red Sails In The Sunset' (Mercury, 1960). The court case wrecked their clean-cut image and, according to Karriem, they lost over $500,000 of bookings and business as a result. The group limped on and went through multiple line-up changes, but their era was coming to an end, blown away by the energy, power and modernity of the new soul music. Of all the characters in the golden-circle seats by the ringside, Karriem was the one most informed about the irremediable acrimony inside the Nation. He suspected that they were all under constant state surveillance. He was right. For over a year now, he had been tracked by FBI agents wherever he went. Without having done anything to warrant the scrutiny, he was a marked man.

After months of logistical problems, financial worries, staged insults and theatrics, when the fight came it was a brief flash of history.

Sports Illustrated described it vividly: 'In the first round, all the smouldering resentment came out in a rush. Bulling from his corner, Liston forgot the instructions of Willie Reddish, his trainer, and he forgot most of what he had learned about boxing. Proud, especially vain of his body and his reputation as a puncher, Liston was a man with but one thought, and it was a dangerously emotional one. He wanted to murder his tormentor, in one minute if possible, more quickly than he had knocked out Floyd Patterson.'

Round 2: it was quieter with Cassius dancing confidently to avoid Liston's assaults.

Round 3: Liston leaked blood from a gash beneath his left eye but he fought on, his formidable battering-ram power undiminished.

Round 4: Cassius panicked. He was smarting and blinking and trying to avoid a barrage of heavy punches. When the bell rang he retreated to his corner screaming, 'Cut the gloves off,' and appealing to the referee that something suspicious was afoot. An astringent ointment from Liston's cut had made its way onto his gloves and it was blinding Cassius, hurting his eyes. But in the febrile atmosphere, many started to suspect underhand tactics. Cold sponges of water were splashed on Cassius's face as his noisy Cuban-speaking corner screamed at Angelo Dundee not to throw in the towel.

Round 5: Liston ploughed forwards with Cassius wheeling and hiding until focus fuzzily returned to his stinging eye.

Round 6: the eye had cleared and Liston began to tire as a barrage of punches stopped him in his tracks.

There is no doubt that Liston's arm was damaged. In the sixth round, he carried it at belt level so that it was of no help in warding off the right crosses with which Clay probed at the cut under his left eye. Still, one expected Liston to come out for the seventh, and for the fight to end with a bang, not a whimper. Whether the left arm was damaged enough for a champion to accept defeat sitting in his corner instead of fighting with one arm until he was knocked out will be a subject of debate among boxing followers for a long time.

Cassius was up early, dancing on his feet and anticipating the seventh round, but it never came. 'I happened to be looking right at Liston as that warning buzzer sounded,' Cassius said, 'and I didn't believe it when he spat out his mouthpiece. I couldn't believe it – but there it was lying there. And then something just told me he wasn't coming out. I gave a whoop and come off that stool like it was red hot. It's a funny thing, but I wasn't even thinking about Liston. I was thinking about nothing but that hypocrite press. All of them down there that had wrote so much about me bound to get beat by the big-fists.'

The arena exploded with confusion and incredulity. The new champion turned his wrath on the newsmen. 'Eat your words,' he screamed above the commotion. Only three of forty-six sports-writers covering the fight had picked him to win, and the odds-on favourite was rooted to his corner seat. The unthinkable had happened: the man mountain who many thought unbeatable could not fight on. Torn shoulder muscles suffered in the first round had hampered Liston's fight, cramping his pounding left hooks, and the pain was so acute he was incapable of continuing. Edwin Pope, the *Miami Herald* sports columnist, stared in disbelief, an unlit cigarette hanging from his gaping mouth. 'The night exploded so fast I never got the match to the cigarette,' he said. 'I remember thinking, "This can't be happening."'

Before the world heavyweight champion title fight on 25 February 1964,
in a poll of forty-six sports writers, three picked Cassius to win . . . After one of the
biggest upsets in boxing history, Liston sits beaten, battered and bewildered,
surrounded by his corner men and disbelieving journalists.

Malcolm X was euphoric in his ringside seat and 'experienced a sweetness unlike any he had felt in some time'. Speaking after the fight, he said, 'The white press wanted him to lose. They wanted him to lose because he is a Muslim. You notice nobody cares about the religion of other athletes. But their prejudice against Clay blinded them to his ability.'

As the ring filled with excited well-wishers, Cassius grabbed microphones, mugged for photographers and hogged television cameras. In his biography of Sam Cooke, *Dream Boogie*, the music historian Peter Guralnick, wrote: 'Cassius was in the middle of an interview with television announcer Steve Ellis and former champ Joe Louis when he spotted Sam, almost dishevelled with excitement, his tie removed, shirt open. "Sam Cooke!" the new champion called out with unabashed enthusiasm. "Hey, let that man up here." Ellis did his best to ignore yet another in a string of uncontrollable developments ("I want justice! I want justice!" the new champ had just been calling out). "This is Sam Cooke!" Cassius shouts. "We see him. We see him," says the announcer, looking utterly bewildered. "Joe, ask Cassius another question." But Cassius is not to be deterred.' It was an iconic moment in the history of soul music, the first time someone of Cooke's status was visible to a global audience of millions – elegant, charming and super-smooth in a cauldron of mayhem. Then Sugar Ray lifted Cassius's hand in triumph and led him through the throng to the sanctuary of his dressing room.

The aftermath was even more dramatic than the fight itself. Klein and the high-rollers from the William Morris Agency had booked a function suite at the Fontainebleau for a celebration party, but neither Cassius nor Liston showed up. Immediately after the bout, Liston had his left shoulder hurriedly taped up, and his manager Jack Nilon drove him to St Francis Hospital, on Allison Island. Surrounded by a congregation of medics and Franciscan nuns, Liston was examined by a physician from the Miami State Boxing Commission. Liston suffered from bursitis in both shoulders and had previously injured the left one in training; he had secretly undergone two weeks of heat and ultrasonic treatment rather than pull out of the fight. His left bicep appeared to have torn in the first round as Liston swung at Cassius's head. The Boxing Commission's medical team unanimously concluded that Liston's injury had prevented him from using his left arm to defend himself. His desire to finish Cassius in the opening round had been his downfall. The muscle damage had caused his arm to swell by almost four inches and his fist was badly inflamed. 'There is no doubt in my mind this fight should have been stopped,' said the lead physician, Dr Alexander Robbins.

The examination was not simply a medical necessity, it was the beginning of a four-week investigation by the Florida State Attorney's office and an even longer dispute about the distribution of the prize money. Rumours of a fix were rife, and the gossip in the bars and on the street corners was that the mob had engineered the most unprecedented of outcomes: the defeat of Sonny Liston. But there was no question that the injury to his shoulder was real and the subsequent investigation uncovered no evidence that the fight was rigged. Moreover, there had been no tell-tale fluctuation in the betting odds anywhere in the country. It was only after publication of the State Attorney's report that Liston's money was released to him, but yet again, the stench of organised crime lingered. From its lofty position in the pulpit of American sport, *Sports Illustrated* published its verdict: 'Almost no one has conceded, so far, that Clay is truly a better fighter than Sonny Liston. Aside from the expectable accusations of a fix, the excuses for Liston have been that he was over trained and heavy-armed, or that he was undertrained, expecting to win in only a couple of rounds and exhausted when the fight went beyond that. There was even one rumour that Liston had suffered a heart attack in the ring. None of these things are true. Liston was trained fine, but not necessarily too fine. His heart was normal. There was no fix. He fought and lost to a quicker, younger and – finally – a much smarter boxer.'

Although he wanted to simply disappear into the night, Liston mustered the courage to attend a post-fight press conference, wearing a sling on his arm. *The New York Times*: 'In a dark suit, black tasselled loafers and with a diamond pinky ring on the sling hand, Liston told how it felt to lose. In the corner between rounds, he said, it felt as if his gloves were filling with water. The pain grew steadily worse, until his arm felt leaden when he tried to fight with it. "In the corner they told me to jab more, but I couldn't jab more," said Liston. Then in a strange analogy that possibly only Liston himself could have conjured he began to explain why he had lost the fight. "If a guy handcuffs you to a tree, why don't you leave? I didn't think I could take him because I couldn't take those handcuffs off. When I threw that left hook in the first round I knew it went out. Yeah, it was a left hook I missed with.'"

Cassius's dressing room was like a fairground. Cubans, bow-tied Muslims, medics, team members and hangers-on clustered around the new champion as he talked incessantly about how his forecast had come true. Dee Dee Sharp was in the crowd, but in later years she described how she'd felt excluded and shunned by the boyfriend she called 'Marcellus'. For much of their romance, she had been the more famous personality, reaching a crossover audience on network television shows and topping the pop charts. But slowly and surely it was Cassius who came to hog the limelight. She had hoped they would marry when he won the title but they had been arguing about her Christian upbringing and religion in general, and many close to the champ claimed the relationship was already over. Cassius swept out of the dressing room without acknowledging her presence. It seemed she was just another one of Cassius's 'foxes' after all.

Cassius had already agreed to join Malcolm X and Sam Cooke at a private party back at the Hampton House Motel in Brownsville. A flotilla of cars took them along I-95 and on to 54th Street where local residents poured out of a warren of low-rise houses to cheer the new champion. The group took over the motel's diner and Malcolm X briefly served behind the bar, photographing Cassius as if he was an excited teenager sitting at the counter. The management brought in ice cream, and the boisterous party, which now included hundreds of fans, scooped it up with long spoons. It was, according to Cassius, the most delicious vanilla ice cream he'd ever tasted.

After celebrating at the diner, the inner circle made its way along the corridor to Malcolm X's room to relax in quieter

Cassius snubs the traditional champion's party and returns to Overtown. Malcolm X, behind the soda fountain, focuses his camera on Cassius, who celebrates his victory with jubilant fans – and a vanilla ice cream.

surroundings. With no witnesses and no journalists present, the scene has been imagined in many ways. Inside the room were Cassius and his brother Rudy, Malcolm X, Sam Cooke and Jim Brown, the running back for the Cleveland Browns, who until that night was the most successful African-American sportsman alive. Journalist Tim Layden once wrote how 'Brown towered over the league, a physical and intellectual force like none other in American sports history'. Under the weight of influence from Brown, Cooke and his spiritual leader, Cassius had grown increasingly ill at ease with his original backers. According to authors Randy Roberts and Johnny Smith, Cassius began to assert quite openly that he was 'going to free himself from the domination of twelve white managers from Louisville'. Bill Faversham, who had shared his concerns with the group, told several investors that their days were almost certainly numbered and that Cassius would almost certainly be terminating their agreement. Within a matter of months, Jabir Herbert Muhammad, the third son of Elijah, became his new manager. He would stay in that role until the boxer retired in 1981.

All that is certain about the confidential gathering is that there was no alcohol, no gambling and no gangsters: it was pure fresh air in the malodorous world of boxing. One man was noticeably absent: Cassius's forceful father. His influence was waning, and Cassius now sought advice and counsel from the Nation. 'They've ruined my two boys,' he told *Miami Herald* journalist Pat Putnam. 'They should run these black Muslims out of the country before they ruin other fine young people. The Muslims tell my boys to hate white people, to hate women, to hate their mother . . . They wanted me to change our last name to X. I laughed at them. I told them I had a good Christian name and it would stay that way. I told them that after a person learns to read and write he don't have to use any X.'

The following day Cassius woke up amidst clouds of suspicion. Some people were having trouble believing he had won the fight fairly. For over two years his antics had dominated the back pages of the Miami news while State Attorney Richard E. Gerstein had dominated the front pages. Gerstein was a boulder of man, a war hero, whose giant frame stood out in the courthouses of the city.

He wore starched white shirt collars and always tucked a silk handkerchief into his top pocket. He was, in the eyes of local press, 'the most powerful, controversial, durable and well-known politician in Dade County'.

Like Cassius, Gerstein had a nose for publicity, and the morning after the fight, he launched a full-scale criminal inquiry into Liston's injury and the conduct of the fight. It was more than simply attention seeking. For over ten years he and his sidekick Doug Kennedy, head of the Miami Vice Squad, had waged war on illegal gambling and on the bolita dens that littered the coastline. Bolita – Spanish for little ball – was a Hispanic lottery game based on a hundred numbered balls. Popular in Cuba until it was outlawed by Castro, the game seeped into Florida, and by the time Gerstein took office the undercover game was rife – predominantly under the control of the infamous Trafficante family. Gerstein led with the legal injunctions while Kennedy and his men kicked down doors, arrested hoods, and burnt the bolita paraphernalia in front of press photographers. It had all the ritualistic trademarks of the Prohibition era, but despite the crackdowns bolita refused to budge. It was too deeply ingrained in the memories of Cuban exiles and was often played as a party game in Hispanic households, enjoyed even more because it was banned back home. There was even a bolita board stashed in a back-room drawer in the 5th Street Gym. Luis Rodríguez and the Cubans had tried to teach Cassius its rules and rituals but it was too much a game of pure chance to excite him. He preferred magic.

Three weeks before the big fight, Gerstein had been in the news again, this time as the victim of a neo-Nazi bomb plot. An employee of Miami's water department named Donald Branch was sentenced to jail for plotting to murder prominent Jewish personalities across the city. He pleaded guilty to the bombing of the home of Don Shoemaker, editor of the *Miami Herald*, and an attempted atrocity at local synagogues. He also admitted to having compiled a death-threat list and being in possession of a stormtroopers' bombing manual. Among the list of targets scrawled under 'Negro' was Cassius Clay and under 'Jew' was Richard E. Gerstein. The cadre of white supremacists at the centre of the plots called themselves 'The

Minute Men' and subsequent trials revealed they were mainly members of the American Nazi party. As Cassius and Liston intensified their training in the run-up to the big fight, Branch was sentenced to forty-two years in jail.

Gerstein's most famous case was yet to come. Not long after Cassius was crowned champion, a gruesome murder in a Key Biscayne apartment brought TV cameras flocking to Miami. It was a tabloid news editor's dream. A beautiful blonde woman was accused of conspiring with her nephew, with whom she was having an incestuous affair, to murder her husband, the millionaire and philanthropist Jacques Mossler. He had been found clubbed over the head and stabbed thirty-nine times. The case was dynamite. Gerstein prosecuted Candace 'Candy' Mossler and her lover Mel Powers, in the process not only revealing a tale of intrigue and murder, but also providing a rare insight into the domestic lives of Miami's super-rich. The supermarket press gleefully described it as 'murder, lubricated by sex, nourished by sex, varnished with sex', and *The New York Times* considered the trial 'so lurid that the judge admitted no spectator under 21. The star performer was the legendary lawyer Perry Foreman, who persuaded a jury to overlook clear motive, bloodstains, palm prints, fingerprints and love letters.' Many saw it as the stage on which Gerstein would demonstrate his credentials to become the state governor, but the jury split and could not deliver a guilty verdict. In scenes of uproar, Mossler and Powers were found not guilty. She joyfully kissed every juror before departing with her nephew in a gold Cadillac. Gerstein's prosecution had failed spectacularly.

In the weeks after the fight, Gerstein invited Miami's citizens to provide evidence that the fight was fixed and, consequently, pursued many false trails. Gossip buzzed like a live electric socket, but any facts supporting a fix were thin on the ground. Under Florida law, Gerstein reminded the populace, persons found 'tampering with an athletic contest can be sent to prison for terms up to ten years'. His inquiry ground to a standstill and he was grasping for possible explanations. Perhaps Liston's injury was a contrivance and he had thrown the fight to benefit his management and himself? The medical reports closed down that line of inquiry.

Perhaps the fight had been a criminal conspiracy between the two camps? There was no evidence to support that proposition. Or could the fight have fallen foul of match fixing? When Gerstein 'followed the money', the most likely match-fixers, the Florida and Philadelphia Mafia, had lost their shirts betting heavily on the favourite. Theories swirled around Miami for months, but no arrests were made, and after four weeks the investigation was discreetly wound down. Case closed.

The FBI, on the other hand, were on a mission. They spent more than a year failing to find any evidence of criminality. Even after regional bureaus told J. Edgar Hoover's office that they had found nothing, the director insisted that they keep going. Much of the FBI's investigation was fanciful. The El Paso office was sent to contact wealthy 'oilmen' about their betting strategies. The Philadelphia office offered a report on Liston's 'over-training' and whether that played a role in his performance. The Denver office talked to people who knew Liston and concluded that 'he is not smart enough to be involved in any fix'. Questions about how the money from the fight was distributed were wrangled over for years to come.

Some financial trails were relatively simple to follow and others maddeningly complicated. Cassius's side of the ledger was straightforward. The fight had generated $4,922,000 from the disappointing live gate, theatre receipts, radio broadcast rights, cable television, advertising, motion picture rights and incidental revenue. Cassius received the smaller share and a purse of $630,000 split evenly between himself and Bill Faversham on behalf of the Louisville Sponsoring Group. By comparison Liston's share was a minefield. The Miami Beach Boxing Commission withheld his purse, and a court case – *Sonny Liston, President of Inter-Continental Promotions Corp. v. Bill MacDonald of Dundee-MacDonald Enterprises* – rumbled on until 1966. Liston was pursuing a missing $400,000 he claimed was due to him from the promoters. For reasons now buried in the hellish history of Liston's life, he shared his purse with Sam Margolis, the Mafia vending-machine boss, and the Philadelphia lawyer Salvatore J.

Avena, an associate of Blinky Palermo. It was a mess that led back to the Philadelphia Mafia.

Cassius's victory had wrong-footed the Nation of Islam's HQ too. Like most Americans, and almost the entire betting industry, they had never seriously believed that their young acolyte might beat Liston. On the morning of 26 February 1964, Cassius woke up late and, despite his lifelong phobia, he boarded a plane to Chicago with the intention of celebrating Saviours' Day, a holiday in the calendar of the Nation of Islam, which commemorates the birth of the organisation's founder, Wallace Fard Muhammad. Cassius finally announced his membership of the Nation and confirmed that he was now to be known officially as 'Cassius X'. When the proceedings ended in Chicago, Cassius hired a car and drove to New York, where he booked two luxury suites at the Hotel Theresa. There he met up with Malcolm X again, which sent waves of panic through the Nation's senior leadership. Rumours spread that Malcolm might use Cassius's global profile to launch a new breakaway organisation. (The rumours were to prove true: after a pilgrimage to Mecca, Malcolm announced the launch of the Organization of Afro-American Unity (OAAU) at a public meeting in the Audubon Ballroom on 28 June 1964. J. Edgar Hoover was incensed, describing it as a threat to national security.) Elijah Muhammad was advised not to over-react: Cassius was a loyal recruit and devoted to his leadership. The anxiety simmered for days and came to the boil on 4 March 1964, when Cassius and Malcolm went on a two-hour tour of the United Nations building together. At an impromptu press gathering, Cassius announced his intention to 'live for ever' in New York. 'I'm so popular I need a big town so all the people who want to watch me can do it,' he joked. The FBI then tailed the two men to Queens, as they drove aimlessly along Grand Central Parkway and up and down side streets, looking at vacant property.

Meanwhile, ensconced on Riker's Island, apoplectic about the outcome of the fight and still profiting from fixing fights through intermediaries, Frankie Carbo was plotting to end Cassius's reign as swiftly and brutally as he could. He had developed a pathological hatred for the boxer. He resented his flamboyance and his arrogance, but most of all he hated the way he had destroyed Liston's reign as champion, thus undermining the mob's leverage on the heavyweight title. A gut-felt racism made him flare up whenever Cassius was in the news and, according to FBI files, Carbo threatened to assassinate Cassius. His threats were taken seriously. In March 1964, less than a month after he had won the title, during his triumphant return to his hometown as champion, FBI agents met Cassius by prior arrangement at Stouffors Hotel. They informed him of a credible Mafia plot on his life and produced a note, purportedly from Carbo. It was scrawled on the back of a flyer for the Cold War film *Seven Days in May*, starring Kirk Douglas and Burt Lancaster, a thriller in which a US military leader plots to overthrow the president. Cassius laughed it off and bid them goodbye.

In his exposé of boxing and the criminal underworld, *Jacobs Beach: The Mob, the Fights, the Fifties*, British journalist Kevin Mitchell described Carbo as a 'charmer, looked after his mum, all that stuff. But he had this split personality; he could be ruthless, aggressive, one of the scariest guys you'd ever meet. They called him "Mr Grey", because he just stayed in the shadows. He didn't want a public profile; he wanted to do things in private, without people knowing his face. That's just how he operated, a nameless face who was arguably the most powerful man in boxing at that time.' He had the background of an assassin and a string of connections with the darkest corners of American crime. Cassius always claimed that the threats never bothered him, but he shared the FBI warning with the Nation, and some of the most formidable characters from the Fruit of Islam paramilitary wing joined his entourage.

These were terrifying times of conspiracy and retaliation, and there are at least three possible explanations for Carbo's assassination threat. One, it could have been a hoax with no roots in reality. Two, Carbo's brooding hatred for Cassius may have worsened as he stewed in jail. Or three, just as plausibly, the FBI had concocted the letter to allow them to get closer to the new champion, whose religious conversion was now national news. The FBI had a long-held policy of attempting to undermine and destabilise what they considered to be radical Black Power organisations, and while their poisonous COINTELPRO programme would not be made public until later in the sixties, many of their techniques had already been tried out on the Nation. One tactic was the sending of bogus letters to individuals deemed a threat in order to either implicate them in conspiracies or sew doubt in the minds of their comrades. Carbo's letter might just as easily have been forged in the Louisville field offices of the FBI, to allow agents to get closer to Cassius and to question him about his contacts.

The apparent death threat was presented to Cassius only months before the most notorious letter in the history of the FBI, the now infamous 'suicide letter' addressed to Martin Luther King and sent to his home address in Atlanta. The letter had been composed in the FBI's Washington headquarters and was written by the head of the Bureau's intelligence division, William C. Sullivan. It was a single sheet, typewritten and tightly spaced, that used foul, derogatory language and accused King of being 'a tom cat with obsessive degenerate sexual urges'. Accompanying the note was an edited tape-recording of King's sexual exploits in a succession of hotel rooms, first at a party in the Willard Hotel in Washington, DC, then in the Hilton Hawaiian Village in Honolulu, and, the most lurid of all, at the Hyatt House Hotel in Los Angeles. To cover their tracks, the FBI arranged for a veteran intelligence agent named Lish Whitsun to fly to Miami and post the package there. The objective of the poison pen letter seems to have been to induce King to commit suicide rather than have his sex life exposed or to pressure him into declining his nomination for the Nobel Peace Prize. King resisted the threats, and on 10 December 1964 he accepted the prize in Oslo saying, 'I accept the Nobel Prize for Peace at a moment when twenty-two million Negroes of the United States of America are engaged in a creative battle to end the long night of racial injustice. I accept this award on behalf of a civil-rights movement which is moving with determination and a majestic scorn for risk and danger to establish a reign of freedom and a rule of justice. I am mindful that only yesterday in Birmingham, Alabama, our children, crying out for brotherhood, were answered with fire hoses, snarling dogs and even death. I am mindful that only yesterday in Philadelphia, Mississippi, young people seeking to secure the right to vote were brutalized and murdered. And only yesterday more than forty houses of worship in the State of Mississippi alone were bombed or burned because they offered a sanctuary to those who would not accept segregation. I am mindful that debilitating and grinding poverty afflicts my people and chains them to the lowest rung of the economic ladder.'

He was given a standing ovation, his speech was circulated around the world, and the damaging letter, which King knew to be the work of the FBI, disappeared into the archives for decades to come.

On returning to his suite at the Theresa, Cassius took a call from Chicago and spoke personally to Elijah Muhammad, who warned him to be cautious of Malcolm X and not to follow any of his directions. And so it was that in a confused spirit of opportunity and deepening anxiety Muhammad pre-recorded an address to his followers, formally announcing a new convert to the cause. The address was broadcast on WVON Chicago and on WWRL New York, two of the towering soul stations of the early sixties. WVON was owned at the time by Chicago's Chess Records and broke, among many, The Dells, Fontella Bass, The Artistics, Jerry Butler and Barbara Acklin. On 6 March 1964, WVON broadcast Elijah Muhammad's message which informed America that henceforth the boxer known to the general public as Cassius Clay, and to his inner circle of confidants as Cassius X, would become known as Muhammad Ali – a man 'worthy of praise'.

Malcolm X was driving his black Oldsmobile 98 in Manhattan when he heard the announcement on WWRL New York. He knew immediately that the Nation of Islam leadership had pulled off a masterstroke. Politically and personally isolated, and fearful for his life, Malcolm tried to make contact with Cassius. He repeatedly rang the Theresa, but the boxer never took his calls. Cassius had taken Chicago's advice and was distancing himself from his old friend. At the time the calls were forwarded to his suite, Cassius was in conference with a group of representatives from the Nation, discussing his future with the organisation. One of the items on their agenda was an arranged marriage and the idea that

Muhammad Ali should take a Muslim bride. Any romance with Dee Dee Sharp was now unequivocally over.

On 8 March, Malcolm X officially announced his break with the Nation of Islam, labelling its leader as 'morally bankrupt'. The following day, *The New York Times* ran the story: 'Malcolm X broke last night with Elijah Muhammad's Chicago-based Black Muslim movement and announced that he was organizing a politically oriented "black nationalist party".' Malcolm told the newspaper that his new party 'would seek to convert the Negro population from nonviolence to active self-defence against white supremacists in all parts of the country'. He said that he remained a Muslim, 'but the main emphasis of the new movement will be black nationalism as a political concept and form of social action against the oppressors. "I have reached the conclusion," he said, "that I can best spread Mr. Muhammad's message by staying out of the Nation of Islam and continuing to work on my own among America's 22 million non-Muslim Negroes."' Viewed from the offices in Chicago, it was the last straw: an act of disobedience and a desecration that sealed his fate.

Malcolm made numerous attempts to contact Muhammad Ali thereafter, but his correspondence and phone calls were rejected. However deep his personal admiration for Malcolm X, it was not enough for Cassius to disobey the leadership. When the April edition of *Muhammad Speaks* hit the streets all doubt disappeared. Cassius appeared on the cover under the headline – 'Walk The Way Of Free Men' – alongside Elijah Muhammad. Inside, the paper carried a lengthy interview with the new champion. The friendship with Malcolm X had suddenly and brutally ended. In a series of press interviews that followed, the champion asserted his right to change his name. 'Cassius Clay is a slave name. I didn't choose it and I don't want it,' he said. 'I am Muhammad Ali, a free name – it means beloved of God, and I insist people use it when people speak to me.' This insistence became his next battle within boxing. Those who for whatever reason still called him Cassius Clay were vilified, and, in the case of Chicago heavyweight Ernie Terrell, brutalised in the ring, with Ali towering over his beaten body, shouting, 'What's my name? What's my name?'

Ironically, an FBI wiretap revealed the background to the name change. In a conversation between Cassius and Elijah Muhammad, probably recorded in either late February or early March 1964, the two men had discussed a new name. Cassius was reluctant to take what the Nation called 'an original name', an honour that had not even been bestowed on top-ranking ministers like Malcolm X, and briefly argued for sticking with Cassius X. But conscious of the propaganda value, the leader overruled him and Cassius agreed to become Muhammad Ali.

The reputation of the charismatic young boxer who had won the greatest prize in boxing was no longer simply that of a braggart and a clown but was now that of a respected member of an organisation many believed to be a threat to race relations in America. Floyd Patterson articulated the change of mood: 'The prize-fighter in America is not supposed to shoot off his mouth about politics, particularly when his views oppose the Government's and might influence many among the working classes who follow boxing.'

The era of Cassius Clay was over and the bell had rung on his remarkable rise to fame. A new champion had emerged from the nervous breakdown of 1963, a self-assertive young man who would dominate heavyweight boxing both inside and outside the ring in ways that no one could ever have predicted. Loathed by the conservative boxing authorities for joining the Nation and refusing to fight in Vietnam, Ali was eventually stripped of his titles and, as the war intensified and major cities descended deeper into race-fuelled violence, he came to personify the era.

Cassius had also witnessed the first hopeful days of soul – it was the music of his youth in the skating rinks of Louisville and in his bedroom at home – and absorbed the rhyming tongues of the radio DJs. As his title prospects blossomed, soul music came to parallel many of the key challenges of the decade: personal respect, tangled personal love affairs, civil rights, social change and, ultimately, the clenched fist of Black Power. In February 1962, when he fought for the first time in Madison Square Garden, precious few had even heard of Aretha Franklin, Otis Redding and Marvin Gaye. But

Cassius's fame rose alongside them and they too grew to iconic status, propelled by the hope of change.

Muhammad Ali's life was one of profound contradictions. He was a supremely gifted boxer who rewrote the rules, using speed, deception and an unorthodox dancing style to defy the stolid, hunched, muscular defence of boxing orthodoxy. He was outwardly a friendly person, fond of the company of children and a witty joker in the company of ordinary folk, but he could also be an icy, calculating man who brushed people away with a glare. His 'psychological warfare' campaign against Sonny Liston began as banter and pantomime but soured into a vindictive, hurtful harassment that revealed a cruelty within his personality that peaked in his blood feud with his greatest rival, Joe Frazier. He was simultaneously capable of lifetime devotion and brutal betrayal. He was a high-school failure but he grew up to become an articulate and passionate symbol of resistance for the sixties generation, courageously condemning racial discrimination in America and the war in Vietnam when he uttered the words: 'No Viet Cong ever called me nigger.' He was acutely conscious of how the media worked and how to manipulate publicity for his own ends yet he joined the Nation of Islam at a time when he knew the allegiance could wreck his career, alienate his parents and bring criticism raining down on him. He was respectful of authority, first with the police officers who introduced him to boxing, then to his white sponsors, and ultimately to Elijah Muhammad, but when confronted by the most powerful authorities in the land – the military, the FBI, the courts and the presidency – he refused to give ground and show them subservience.

When Muhammad Ali – by then infirm with Parkinson's disease – lit the flame at the Olympic Games in Atlanta in 1996, the music he had embraced as a young man had become a global pop phenomenon. That year, the charts were dominated by R&B, house and hip-hop, by 2Pac, Dr Dre, R. Kelly, LL Cool J, Keith Sweat and Whitney Houston. Whitney, the offspring of gospel soul singer Cissy Houston, was a three-month-old baby when Cassius fought Sonny Liston. An epic transformation had taken place. A form of music once marginalised and discriminated against by mainstream radio and the recording industry had risen to become the pre-eminent form of popular music in the world. In the battle for commercial visibility – the prize that Cassius X had once described to Tom Wolfe – black music had won.

Cassius's life was a series of twists and turns that defy a simple narrative, but he once said that he was driven by a single over-whelming ambition: 'My mission was simple. I had to prove I could be a new kind of black man.' It is to his eternal credit that he did.

A requiem for Sam, 17 December 1964. Cassius views the body of his friend, Sam Cooke, at the A. R. Leak Funeral Home in Chicago. Behind him is Cooke's road manager, S. R. Crain. Later the same day, in freezing temperatures, a crowd of 15,000 gathers at the Tabernacle Baptist Church on the South Side to pay their respects and radio station WVON broadcasts the entire memorial service.

REQUIEM

On a freezing-cold day in December 1964, ten months after he became heavyweight champion of the world and by which time he was universally known as Muhammad Ali, Cassius took a limousine to the A.R. Leak & Sons Funeral Home, on Cottage Grove Avenue, in Chicago's South Side. The body of his friend and one-time mentor Sam Cooke lay in an open coffin, under a protective glass cover. Cooke's body had been flown home to Chicago from Los Angeles, where he had been shot by a hotel manager. She claimed in a subsequent court case that Cooke had burst into her office threateningly, she'd pulled a gun and Cooke died in the confrontation. It was a moment of collective grief for Chicago's African-American community as their city's most famous singer lay dead, his still-beautiful body embalmed by the hands of Bernard Slaughter Sr. On completing the embalming, Slaughter laid Sam's body to rest in a $5,000 bronze casket with a beige silk interior. Cooke's brother, the gospel soul singer L.C. Cooke, was invited to make the final cosmetic adjustments. He combed Sam's hair and sprinkled the sandalwood aftershave Aramis into the coffin.

Muhammad Ali was one of the first mourners. He was pictured wearing a slimline iridescent suit and a dark tie with a jewelled tie pin, looking down reflectively on the body. They had shared so much: the meetings in Miami around the pool at the Sir John, excited conversations about taking control of business, horseplay as they recorded together in the studio, and most recently of all, the private gathering in Malcolm X's room in the Hampton Motel after Liston's defeat, when they had discussed their different versions of the same core belief: that a mighty change was gonna come.

Traffic gridlocked the main roads on the way to the funeral. Many hundreds gathered in the bitter cold, sheltering in the doorways of convenience stores along the block beside the funeral home. The crowd was so desperate for a glimpse of Cooke that pressure from bodies on the street outside cracked the funeral home's plate-glass windows. A crowd estimated at 15,000 at its height had also gathered around the Tabernacle Baptist Church nearby. Only a third of the crowd could be accommodated in the church, and squads of police officers, screeching through bullhorns, tried vainly to manage the overflow as it stopped the traffic on South Indiana Avenue.

Despite a tension in the air, the bottled-up emotions inside the church were largely kept in check by hallelujahs and streaming tears, but outside and in front of the scrum of cameras and microphones, emotions were uncontrollable. The comedian Dick Gregory, never shy of pointing the finger, eviscerated the LAPD for their failure to protect Cooke, and Muhammad Ali raised his suspicions too. 'I don't like the way he was shot. I don't like the way it was investigated. If Cooke had been Frank Sinatra, the Beatles, or Ricky Nelson, the FBI would be investigating yet and that woman would have been sent to prison.' He was not the only person to raise questions about Cooke's death, the circumstances of which remain unexplained to this day.

Malcolm X's recent announcement about a new 'black nationalist party' and Cassius's conversion threw a bomb into mainstream conservative journalism. The *Saturday Evening Post*: 'For a time, when he was confining himself to bad poetry, Cassius was a loudmouth but a likable character who seemed to be harmless in and out of the ring. Then he won the championship and became, in his own estimation, "The Greatest". After the fight, he acknowledged that he was a Black Muslim, converted by the arch-extremist, Malcolm X, the man who crowed that President Kennedy's assassination was "a case of the chickens coming home to roost". Malcolm X was separated from the Black Muslim movement after that remark and is now attempting to organize his own black nation. He wants to arm all the Negroes in the U.S. and ultimately take them back to Africa.'

Malcolm X's Organization of Afro-American Unity (OAAU) was keen to recruit but was not diligent enough about who it attracted. Sometime in the spring of 1964, with FBI clearance, an undercover New York police office called Eugene Roberts successfully infiltrated the OAAU. To deepen the deceit, he assumed the name Gene X Roberts and pursued a course of religious study that he hinted might lead to full conversion. A quiet, unassuming fellow, with the fake identity of a happily married warehouseman, he came to be trusted within the OAAU and was promoted to the inner circle role as Malcolm X's personal bodyguard, regularly standing beside his leader at rallies and huddling with street militants whenever a protest erupted.

By this time, Malcolm X was imbued with fatalism. 'I live like a man who's already dead,' he told *The New York Times* journalist Theodore Jones in the OAAU's office in the heart of Harlem. 'I'm a marked man.'

Roberts was on security duty at the rear of the Audobon Ballroom in Manhattan on the day that Malcolm X was murdered. A young nineteen-year-old woman from Bedford-Stuyvesant, who had signed up to the OAAU and called herself Sharon Six X Shabazz, told reporters: 'I think he had only said the words "Brothers and Sisters" when there was a commotion in the back of the room. I thought it was some rowdy drunks.'

The disturbance had been caused by an assassination squad from the Nation of Islam. According to Manning Marable, in *Malcolm X: A Life of Reinvention*, 'an incendiary smoke bomb ignited at the extreme rear of the ballroom, instantly creating panic, screams and confusion. It was only then that Willie Bradley, sitting in the front row, got to his feet and walked briskly toward the rostrum. When he was fifteen feet away, he elevated his sawed-off shot gun from under his coat, took careful aim, and fired. The shotgun pellets ripped squarely into Malcolm's left side, cutting a seven-inch-wide circle around his heart and left chest. This was the kill shot, the blow that executed Malcolm X . . .'

Roberts fought his way to a stage littered with drum kits and amplifiers and up to the bullet-ridden lectern, evading gunfire as he ran, and attempted to give Malcolm X mouth-to-mouth resuscitation. But it was too little, too late. The autopsy recorded that he had died of 'multiple gunshot wounds' from three different weapons.

Despite having at least one undercover officer close to Malcolm X, the NYPD were quick to shake off any suspicion that they might have been implicated. They reported that they had offered Malcolm police protection on seven separate occasions but he had always turned them down.

Although the assassination has led to countless conspiracy theories, it is now the settled presumption that the assassins were a gang of conspirators from Newark's Mosque No. 25, working on assignment for Elijah Muhammad. They were: Benjamin Thomas, Leon Davis, Wilbur McKinley, Talmadge Hayer and William Bradley. The five assailants all had criminal records and hailed from the East Orange area near Newark. But did they operate independently of the secret state?

It is estimated that anywhere between 14,000 and 30,000 mourners paid their respects when Malcolm X's body was presented at a public viewing at the Unity Funeral Home in Harlem. A funeral service followed at the Child's Memorial Temple Church of God in Christ, on Amsterdam Avenue. The church was filled to capacity with more than 1,000 people, loudspeakers were set up outside so the overflowing crowd could listen, and a local cable television station broadcast the funeral live. Standing on the stage of the converted old cinema still known locally as the Bluebird, framed by an old theatrical proscenium arch and only

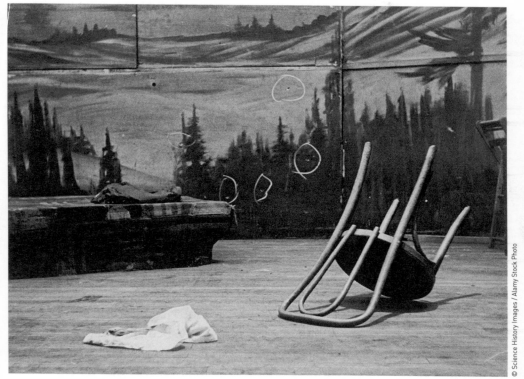

Malcolm X was shot dead on 21 February 1965, in Manhattan's Audubon Ballroom.
An upturned chair next to the podium and a series of chalked bullet holes in the canvas
backdrop convey the bleak aftermath of the killing.

It is a time for martyrs now, and if I am to be one, it will be for the cause of brotherhood.
That's the only thing that can save this country.
—Malcolm X, two days before his assassination

periodically glancing down at his handwritten notes on the pulpit, the actor and activist Ossie Davis delivered the eulogy.

In the front row, a man in a brilliant-white Arabic headdress stood erect. Next to him was an anonymous character in a sharp black suit and dark shades, and behind them were row upon row of men in starched collars and overcoats, and women in mink bucket hats. Muslim preachers, civil-rights leaders, gangsters and the ordinary folks of Harlem had come together.

Despite the tense atmosphere and the shrieking speaker system, Davis's mellifluous baritone flowed over the heads of the crowd. He spoke with an actor's training and a preacher's self-confidence, as if everyone within miles of the church was bearing witness to the body of Malcolm X. 'Here – at this final hour, in this quiet place – Harlem has bid farewell to one of its brightest hopes – extinguished now, and gone from us forever.' It was a powerful eulogy, directed not only to the crowds but to the killers and those who unjustly vilified Malcolm X. This, by his own reckoning, was his greatest ever performance, a Shakespearean panegyric to black militancy. 'Consigning these mortal remains to earth, the common mother of all, secure in the knowledge that what we place in the ground is no more now a man – but a seed – which, after the winter of our discontent, will come forth again to meet us. And we will know him then for what he was and is – a Prince – our own black shining Prince! – who didn't hesitate to die, because he loved us so.'

Malcolm X was finally laid to rest in Ferncliff Cemetery, in Hartsdale, New York.

It was exactly a year since Cassius had celebrated with Malcolm X in Miami, but they had not spoken for months and Cassius was conspicuously absent from the funeral. The last time they had set eyes on each other had been in Ghana, the newly liberated British colony in West Africa. It had become a magnet for independence fighters and anti-colonial activists. The writers Maya Angelou and Richard Wright had been there, so too had Martin Luther King. For many it was their first time in Africa, so the country held a special romance: it was a place of homecoming.

By chance Malcolm X and Muhammad Ali bumped into each other for a final time outside the Ambassador Hotel in Accra.

'I was on a tour of Egypt, Nigeria, and Ghana,' Ali said later in life. 'I saw Malcolm in Ghana where he stopped on his way back to America. He'd just finished a holy journey to Mecca that devout Muslims are required to make once in their lives, and he was wearing the traditional Muslim white robes, further signifying his break with Elijah Muhammad. He walked with a cane that looked like a prophet's stick and he wore a beard. I thought he'd gone too far. When he came up to greet me, I turned away, making our break public.'

It was a moment burdened by different emotions: loss, betrayal, and false memory. Much later, Ali confessed to regretting the way he had dismissed his former mentor. 'Malcolm X was a great thinker and an even greater friend,' he wrote in his autobiography. 'I might never have become a Muslim if it hadn't been for Malcolm. If I could go back and do it all over again, I would never have turned my back on him.' But he did – an unfaithful friend.

A contractual clause common in boxing contracts in the sixties permitted Sonny Liston a rematch, and after much haggling and commercial skulduggery, it finally came to pass. On the night of 25 May 1965, the two boxers entered the ring in a most unlikely venue, the tiny Central Maine Youth Center, known locally as St Dominic's Arena, in Lewiston, Maine. Several states had refused to stage the fight, and from the outset it was clouded in suspicion. A comedy of errors unfolded, including Robert Goulet, a Canadian-American singer signed as a crooner to Columbia, forgetting the words to the National Anthem. According to the veteran British heavyweight Tommy Farr, it was 'the blackest night in boxing'. Within a minute of the opening round Ali floored Liston with a short right. Liston crumpled to the canvas, all but knocked out. Ali was at first mystified and then enraged. He loomed over Liston, staring at him with contempt and then urging him to get up. Liston stayed where he was.

Herbert Goldman of the boxing encyclopedia *The Ring* has since described the fight as one that 'marked a loss of innocence for the old-time fight fans' and it is still called 'the fight with the phantom punch'. Did Liston take a dive? Was he just too old? Or had he just had enough? A cloud of corruption hung over the fight, and while it did not end Liston's career, it brought his credibility yet again into question.

Charles 'Sonny' Liston died on 6 January 1971. His body was found in his Las Vegas home by his wife Geraldine when she returned home from visiting her mother. The doorstep was cluttered with unopened milk bottles and a stack of unread newspapers. The BBC reported: 'Once the most feared fighter in America, he was sprawled at the foot of their bed wearing only his underwear. His body was bloated – he had been dead for at least six days – and there was dried blood streaking from his nose. There were no visible wounds and no weapons were found.' Sergeant Dennis Caputo of the Las Vegas Police Department discovered a small amount of heroin in the kitchen but no syringe. 'The kitchen was spotless except for a penny balloon on the counter,' he said. 'It was common knowledge that these kind of balloons were used to transport illegal narcotics. I will also say that it was pretty well-known that Liston was a part-time user.'

Sadness and mystery pursued Liston to the bitter end. In life, he was often his own worst enemy, repeatedly compromised by a temper that flared up in the face of uniformed authority, but he was also a victim, scarred by a bleak and traumatic childhood and a precarious adolescence spent on the streets of St Louis. Jail gave him a flint-like toughness and introduced him to the discipline of boxing, but as soon as he was out of the protective reach of the priests who moulded him, parasitic criminals dug their talons into him and exploited him at almost every turn. It remains unclear whether it was naïvety or greed that kept drawing Liston back, time and time again, to some of the most pernicious and manipulative people on earth.

Despite the ignominy of his life and death, Liston was one of the greatest boxers of all time. He was for many 'the greatest', but that title had already been taken. Yet without his pounding contribution to a golden era, Cassius X's reputation might never have soared so high.

BOXING AND SOUL: A PLAYLIST

1. 'Night Train' by James Brown and the Famous Flames (King, 1961)

A blistering R&B reworking of Jimmy Forrest's St Louis jump-jazz classic from 1951, this was Sonny Liston's signature tune.

2. 'You Beat Me To The Punch' by Mary Wells (Motown, 1962)

Writers Smokey Robinson and Ronald White of the Miracles used the metaphors of boxing to enrich this early Motown love song.

3. 'Sweet Potatoe, Collard Greens' by Sweet Les and Joe Frazier's Knockouts (P.I.P., 1972)

Soul food funk by Sweet Les featuring heavyweight champion Joe Frazier and his Philly backing band The Knockouts.

4. 'The Gang's All Here' by Sam Cooke and Cassius Clay (Columbia, 1963)

Sam Cooke and Cassius Clay double up to rework the old American popular song, set to a tune originally from *The Pirates of Penzance*, turning it into a soulful party song.

5. 'First Round Knockout' by Joe Frazier (Motown, 1975)

Disco king Van McCoy oversees the northern soul rarity by heavyweight champion Smokin' Joe Frazier.

6. 'Love T.K.O.' by Teddy Pendergrass (Philadelphia International, 1980)

A master vocalist sings this great Philly love song written by Cecil Womack. Surely the only time that the boxing term for technical knockout has made it into music.

7. 'Doin' The Ali Shuffle' Alvin Cash (Mar-V-Lus, 1967)

Chicago funk maestro Alvin Cash pays homage to Muhammad Ali's trademark canvas dance – the Ali shuffle.

8. 'Mama Said Knock You Out' LL Cool J (Def Jam, 1990)

From the album of the same name by rapper LL Cool J, this is one of the big entrance songs in professional boxing – hip-hop's answer to Foreigner's 'Eye Of The Tiger'.

9. 'I'm A Lover' by Sonny Liston (Palamino, 1970)

A growling slice of St Louis funk featuring the most feared man in boxing on vocals backed by local funk visionary Gene Anderson and His Dynamic Psychedelics.

10. 'Knock Out' by Margie Joseph (HCRC, 1982)

The great Mississippi soul singer who was often compared to Aretha Franklin survived the shift into disco and club music and this was one of her best-selling records.

11. 'Heart Breaking Man' by Sonny Fishback (Out-A-Site,1966)

Muhammad Ali's high-school friend leads on this cranking northern soul rarity.

12. 'Soul Power' by James Brown (King, 1971)

The Godfather of Soul powers through this funk anthem, the title track of the famous concert that supported Muhammad Ali v. George Foreman's 1974 Rumble in the Jungle in Kinshasa, Zaire.

13. 'Linger On' by Prince Buster (Prince Buster, 1964)

The king of Jamaican ska pays tribute to the newly crowned champion of the world – Cassius Clay.

14. 'I Believe' by Jimmy Ellis and the Riverview Spiritual Singers (Atlantic, 1970)

Muhammad Ali's high-school friend, sparring partner and heavyweight contender Jimmy Ellis leads his Louisville gospel group in a spiritual rendition of the old Mahalia Jackson classic 'I Believe'.

15. 'Road To Glory' by 2Pac (unreleased mixtape, recorded 1996)

Written for one of 2Pac's closest friends, Mike Tyson, the lyrics refer to the boxer's fight with the UK heavyweight Frank Bruno.

16. 'I Can't Wait' by Ernie Terrell and His Heavyweights (Argo, 1965)

Charmingly dated family soul song by the Chicago heavyweight who was battered by Ali in the now infamous 'what's my name?' title fight. Ernie's sister Jean replaced Diana Ross in The Supremes in 1970.

17. 'Night Train' by Georgie Fame and the Blue Flames (Columbia, 1964)

The organ-led Mod version of Sonny Liston's signature tune from Fame's live album *Rhythm And Blues At The Flamingo*.

18. 'I'll Be Around' The Spinners (Atlantic 1972)

Not boxing-themed, but a standout track from the soundtrack to *When We Were Kings*, the 1996 Oscar-winning documentary about Ali and Foreman's Rumble in the Jungle in 1974.

19. 'Knock Him Down Whiskey' by Sugar Ray Robinson (King, 1953)

The legendary boxer leads a jazz and R&B tribute to whisky. Sugar Ray is supported by Earl 'Fatha' Hines and His Orchestra.

20. 'The Bigger They Come (The Harder They Fall)' by Joe Frazier (Cloverlay, 1970)

Another soul release from Frazier, who became undisputed heavyweight champion in Ali's absence. Released on his own indie label Cloverlay, also the name of his management agency.

BIBLIOGRAPHY

Primary Sources

Amsterdam News, Special Collections, Columbia University
    Library.
Black Power Records RG 65, Records of the Federal Bureau of
    Investigation (Class 157), National Archives, Washington, DC.
    (Note: the FBI established Classification 157 (Civil Unrest) on
    23 January 1959, initially calling it 'Racial Matters/Bombing
    Matters'.)
The Jean Blackwell Hutson Research and Reference Division,
    Schomburg Center for Research in Black Culture, 515
    Malcolm X Boulevard, New York, NY, 10037.
Blues & Soul magazine, 1968–1975, author's own collection.
COINTELPRO Papers, The FBI Education Center, Pennsylvania
    Avenue, NW Washington, DC.
The FBI Vaults, released and partly redacted files of FBI
    investigations on Cassius Marcellus Clay, Charles 'Sonny'
    Liston, Malcolm X and the Nation of Islam.
The House Select Committee on Assassinations (HSCA), 1976–
    1979, Library of Congress, Washington, DC.
*The Papers and Correspondence of the Reverend Martin Luther
    King Jr*, The Martin Luther King, Jr. Center for Nonviolent
    Social Change, Atlanta, GA.

Miami Herald, 1962–64, University of Miami, Richter Library.
Michigan Chronicle, 1962–72, Detroit Public Library, Detroit.
Newsweek, vols 68–88, 1967–69.
The New York Post, 1965–75, New York Public Library, New York.
The New York Times, 1965–75, Columbia University Library.
Sports Illustrated magazine.
Wax Poetics magazine, Brooklyn 2007–10, author's own collection.

Secondary Sources

Ali, Rahaman, *That's Muhammad Ali's Brother: My Life on the Undercard*, New York: Page Publishing, 2014.

Ali, Rahaman with Rafiq, Fiaz, *My Brother Muhammad Ali: The Definitive Biography*, London: John Blake, 2019.

Baker, Rob, *Beautiful Idiots and Brilliant Lunatics: A Sideways Look at Twentieth-Century London*, Stroud: Amberley Publishing, 2015.

Blackstock, Nelson, *COINTELPRO: The FBI's Secret War on Political Freedom*, New York: Pathfinder Books, 2000.

Bowman, Rob, *Soulsville U.S.A.: The Story of Stax Records*, New York: BWA Ltd, 1998.

Boyd, Herb (ed.), *The Harlem Reader: A Celebration of New York's Most Famous Neighbourhood, from the Renaissance Years to the 21st Century*, New York: Three Rivers Press, 2003.

Branch, Taylor, *At Canaan's Edge: America in the King Years 1965–68*, New York: Simon & Schuster, 2006.

Carlin, Richard, *Godfather of the Music Industry: Morris Levy*, Jackson: University Press of Mississippi, 2016.

Carpenter, Bil, *Uncloudy Days: The Gospel Encyclopaedia*, San Francisco: Backbeat Books, 2005.

Chambers, Jason, *Madison Avenue and the Color Line: African Americans in the Advertising Industry*, Philadelphia: University of Pennsylvania Press, 2007.

Delmont, Matthew F., *The Nicest Kids in Town: American Bandstand, Rock 'n' Roll and the Struggle for Civil Rights in 1950s Philadelphia*, Los Angeles: University of California Press, 2012.

Didion, Joan, *Miami*, New York: Simon & Schuster, 1987.

Donner, Frank J., *The Age of Surveillance: The Aims and Methods of America's Political Intelligence System*, New York: Alfred A. Knopf, 1980.

Edgecombe, John, *Black Scandal*, London: Westworld International, 2002.

Eig, Jonathan, *Ali: A Life*, New York: Simon & Schuster, 2017.

English, T. J., *The Savage City: Race, Murder, and a Generation on the Edge*, New York: William Morrow & Co., 2011.

Felber, Garrett A., *Those Who Say Don't Know: The Nation of Islam, the Black Freedom Movement, and the Carceral State*, Chapel Hill: University of North Carolina Press, 2019.

Fishback, Sonny, *Plant a New Seed*, Bloomington: Trafford Publishing, 2005.

Freeman, Scott, *Otis!: The Otis Redding Story*, New York: St. Martin's Press, 2001.

Gallender, Paul, *Sonny Liston: The Real Story Behind the Ali–Liston Fights*, Pacific Grove: Park Place Publications, 2012.

Gentry, Curt, *J. Edgar Hoover: The Man and the Secrets*, New York: W.W. Norton & Co., 1992.

George, Nelson, *Where Did Our Love Go?: The Rise and Fall of the Motown Sound*, New York: St. Martin's Press, 1985.

George, Nelson, *The Death of Rhythm and Blues*, New York: Random House, 1988.

Gordon, Robert, *Respect Yourself: Stax Records and the Soul Explosion*, New York: Bloomsbury, 2014.

Gordy, Berry, *To Be Loved: The Music, the Magic, the Memories of Motown*, New York: Grand Central Publishing, 1994.

Gordy Singleton, Raynoma, *Berry, Me and Motown: The Untold Story*, New York: McGraw Hill, 1989.

Guralnick, Peter, *Dream Boogie: The Triumph of Sam Cooke*, London: Abacus, 2006.

Haley, Alex, with Malcolm X, *The Autobiography of Malcolm X*, New York: Grove Press, 1965.

Hamilton, Marybeth, *In Search of the Blues*, London: Jonathan Cape, 2007.

Hauser, Thomas, *Muhammad Ali: His Life and Times*, London: Simon & Schuster, 1991.

Hegarty, Neil, *That Was The Life That Was: Frost – The Authorised Biography*, London: W.H. Allen, 2015.

Howard, Josiah, *Blaxploitation Cinema: The Essential Reference Guide*, Godalming: FAB Press, 2008.

Jones, Thom, *Sonny Liston Was a Friend of Mine*, London: Faber, 1999.

Kahn, Ashley, *The House That Trane Built: The Story of Impulse Records*, New York: W.W. Norton & Co., 2006.

Kempton, Murray, *The Briar Patch: The Trial of the Panther 21*, New York: Da Capo Press Inc., 1997.

Kindred, Dave, *Sound and Fury: Two Powerful Friends, One Fateful Friendship*, New York: Free Press, 2006.

Kot, Greg, *I'll Take You There: Mavis Staples, the Staple Singers, and the March Up Freedom's Highways*, New York: Scribner, 2014.

Kotz, Nick, *Judgment Days: Lyndon Baines Johnson, Martin Luther King Jr., and the Laws That Changed America*, Boston: Houghton Mifflin, 2005.

Lucas, Frank, *Original Gangster: My Life as NYC's Biggest Baddest Drugs Baron*, New York: St. Martin's Press, 2010.

Marable, Manning, *Malcolm X: A Life of Reinvention*, New York: Viking, 2011.

Marqusee, Mike, *Redemption Song: Muhammad Ali and the Spirit of the Sixties*, London: Verso, 1999.

Mayfield, Todd, *Travelling Soul: The Life of Curtis Mayfield*, Chicago: Chicago Review Press, 2016.

McRae, Donald, *A Man's World: The Double Life of Emile Griffith*, London: Simon & Schuster, 2015.

Newsday staff and editors, *The Heroin Trail*, London: Holt, Rinehart & Winston, 1975.

O'Reilly, Kenneth, *"Racial Matters": The FBI's Secret File on Black America, 1960–1972*, New York: The Free Press, 1991.

Pepper, William F., *An Act of State: The Execution of Martin Luther King*, New York: Verso, 2003.

Posner, Gerald, *Motown: Money, Power, Sex, and Music*, New York: Random House, 2002.

Rasenberger, Jim, *The Brilliant Disaster: JFK, Castro, and America's Doomed Invasion of Cuba's Bay of Pigs*, London: Robert Hale, 2011.

Ribowsky, Mark, *Dreams to Remember: Otis, Redding, Stax Records, and the Transformation of Southern Soul*, New York: Liveright, 2015.

Ritz, David, *Divided Soul: The Life of Marvin Gaye*, New York: McGraw-Hill, 1985.

Roberts, Randy & Smith, Johnny, *Blood Brothers: The Fatal Friendship Between Muhammad Ali and Malcolm X*, New York: Basic Books, 2016.

Salvatore, Nick, *C.L. Franklin, the Black Church, and the Transformation of America*, New York: Little Brown & Co., 2005.

Schulke, Flip, *Muhammad Ali: The Birth of a Legend*, New York: St. Martin's Griffin, 2001.

Smiley, David L., *Lion of White Hall: The Life of Cassius Marcellus Clay of Kentucky* volume 1, Madison: University of Wisconsin, 1953.

Smith, Suzanne, E., *Dancing in the Street: Motown and the Cultural Politics of Detroit*, Cambridge: Harvard University Press, 1999.

Sugrue, Thomas, *The Origins of the Urban Crisis: Race and Inequality in Post-war Detroit*, New Jersey: Princeton University Press, 2005.

Tosches, Nick, *Night Train: A Biography of Sonny Liston*, New York: Little Brown & Co., 2000 (also known as *The Devil and Sonny Liston*).

Ward, Brian, *Just My Soul Responding: Rhythm and Blues, Black Consciousness, and Race Relations*, London: UCL Press, 1998.

Warner, Jay, *Just Walkin' in the Rain*, Los Angeles: Renaissance Books, 2001.

West, David (ed.), *The Mammoth Book of Muhammad Ali*, London: Constable & Robinson, 2012.

Wexler, Jerry, *Rhythm and the Blues: A Life in American Music*, New York: Alfred A. Knopf, 1993.

Williams, John L., *Michael X: A Life in Black and White*, London: Century, 2008.

Wolff, Daniel, *You Send Me: The Life and Times of Sam Cooke*, New York: William Morrow & Co., 1995.

INDEX